D1035527

THE FIRST DUCE

Gabriele D'Annunzio

THE FIRST DUCE
D'Annunzio at Fiume

Michael A. Ledeen

The Johns Hopkins University Press · Baltimore · London

This book is dedicated to my teachers

Alvin Frank

Richard Heffner

George Mosse

Richard Popkin

Julius Weinberg

Other Books by the Author

Universal Fascism: The Theory and Practice of the Fascist International, 1928–1936

Fascism: An Informal Introduction to Its Theory and Practice (with Renzo de Felice)

Copyright © 1977 by The Johns Hopkins University Press

The Johns Hopkins University Press, Baltimore, Maryland 21218
The Johns Hopkins Press, Ltd., London

Originally published as *D'Annunzio a Fiume* (Bari: Giuseppe Laterza & Figli, 1975). English-language edition prepared by the author.

Library of Congress Catalog Card Number 76-47376
ISBN 0-8018-1860-5
Library of Congress Cataloging in Publication data will be found on the last printed page of this book. *1 - 19 - 79*

Contents

Preface

The First Duce deals with the sixteen months when Gabriele D'Annunzio ruled the city of Fiume and held it against the world. This is not only a fascinating and entertaining story in its own right (and worth retelling for that reason alone) but also a highly revealing and suggestive model for much of the West today, for Fiume under D'Annunzio was a microcosm of the modern political world. An analysis of D'Annunzian Fiume goes a long way toward accounting for much of the puzzling political behaviour that has characterized Western society ever since the Great War.

The colorful style of political manipulation that D'Annunzio developed at Fiume was the harbinger of the successful mass movements later in the twentieth century. Some scholars have tended to deal with both D'Annunzio and the Fascist movement that followed as examples of "aberrant" politics, diseases of the social body. Yet "D'Annunzian politics" have unfortunately become the norm for the West in this century, and we are the heirs of a political tradition that was developed in part during the sixteen months when Fiume came under the poet's control. The age of mass politics has become a reality because of those men and women who learned how to shape the masses into a coherent political body, and D'Annunzio occupies a prominent place in their ranks.

The connection between D'Annunzio and Fascism lies at the center of this story, for D'Annunzio has often been described as the John the Baptist of Italian Fascism. There is much truth in this label, for without D'Annunzio the Fascist seizure of power would most likely not have taken place. Virtually the entire ritual of Fascism came from the "Free State of Fiume": the balcony address, the Roman salute, the cries of "aia, aia, alala," the dramatic dialogues with the crowd, the use of religious symbols in a new secular setting, the eulogies to the "martyrs"

of the cause and the employment of their "relics" in political ceremonies. Moreover, quite aside from the poet's contribution to the form
and style of Fascist politics, Mussolini's movement first started to attract
great strength when the future dictator supported D'Annunzio's occupation of Fiume. The forces that supported the poet were often captured
by fascists, even though there were fundamental conflicts between
Mussolini and D'Annunzio. Both men spoke for a "new" Italy and
eventually a new world. Both attempted to transform their countrymen
into more heroic types, rejecting the Italian tradition of civility in favor
of an ethic of violence and imperialism.

D'Annunzian Fiume gave expression to a dynamic element in
Italian society which had taken form during the First World War and
which would eventually constitute an important component of Fascism.
Renzo De Felice has recently called this component "fascism-movement";[1] it was the expression of the desires of an emerging lower middle
class that had been mobilized by the war yet excluded from effective
political participation. This emerging middle class, both at Fiume and
within Fascism, attempted to assert its demands against both the established bourgeoisie and the proletariat. Of necessity these demands
were vague and poorly defined, but they were not less revolutionary
because of their vagueness. In time, Mussolin would be forced to
suppress "fascism-movement" in order to establish a viable Fascist regime,
and many of the conflicts between D'Annunzio and the future Duce
prefigured the later struggle between movement and regime within
Fascism itself.

There were, then, important linkages between D'Annunzian Fiume
and Mussolini's Italy, but there were also profound differences, above
all in the realm of ideology. The constitution that D'Annunzio and
Alceste De Ambris drafted for the new state was a radical document,
whose goal was very different from the totalitarian state created by
Mussolini. Indeed, D'Annunzian Fiume virtually defies attempts to
classify it as a phenomenon of either the political Right or Left. One
of the most brilliant aspects of D'Annunzio's politics was his ability to
enlist the passionate support of the most diverse elements of the political
world. The government of Fiume contained American journalists and
poets, Belgian writers, and Italian businessmen, in addition to representatives of radical trade unions, anarchist groups, and the armed forces.
Fiume was one of the first governments to arrive at a form of "consensus politics," and D'Annunzio managed to convince all these apparently conflicting forces that his government served their best interests.

In many ways D'Annunzio's Fiume was a revolutionary phenomenon
in the West, and the poet's commitment to organizing an "anti-League
of Nations" adds to this claim. Already in 1919 he was speaking of an

alliance between Arabs, the Irish, and Palestinian Jews, in order to confront the colonial powers with the forces of the "new world" he was trying to rally to his cause.

The Constitution of Fiume (la Carta del Carnaro) constituted a major contribution to political theory, for it blended both the radical elements of the "new politics" and the quasi-religious qualities of D'Annunzio's eloquent rhetoric into a unique political document. Drafted in collaboration with De Ambris (a leading anarchosyndicalist), the Carta del Carnaro provided for the complete equality of women, total toleration of religion and atheism, and a thoroughgoing system of social security, medical insurance, and old-age care, in addition to a method of direct democracy. Furthermore, it provided for a constant change in political leadership in order both to protect against an entrenched bureaucracy and to guarantee a constant infusion of new elements into the government of the city. These specifically political elements were combined with an elaborate system of mass celebrations and rituals designed to guarantee a high level of political consciousness and enthusiasm among all the citizens of the state. Culture was combined with politics and art in a unique synthesis, and one critic has called the Carta del Carnaro a kind of Napoleonic Code rewritten by an Ezra Pound.

At the core of D'Annunzian politics was the insight that many conflicting interests could be overcome and "transcended" in a new kind of movement. With the passage of the old ruling class the alignments and alliances that had been dominant during the previous century would pass away, and the colonial peoples could come to the fore on an international scale, just as the previously powerless forces of Western society could now seize power in their own countries. D'Annunzio's vision was that the new order would be based on personal qualities of heroism and genius, rather than upon traditional criteria of wealth, heritage, and power. Armed with this belief and his instinctive insight into the nature of mass politics, D'Annunzio managed to flourish in Fiume despite the almost unanimous opposition of the victorious Allies of the Great War. He was finally overthrown when the Italian armed forces drove him from the city, but he remained a force of tremendous importance in Italian domestic politics. Perhaps the most eloquent tribute that could be paid him was the great respect and fear demonstrated by Mussolini in the years following the Fiume adventure.

The leaders of post-War Italy recognized the potential strength of the poet and were deeply concerned about his intentions. Everyone from Mussolini to Premier Francesco Saverio Nitti realized that D'Annunzio could have led a successful march on Rome during his reign at Fiume, and an analysis of the diplomatic correspondence of the period shows that this concern was exceedingly widespread throughout the Western world. Even the American diplomats in Europe, who often could not even spell the names of Italian politicians, recognized the explosive nature of D'Annunzio's adventure, and it was only the poet's lack of political acumen that prevented him from eventually seizing power in Italy. The significance of D'Annunzio as a political phenomen lies then more in the forces to which he appealed and the vision of society which he presented than in any durable state or extended period of rule.

The history of D'Annunzian Fiume presents us with many of the developments we consider novel and unsettling today: clergymen abandoning the cloth in favor of marriage and secular activities; women demanding an equitable status in a male-dominated society; youth calling for the elimination of the old and corrupt political leadership; military men calling for a democratic army; artists suggesting that aesthetics should be the proper basis for political decisions; poets demanding a beautiful world instead of a utilitarian one; minorities clamoring for their fair share of political power. Seen from a distance of over half a century, it is perhaps easier for us to analyze these problems in the microcosm of Fiume than in the larger chaos of today's world.

The revolt D'Annunzio led was directed against the old order of Western Europe and was carried out in the name of youthful creativity and virility, which would hopefully create a new world in the image of its creators. The essence of this revolt was the liberation of the human personality, what we might call the radicalization of the masses of people who had been systematically exploited for so many centuries. The symbol of this transformation of mankind was D'Annunzio himself, and the uniqueness of his own personality was taken as living proof that such a revolution could succeed. Those who came into contact with him were invariably inspired and intoxicated by the experience, and the men who participated in the Fiume adventure were deeply moved by it, and wrote of it as if it were a spiritual catharsis. This spiritual element was of enormous importance in D'Annunzio's success, for he incorporated it into his political practice as well as his political theories.

In the end, it was D'Annunzio's ability to convince his followers that they were part of a spiritually "higher" realm of the world that made him such a potent and important political phenomenon. He thus stands as one of the great innovators and the occupation of Fiume as one of the watersheds of the modern world.

Acknowledgments

Most of the research for this book was done during the academic year 1972-73 thanks to a fellowship from the American Council of Learned Societies. There was additional support from the Graduate School of Washington University. During that year I had the good fortune and great pleasure of working in numerous archives and libraries in Italy, all cited in the notes. I would like to express my appreciation for the enthusiastic collaboration and assistance given me by Dr. Costanzo Casucci and Mario Missori of the Archivio Centrale dello Stato, Dr. Andrea Petrich and Renato D'Ancona of the Archivio-Museo Fiumano, and Professor Alberto Arpino of the Archivio Centrale del Risorgimento, all in Rome.

In addition, I received help and encouragement from several other persons whom I wish to thank publicly: Professor Giorgio Radetti, Dr. Elvio Sciubba, Father Giovanni Caprile, Ferdinando Gerra, the Honorable Ettore Viola, Colonel Luigi Corrado, Dr. Pietro Blayer, His Excellency Ambassador Giorgio Ciraolo, and Professor Emilio Mariano.

I wish to express my particular appreciation to Professor Renzo De Felice, who encouraged, helped, and criticized me from the inception of this project to its completion.

Finally, and above all, my thanks to Barbara, for making it all happen.

THE FIRST DUCE

1

The Star

On the ninth of August 1918 the citizens of Vienna were subjected to a unique aerial bombardment. The skies were filled with pieces of colored paper, which were tinted red, white, and green, the colors of the Italian flag. They were propaganda leaflets, and the text began in a spectacular manner: "Viennese! We could now be dropping bombs on you! Instead we drop only a salute." This masterpiece of wartime propaganda reads like a contemporary document. "We Italians do not make war on women and children," the Viennese read, "we are making war on your government, which is the enemy of your national liberty." This distinction, suggesting that the government was unworthy of the people it purported to lead, has become a commonplace in attempts to provoke mass public dissatisfaction. At the time, however, it was something of an innovation, as was the final flourish of the text. "You have turned the world against you. If you wish to continue the War— continue it! You will thereby commit suicide. What have you to gain? The decisive victory promised you by the Prussian generals? Their decisive victory is like Ukrainian bread. You will starve waiting for it. . . ."[1]

The pilots who dropped this message on Vienna had risked their lives (the flight itself was exceedingly dangerous in that early period of air travel, quite aside from the menace of Austrian planes and antiaircraft) in order to make what was, after all, simply a glorious gesture. This enterprise stood in stark contrast to most of the actions of the "Great War," which was notoriously a war without heroes, a faceless trench battle in which masses of soldiers slaughtered one another for territorial advantage. To be sure, there was no lack of genuine heroism on the battlefields of Europe, but the image of the war that has come down to us is one of a plodding and methodical war of tactics and attrition. In the literature of the war there is relatively little refer-

1

ence to the exploits of individuals, and although the figure of the
Prussian "Red Baron" has recently been elevated from relative obscurity
to the level of camp hero, there were few such figures. One of the most
revealing comments about the Great War is to be found in the movies
about it, for, unlike other conflicts, movies about this war have virtually
no heroes. The great classic *All Quiet on the Western Front* is typical;
the film stressed the almost mechanical nature of the struggle, portray-
ing the war as an alternating slaughter of French and German troops,
moving back and forth between lines of trenches. In America, the most
famous hero in the films of the war was Sergeant York, a boring country
boy whose only distinguishing quality was his remarkable accuracy with
the weaponry of the period. But York was an obedient soldier who
followed orders and did his duty, not an enterprising individual.

Gabriele D'Annunzio, author of the pamphlet that fell on Vienna
on August ninth and leader of the squadron that risked death to *fare la
bella figura* ("cut an elegant figure"), was one figure who towered over
this scene of trench warfare. While there were other groups of soldiers
noted for their heroic enterprises (such as the various stormtroopers),
it would be hard to find anyone to match D'Annunzio for sheer bravado
and color. His field of activity was not limited to the air; he left his
mark in sea battles and land actions as well. Whether it was bombing
Trieste from the air twice in one day (first with pamphlets, then with
bombs), charging Austrian trenches in the middle of the night with
pistols and knives, dressed in a flowing cape, or sailing torpedo boats
into the middle of the Austrian fleet at anchor and blowing up a torpedo-
boat in the Bay of Buccari, D'Annunzio achieved a reputation as the
great poet-warrior of the war. All this was accomplished by a man who
was fifty-two years old when he enlisted and who lost an eye during the
course of hostilities. Furthermore, D'Annunzio had not had much experience in military activities before the outbreak of fighting (with the exception of a few duels), but was noted in the fields of romance and literature.
His reputation had been that of a flamboyant and decadent poet, play-
wright, and novelist and, above all, one of the great lovers of his day.

It is rare for a poet to achieve such stature during wartime. The only
other literary figure who comes to mind in this connection is not a real
man, but a fictional one—Cyrano de Bergerac, and Cyrano is a rather
farcical character. Yet many of the social upheavals of the early twentieth century involved the active participation of poets (the most famous
case is Kurt Eisner's leadership of the revolutionary socialist republic of
Bavaria in 1919), and it is in this context that D'Annunzio's dramatic
role in twentieth-century politics must be viewed.

THE POET AS WORLD-SHAPER

We do not commonly think of poets as world-shapers, despite their influence over the world in which we live. Yet the men and women who dictate style and taste possess enormous power. Given the high degree of organization of all means of communication today, we are more likely to find powerful poets working for an advertising agency or a political party than living in a loft on the fringes of a city, yet the role remains the same: whoever defines the language of politics wields great power. D'Annunzio gained control over the political rhetoric of Italy at a moment of chaos and crisis, and he mastered the emotions of those who filled Italy's piazzas to listen to his speeches. His heroism during the war made it possible for D'Annunzio to bridge the chasm between intellectuals and the masses, for he had demonstrated that his bravado was more than a verbal facade. People believed D'Annunzio when he spoke of reviving the glory of Italy's Roman days and of leading a civilizing mission through the Western world. Few others were so credible in the political arena of postwar Italy.

D'Annunzio was born on the Italian Adriatic coast in the town of Pescara on 12 March 1863. His own personality was foreshadowed by that of his father, a one-time mayor of the city, who was noted for his lechery and his fiscal profligacy. Gabriele was a true D'Annunzio in both his frenetic search for new women to conquer and his constant flirtation with bankruptcy. His education was good, acquired at the famous Cicognini college in Prato, and his verbal flair developed at an early age. When only thirteen, D'Annunzio composed an intensely chauvinistic poem celebrating a visit by King Umberto to Pescara.

His literary career began in the period when Rome started to become a European center; D'Annunzio moved there in 1881, about the time that the city's first publisher was setting up business. D'Annunzio soon became the Father Knickerbocker of Rome, filling the pages of the *Fanfulla* with exotic and erotic tales of high society, beautiful women, and dramatic exploits. He was perhaps the first figure of a type that later became celebrated in *La Dolce Vita*. Many of his columns for the *Fanfulla* were quite transparently autobiographical, and often downright obscene, but in the turbulent atmosphere of Rome at the end of the century, this licentiousness served to enhance his reputation, his charisma, and his appeal to Roman women. His tastes were similar to those of other decadent artists of the period in other European capitals. Like so many other figures of the *fin de siècle*, D'Annunzio found himself torn between two desires: one for a "pure spirit," the other for material acquisitions. "My aesthete's feeling draws me inevitably toward the acquisition of fine things. I could have eaten quite well in a modest home, sat on a simple wooden chair, eaten off common plates, walked about on carpets made in Italy. . . . Instead, fatally, I have desired divans, Persian carpets, precious materials and stuffs, Japanese plates, all those beautiful and useless things which I love with a deep and ruinous love."[2]

Much of D'Annunzio's writing was exaggerated, especially when the subject was the poet himself, but this particular passage is an understatement. If one visits his last home, the famous Vittoriale in the hills overlooking Lake Garda (where his apartment has been meticulously conserved as it was when the poet lived there), one finds ample evidence of D'Annunzio's "deep and ruinous love" for the artifacts of the world. His taste was thoroughly eclectic, for the rooms of the Vittoriale are filled with paintings, wall-hangings, masks, bric-a-brac, sculptures, figurines, vases, rugs, china, medals, bells, musical instruments, and books thrown together in a chaotic mixture of styles and cultures. The ceilings are either draped with chamois hangings or inscribed with various slogans, epithets, or erotic phrases. The walls are covered with dark tapestries and paintings of every imaginable description. It is, in short, quite in keeping with the mentality of its poet-in-residence. D'Annunzio was never a great admirer of the sun, living at a time when a pallid complexion was considered more beautiful than a sun tan, and most of his work was done during the night. Hardly a sunbeam enters the Vittoriale, and its heavy, oppressive atmosphere conjures up images of an opium den, even on a sunny day. In his later years, the poet did most of his writing between ten o'clock at night and four or five o'clock in the morning, and within the Vittoriale this nocturnal atmosphere is constantly maintained.[3]

The style of life that D'Annunzio led, as symbolized by his home, set him apart from his countrymen. In his often frantic search for uniqueness, and for a life-style totally removed from "normality," D'Annunzio reflected a widespread conviction that artistic creativity could not take place within the confines of bourgeois society. Modern society was viewed as stultifying, artificial, and boring, capable of producing enormous quantities of machines and consumer goods but unable to generate the creative spark that characterizes great artists. Thus, for D'Annunzio and many other creative figures, a spiritual transformation of the world was absolutely necessary, in order that modern man might reestablish contact with the sources of his own natural creativity.

D'Annunzio recognized that his fatal attraction to material things was proof positive of the corrupting influence of modern society, for one could hardly be a true creator if one dissipated one's energies in the pursuit of baubles and trinkets. Thus, at the same time that he was confessing his weakness for imported rugs, D'Annunzio was calling on his fellow Italians to rebel against the superficiality and the artificiality of the modern world and to express their "Latin creativity" in acts of violence. In one of his most famous novels, *The Virgins of the Rocks* (1894-95), D'Annunzio described his spiritual ancestors as "an ancient and noble race of warriors," and he hailed their acts of savagery in the past, "their victories, the beautiful women they raped, their drunken-nesses, their magnificence." He was an Italian Nietzschean, viewing modern civilization as a thin veneer that barely covered up the savage and violent human instincts. D'Annunzio wanted to uncover these in-stincts so that his fellow Italians could become "natural," "whole" beings.

This search for "the man within" (or the "new man," as it was often stated) was typical of the *fin de siècle*, and D'Annunzio was one in a long list of writers who became obsessed with discovering the essence of human nature and human originality at a time when the entire direction of civilization seemed destined to submerge such originality in a sea of conformity and "massification." The late nineteenth century was, after all, the moment of the great triumph of the industrial revolution and all its accompanying dislocation. For the artists of the period, the most painful change was in their economic base. Instead of being supported by elegant patrons, they became increasingly subject to the whims of a literary marketplace. Intellectuals rebelled against this change, for they often despised "the public," preferring to be judged by their own peers. As their own concepts of style and creativity were increasingly rele-gated to a secondary position and the worth of an artist increasingly judged by his "marketability," artists became alienated from the process of modern culture, preferring to think of themselves as men apart. For some, this separation was a purely intellectual act, while for others it took a more total form. For an Italian, however, separation from his society is one of the cruelest of all fates, and for someone as convivial as D'Annunzio, isolation from the world was unthinkable (although he did experience extended periods of intense depression, when he cut himself off from most human contact). D'Annunzio needed an audience and was unwilling to be alone. Like a true dramatist, he surrounded himself with highly diverse types so that he could be sure of finding the response he desired. Instead of "opting out" of modern society, D'Annunzio eventually undertook to change it.

The notion of transforming the masses of the modern world from the "great unwashed" into a cultured body of men and women of good taste has long fascinated intellectuals. One of the most appealing aspects of this dream is that the intellectuals themselves would clearly be the ones to effect the transformation, and D'Annunzio was not one to shrink from such a task. In this way, the problem of the artist's rela-tionship to society became transformed into that of the salvation of society itself, for the artist was to be the ultimate arbiter of society's ills. D'Annunzio put this into typically fiery prose when he spoke of his own mission to his countrymen (long before he conceived of a specifically *political* role for himself): "I want to write a volume of poetic prose which will be a war-cry for the Latin people,"[4] he wrote. D'Annunzio hoped to inspire his countrymen by the force of his prose and the drama of his example. He believed that Italians had become soft, and he wanted to awaken a spirit of aggressiveness in them. Thus, he became an advocate of colonial adventures in Africa (coining the term *mare nostrum* for the Mediterranean) in order to stress what he felt was Italy's properly paternalistic and dominating attitude toward the other countries on the shores of the ocean. Ironically, he suffered for years from severe seasickness and was unable to make a grand tour of the Mediterranean. Nonetheless, he overcame this disease to carry out one of his most famous feats, the *Beffa di Buccari*, at sea during the First World War.

Like virtually all members of the European literary elite at the turn of the century, D'Annunzio was at first anything but a democrat. He felt that decisions should be made by the chosen few who could alone elevate the tastes and lives of the multitudes. A state based on universal suffrage, he said, was an ignoble institution, since a truly great state would favor "the gradual elevation of a privileged class toward its ideal form of existence."[5] In order to advance his own elevation, D'Annunzio entered Parliament in the last year of the century, sitting on the right side of the chamber. But shortly thereafter (on March 27th) the poet announced that he had undergone a political conversion. Henceforth, he proclaimed, he was a man of the Left, having moved "from death to life, from Right to Left."[6] In actuality these terms were virtually meaningless to D'Annunzio, for he was no more allied with the traditional Italian Right than with the Socialists. His thought rarely focused on traditional political ideas like taxation, governmental institutions, or class conflict. Instead, D'Annunzio's "political" thought was concerned with national greatness, the aesthetics of Italian cities, the creativity of the Italian people, and the virility of Italian men. His notion of "politics" was an essentially spiritual one, and this was quite in keeping with the temper of the age. Many agreed with D'Annunzio that parliamentary politics were banal or ignoble. Many sought, with him, some form of political activity that could restore excitement to government and that would enlist the passions of the people in the enterprises of their nation. By the early twentieth century, such groups as the Futurists were calling for a massive war to cleanse the world of the rotten elements that were destroying it. War, in their view, was the only "hygiene" capable of restoring Western civilization to a state of health.[7] The First World War, probably the most ruinous event in modern European history, was welcomed with open arms by such people.

It is unlikely that D'Annunzio conceived of the Great War solely in such terms, at least at the beginning of the struggle. For the poet, war was both an outlet for his own unique abilities and an experience that would purify the Italian people. Further, D'Annunzio hardly believed that war was the only way to achieve greatness, and for most of his life he preferred love to battle. His great notoriety as a lover was achieved through a succession of passionate affairs with some of the most beautiful and fascinating women of the day. The most famous of these was his extended romance with the great Italian actress Eleonora Duse, the only real challenger to Sarah Bernhardt for the title of First Lady of the European stage. D'Annunzio and Duse were together from 1897 to 1904, living in rural splendor, wearing outlandish clothes, staging wild parties, and capturing the imaginations of thousands of jealous onlookers. Rumors of their joint activities could fill volumes. One of the most innocent, but telling, rumors was that each evening at sunset D'Annunzio swam naked in the Mediterranean and that Duse waited for him at the shore with a purple robe to throw over his shoulders as he emerged from the waves.

This was the period during which D'Annunzio raised his own eccentricities to the level of an art form, cultivating his own habits in order to set himself completely apart from the humdrum world of bourgeois Europe. Others were enchanted with modern technology; D'Annunzio always wrote with a quill pen. Others were fascinated by the progress of science; D'Annunzio became a mystic, "reading" the cards in the evening, spending hours on end with witches and soothsayers, studying the secret meanings of numbers, learning the "wisdom of the Orient."

D'Annunzio was, further, a totally captivating personality, one of the few characters whose charm and charisma extended to both men and women. His success with women is legendary, but he also achieved great fame as a leader of men. It has been suggested that his romantic attraction was not limited to females and that he was, in fact, bisexual.[8] If true, it would be remarkable, for he had very few male friends and seems not to have been deeply involved even with his closest associates. The most important aspect of his relationship with men was his ability to convince them to follow him, an ability that was almost hypnotic. He cultivated conversation, always seeming to know the right words to win over an opponent or reinforce a wavering will. He had a prodigious memory for the most insignificant details and was able to remember an encounter years before with someone whom he had not seen in the interim. In his contacts with other men, D'Annunzio had a rare ability to convince his acquaintances that he was immensely concerned with their problems, fascinated by their stories, and involved in their lives.

In reality, his egotism was so great that his real feeling was invariably almost total indifference to other people.

If direct contact with D'Annunzio was hypnotic, what can be said about his powerful influence as an orator? D'Annunzio was one of the greatest public speakers in an age noted for its oratory. In addition to his great gift for language, D'Annunzio understood the way a human multitude functioned, and he worked on the crowd, shaped it, inspired it, until he had completely bent it to his will. D'Annunzio made the crowd an active element in his speeches, calling out to the people, asking them questions, calling for their participation. When he asked a crowd, "Are you prepared to sacrifice your lives for this great enterprise?" their screamed Yes echoed for miles. D'Annunzio likened the relationship between the speaker and the crowd to that between the artist and his creation. "The crowd contains a concealed beauty from which only the poet and the hero can obtain flashes [of inspiration]. When that beauty reveals itself in the unexpected noise that surges forth in the theater or the piazza or the trench, then a torrent of joy swells the heart of the man who has inspired it with his verse, his oratory, or his sword. The word of the poet communicated to the crowd, like the gesture of the hero, is therefore an act that creates an instantaneous beauty in the obscurity of the soul, just as a great sculptor can draw forth a divine statue from a block of stone. . . ."[9]

These lines were written in 1896, years before the poet became known as a great public speaker. As a matter of fact, D'Annunzio was talking about theater, not politics, and here the connection between D'Annunzio's notion of artistic creativity and his involvement in mass politics becomes clearer. There was no line of demarcation between the two realms for him, since great political leaders were by definition great artists, and great art served a political function by elevating the spirits of the people. When he attempted to create a new national theater for Italy around the turn of the century, he did so in part because he believed it would help create a new national consciousness. And, as the citizens of Vienna discovered, he carried his artistic flair into the practice of war.

As D'Annunzio effectively obliterated the boundary between art and politics, he similarly transcended the distinction between the sacred and the secular. D'Annunzio was deeply interested in the nature of the sacred. The language of his speeches and books reveals the extent to which he was functioning within a quasi-religious or mystical framework. One of the finest examples of this sort of D'Annunzian prose is "Italian Pentecost," written on 8 June 1919. The essay deals with the question of the redemption of Fiume, and D'Annunzio elevated Fiume to the status of a religious symbol: "'He breathed in their faces and said to them: receive the spirit.' This is the word of the apostle John. Today

Fiume breathes in the faces of all us Italians, it sets our faces ablaze with its breath, and it says to us: receive the flame. . . . Today we celebrate, in the glory of Fiume and in the glory of that young lion of Italy, the feast of the spirit."[10]

This is D'Annunzian oratory at its finest: a striking mixture of sacred and profane elements, invoking the emotional force of the sacred symbols, while linking them unexpectedly with more earthly tasks. The effect on his audience, thoroughly familiar with the Christian symbolism, was enormous. His voice was unusually beautiful, and he was able to deliver long speeches without losing his audience. Above all, as a dramatist he knew all the secrets of keeping the attention of a crowd, and he was indeed like an artist carving a sculpture out of a piece of rock when he spoke to thousands of people. He was so effective that the Italian government on more than one occasion forbade him to speak in public, fearing the effect he might have on national politics.

D'Annunzio's use of religious symbols in traditionally secular contexts enabled him to convince his allies that they were participants in a holy enterprise. Throughout his career, even before he became famous as a soldier or a political activist, D'Annunzio had divided the people of the world into two rough categories: those members of the spiritual elite who were his friends and allies, and those reprobates who opposed his will. This contrast became even clearer during the war, when the history of Italy was added to the realm of the sacred. The poet's greatest speech on behalf of intervention was a blasphemous parody of the Sermon on the Mount, the famous "Oration of Quatro":

> O blessed be those who have more, for more will they be able
>   to give, more ardent shall they be.
> Blessed be those who are twenty, chaste of mind, temperate of
>   body, whose mothers are brave.
> Blessed be those who, waiting and trusting, waste not their
>   strength but preserve it with a warrior's discipline.
> . . . .
> Blessed be the young who hunger and thirst for glory, for they
>   will be sated.
> . . . .
> Blessed be the pure of heart, blessed those victorious returning,
>   for they will see the youthful face of Rome, the brow recrowned
>   by Dante, Italy's triumphal beauty.[11]

This type of parody was properly regarded with antipathy by men of the cloth, but its cultural significance was nonetheless considerable. D'Annunzio was among the first to destroy the traditional boundaries between the religious and political spheres of Italian life, and he managed to create a new form of discourse in which the two elements

were fused together in a kind of political passion play. The emphasis
upon youth in the Quatro oration was also a theme that became very
important in D'Annunzian politics, for the contrast between the sacred
and the profane was often accompanied by a parallel division between
those who defended the old order and those who were prepared to
create a new, "young" world in the future. D'Annunzio, despite his
advancing age, spoke for the forces of national rejuvenation, and his
constant stress on vitality and virility, coupled with his own well-known
vigor, enabled him to pose as the leader of a youthful army. After his
seizure of Fiume, this often abstract notion became formalized in the
institution of the League of Fiume, an anti-League of Nations that
undertook to represent the interests of the young, emerging nations of
the world, which were coming out from underneath the oppression of
the colonial powers of an aging Western civilization.[12] D'Annunzio thus
became one of the first leaders of what we call today the Third World
revolution, although he did so in the name of his own peculiar brand of
cultural imperialism, for he was entranced by the idea of a revolution of
the oppressed peoples of the world under his own leadership.

Had it not been for the war, D'Annunzio might well have remained
an interesting and colorful figure of the Victorian era, but his exploits
in battle transformed him into something special. To be sure, he had
already demonstrated a great ability to make his fantasies come true,
but few expected that this would happen in the context of the Great
War. D'Annunzio had long dreamed of participating in a drama of
national heroism, of arousing his fellow Italians to greatness on the battlefield, and of protecting Italy against a barbarian invasion from the north.
The outbreak of the Great War gave him such an opportunity, and the
peculiarities of the leadership of the Italian forces enabled him to participate in the struggle in a unique way.

It was not easy for the poet to gain entry into the armed forces, and
it was rare for a man of fifty-two to serve at the front. Fortunately,
D'Annunzio was well connected, and he managed to pull enough strings
to get into a cavalry division. Soon thereafter he became a free-floating
spirit among all the armed forces, choosing, according to his whim, the
army, the navy, and the air forces for his exploits. The stories about his
actions during the war would fill a volume by themselves, but suffice it
to say that D'Annunzio amply lived up to his own expectations. He was
fearless, flying for hours through enemy antiaircraft fire, sailing for
hours in pitch darkness through enemy waters, sitting for hours in
trenches under heavy fire. Furthermore, he managed to transcend the
banality of the war by improvising exploits that were uniquely his own.
Following the flight over Vienna, the *Arbeiter Zeitung* ruefully asked
its readers if there were not any Austrian poets who might carry out

similarly adventurous raids over Italian cities.[13] The clearly negative answer only served to enhance D'Annunzio's growing reputation, and the Hapsburgs offered a special reward for the poet's capture or death.

By the war's end, D'Annunzio had become a legendary figure. Almost alone among the men of his time, he had not only created an exciting vision of life and of his role in the world but also managed to impose his own poetic vision upon reality itself. If this was not a definition of heroism, at least there were few at the time who could lay claim to the hero's mantle with credentials as good as his. Since the war had awakened dreams in the souls of many men, D'Annunzio became a national symbol for those who believed that the heroism born of war must find fulfillment within the nation.

D'Annunzio's political effectiveness derived from a variety of elements of his own personality. His love affairs made him a symbol of virility, a crucial element for success in the Latin political world. His use of language and his oratorical skill made him an effective campaigner and an inspirational leader. His exploits in the war made him a national hero. His poetic skill, further, was of the utmost importance in his political enterprises, for he created the symbols of the new politics of the postwar world.

This is not to say that D'Annunzio was composed entirely of the stuff of heroes. While his gifts were considerable, he also had substantial defects for a potential leader. In the first place, he was not a good-looking man, and as time passed he became uglier. His nose was bulbous, his eyes were too close together, and he had bad teeth. Indeed, his teeth were not only unpleasant to look at, but they caused D'Annunzio considerable suffering in his later years. Like so many of his countrymen, the poet did not believe in the usefulness of dentists, and he seems to have hardly ever visited one. The result was great pain and a mouth that contained ever fewer teeth. But his teeth were not his only pronounced physical defect, for D'Annunzio was very short, and completely bald by the time of the Fiume enterprise (the result of an over-zealous application of antiseptic to a scalp wound incurred in a duel). He evidently felt uncomfortable with his shiny pate, for his friends have written of an almost compulsive boasting of the beauty of his cranium. The skin was drawn so tightly over his skull that its "seams" were clearly visible, and he bragged of the uniqueness of this visual impression. He claimed to possess the most beautiful skull in the world and said that his own shining head would set a new style. In the world of the future, he suggested, all the "beautiful people" would be completely bald.[14]

The loss of an eye during the war greatly hindered D'Annunzio in public, and he was always careful to arrange the seating at his dinners so that he could survey the table with his one good eye. Further, the strain to which the good eye was subjected by long hours of work during the night produced frequent headaches, and the poet was often forced to rest for days on end until the pain abated enough for him to resume his labors.

Above all the obsessions of his life, D'Annunzio's constant pre-occupation with money was among the most celebrated. This is a curious thing to say about a man who lived for the most part in an opulent atmosphere, surrounded by elegance and a surfeit of material good; but while D'Annunzio never lacked for *things*, he almost never had any substantial financial resources. An inordinate amount of his time was spent in beating away his creditors, and he complained continually about his never-ending need for money. At one point, while he was in France in the early years of this century, the Italian government was forced to place his home and belongings on public auction to raise enough money to pay his bills. The situation did not change much during the course of his life. This is hardly the most propitious state of mind for one who would become a great political leader, although it might well account for a good deal of his energy. Anxiety over personal status is frequently linked to spiritual beliefs, and it may well be that D'Annunzio's compulsive drive to create a new state of spiritual values for his time was related to his endless anxiety over his fiscal condition.

THE DRAMATIST OF THE POSTWAR WORLD

After the war the king awarded D'Annunzio a gold medal for valor, and it is not an exaggeration to say that the poet could rightfully claim to be the symbol of his country's struggle in the war. His audience was guaranteed, and his influence was as great as that of any man in the Italian political arena. Predictably, at the end of the war, D'Annunzio became the focus of an extraordinary series of political maneuvers designed to place him at the center of attempts to seize control of Italy. As we shall see, representatives of virtually every political party and movement in the country approached him at one time or another, for D'Annunzio's politics were such as to permit almost anyone to imagine himself in league with the poet.

The problems that brought D'Annunzio to the center of the political stage were those produced by the Peace Conference that followed the war. Italy had entered the Great War with a carefully defined set of promises from her Allies, codified in the Treaty of London (a secret document that promised the Italians a series of territorial gains, mostly along her northeastern borders and on the Adriatic coast).[15] However, with the entry of the United States into the war, it became necessary for the participants to gain Wilson's approval for the projected peace settlement, and the American president refused to recognize the validity of such secret compacts as the Treaty of London. Consequently, the representatives of the victorious nations met at Versailles to reconsider the complicated question of dividing the spoils with Wilson holding a virtual veto power over the final settlement.

Like the other members of the victorious alliance, the Italians were enthusiastic supporters of America, and they felt considerably inferior to the Americans. Hence, Vittorio Emanuele Orlando, Sidney Sonnino, and their colleagues at Versailles, while trusting in the eventual benevolence of Wilson, hesitated to press their case with great vigor. The Italian diplomats at Versailles chose to delay discussing their territorial demands until the other, more important issues had been settled: the questions of Germany and the remains of the defunct Austro-Hungarian Empire. To their great chagrin, Wilson was utterly opposed to several of the concessions that had been granted the Italians in the Treaty of London, and when they attempted to discuss the question with the American representatives, they were unable to budge them from their position. Wilson believed that the entirety of the Adriatic coast, with the exception of Trieste, should be part of the new nation of Yugoslavia. Even worse, it became clear early on that the Americans simply did not trust the Italians, whose "image" in America was not the same as it was in D'Annunzio's fiery rhetoric. Most Americans, Wilson included, believed that Italians were untrustworthy and morally corrupt, that if they did not have criminal tendencies they were, at best, congenital liars. The America of Woodrow Wilson was the America of the Sacco and Vanzetti trial, and this America was hardly disposed to make significant concessions to Orlando's representatives at Versailles.[16]

This mixture of Italian diffidence and American suspicion and hostility produced serious diplomatic problems for the members of the Italian Foreign Ministry who were involved in the actual negotiations at Versailles. The problems were sufficiently severe to preclude any quick solution, and there were numerous other issues on the agenda that demanded the time and energy of the diplomats. To the Italian representatives, it was simply wise diplomacy to proceed cautiously, taking care to convince the Americans of the good intentions of Italy, and not precipitate a crisis.

The chances for a satisfactory settlement of Italy's claims were weakened by the rise of a new irredentist element within Italy, a group that demanded not only all of the territories promised by the Treaty of London but also a small town on the Western coast of Yugoslavia that had not been part of any of the treaties or proposals worked out before or during the conflict: Fiume. Ironically, the grounds for the Italian claim to Fiume were those advanced by Wilson to deny Italy's demands in Dalmatia: the right of the self-determination of peoples. For while the "Italianness" of the Adriatic coast around Split was dubious at best, it was possible to argue that the majority of the population of Fiume was Italian and wished to join the Italian nation; indeed, the government of the city had formally declared its desire to be annexed to Italy the previous autumn. The situation was further complicated by the fact that Fiume was under joint Allied occupation, and French, Italian, British, and American troops were quartered there pending the resolution of the question at Versailles.

As months passed, it became increasingly clear that Italy was having a difficult time convincing the Allies to cede territory along the Adriatic coast, whether the Italians claimed it by right of contract (the Treaty of London) or by right of self-determination (the case of Fiume). With the passage of time a wave of righteous indignation grew within the country. Had Italy not won the war? Was she not entitled to territorial rewards for her participation in the conflict? Why, then, was she being forced to behave like a beggar, pleading for crumbs from the tables of the rich nations of the West? The man who gave voice to these sentiments with the greatest passion and the greatest eloquence was D'Annunzio, who coined the impassioned slogan of the day: "Oh, victory, you shall not be mutilated."[17]

At first, D'Annunzio's rhetoric served the interests of Sonnino and Orlando, who remained firm in their demands at the peace tables. Like the poet, these statesmen believed that it would be disastrous for the country if they left Versailles without substantial rewards for the effort of the Great War. In particular, they feared serious domestic consequences, even a form of civil war, if Italian aims were frustrated by Wilson and the other Allies. Ironically, they feared such upheavals from men like D'Annunzio, impetuous enough to launch some mad scheme designed to overturn the peace. These fears were well grounded, for D'Annunzio had been sounding like a man loath to abandon his role of Italy's leading warrior. He was evidently yearning for some new and dramatic action, and he was deeply concerned over the destiny of Italy's Adriatic desires. This concern was voiced in an essay in January 1919 entitled "Letter to the Dalmatians." "Those of us who flew over Trieste, passing between fires, took possession of Trieste. Whoever challenged the inferno of Pola seized the port for Italy. He who directed the miracle of Premuda took command of the entire archipelago. . . . He who violated the Carnaro in the night of Buccari desired to fill the void in the Treaty of London. From the beginning to the end, I was of that breed. . . ."[18]

These heroic efforts, D'Annunzio said, should have been crowned by a triumphant peace, but instead Italy seemed to be suffocated by her victory. Indeed, this victory seemed to produce more problems than had the war itself. Above all, Italy now found herself facing a new enemy, and D'Annunzio portrayed his new opponent as the group that had been corrupted by Wilson's words and America's dollars. He warned his countrymen not to listen to those who counseled patience, moderation, and compromise. What peace, he asked, would finally be imposed upon the Italians? *"Pax gallica? Pax brittanica? Pax stelligera? Miserere nostri. . . ."* This, he insisted, was not the destiny for which so many had fought and died. Italy must have her own just peace, a Roman peace: "We fought for a greater Italy. We want a greater Italy. I say that we have prepared the mystic space for her ideal appearance."

As in all his great speeches and patriotic writings, D'Annunzio blended the political with the religious, creating a mixture of the two that was uniquely his own. It was, he said, for this "divine Italy" that he and his comrades had fought, and it was this divine Italy they now demanded at the peace tables of Versailles. "My comrades and I do not desire to be Italians in an Italy enfeebled by transatlantic purgatives from Doctor Wilson and amputated by the transalpine surgery of Doctor Clemenceau."[19]

These words were calculated to bring joy to the hearts of the Italian delegation at Versailles, but D'Annunzio made it clear that if Italy failed to emerge from the conference with the "divine Italy" duly safeguarded, he would take matters into his own hands. "I am ready today," he told the Dalmatian patriots to whom he addressed his message, "to sacrifice every love and friendship, every comfort to your cause . . . you will have me with you *to the end*. And you know what I mean by this promise."[20]

All Italy knew what he meant. The country was exhausted by war and anxious to return to a peacetime world. But there were many Italians who would not accept a peace of the sort Wilson envisaged. D'Annunzio was speaking not only for himself and other patriotic veterans of the war but also for a large and potent sector of the Italian political and industrial spheres. Should Orlando and Sonnino fail to obtain their goals in France, there were wealthy and powerful men who were prepared to support D'Annunzio, or others like him, who would simply take what they felt was rightfully theirs.

If the situation was alarming to a government that shared the annexationist desires of D'Annunzio and his allies, it was positively menacing to Francesco Saverio Nitti, who formed a new government in the middle of June. Nitti, who was no imperialist, believed that peace and tranquillity were far more important for his country than were islands in the Adriatic or control over the port and railroad lines of Fiume. Further, Nitti was terrified by the prospect of open conflict with America, particularly since the Americans had threatened to withdraw their support of the Italian lira.[21] If this were done, as the United States' representatives in Rome and Versailles had been at great pains to explain to the Italians, it was doubtful that American grain would continue to pour into Italy. Since many areas of the peninsula were already on the verge of starvation and since warehouses containing foodstuffs had already been the objects of rioting and sacking, these threats carried considerable weight.

Nitti thus found himself in a delicate position, forced to deal both with an America that was unwilling to permit Italy to feast off the spoils of the war and with a growing movement within his own country that threatened to take matters into its own hands if Nitti yielded to Wilson on questions concerning Dalmatia and Fiume. The Fiumans themselves proved to be able propagandists in their own behalf, and they managed to make Fiume into a great symbolic issue for the entire nation. By mid-summer of 1919, many Italians who had never heard of Fiume a year before had become convinced that the honor of their country was involved in the resolution of the Fiume question. D'Annunzio summarized these emotions on the twenty-fifth of April in a speech to thousands of ecstatic Venetians in Piazza San Marco: "'Today, the book is closed on all the maritime ports of the Dalmatian cities, on all the walls of that most ardent Fiume. If we reopen it, we will reopen it to the page where there is written, with the blood of Montello, with the blood of Vittorio Veneto, as it is over the gate of Rovigno: VICTORIA TIBI, MARCE. VICTORIA TIBI INTEGRA, ITALIA.' (Wild Applause)"[22]

The Stage

Fiume was a port of considerable strategic importance. By the time of the outbreak of the Great War, it was the major hub for the railroad lines leading to Belgrade, Prague, Budapest, and Zagreb, and was the natural outlet for commerce flowing between these cities and the West. D'Annunzio's City of the Holocaust was a commercial and industrial center of some importance in its own right, and one of the most prosperous cities in the Austro-Hungarian Empire.

Although Croatian domination would have been quite logical, given the location of Fiume, the city was in fact more often under Magyar influence. While the remoteness of Fiume's Hungarian governors gave the city a degree of independence it could hardly have achieved under Croatian domination, Magyar control also produced a virtually constant conflict with the Croats, an ongoing struggle for control that was one of the major themes of Fiuman history. On more than one occasion, the Croats occupied Fiume, but never for very long, and over the course of the eighteenth and nineteenth centuries the Fiumans managed to achieve a unique judicial status within the Dual Monarchy: while formally part of Hungary, Fiume was considered to be a *corpus separatum*, a separate political body, for many of its functions.

A brief survey of the history of the city helps to understand many of the attitudes that Fiumans carried into the postwar world.[1] In 1717 the Emperor Charles VI created two free ports for the empire: Trieste and Fiume. His intention was that Trieste would serve as the main port for commercial communication with the north and the west, while Fiume would serve the south and the east. To that end, new roads were built linking Fiume with Budapest, and during the course of the century, Fiume substantially expanded both its population and its commercial activity. Toward the end of the century, the Empress Maria Theresa granted Fiume the special status of *corpus separatum* upon which the

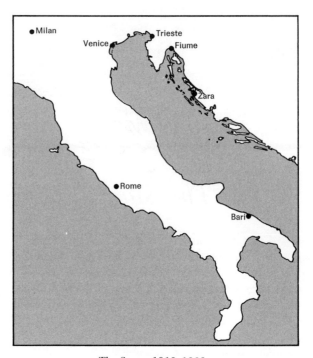

The Stage, 1919–1920

city eventually based its claim to self-determination. The last quarter of the eighteenth century was one of the best periods in the city's history, for it was then that the first major expansion of the port took place, that shipbuilding became a major industry, and that the city expanded outside the old Roman walls. This happy period came to a violent end when Napoleon's armies marched across Italy. With the substitution of the Napoleonic Code for the Hungarian laws that had theretofore governed the city's affairs, Fiume lost not only her special political status but also the economic benefits that stemmed from her status as a free port. Commercial activity dropped sharply, and Fiume continued to suffer, even after the end of the occupation in the summer of 1813, when the French were replaced by the Austrians. This unhappy situation ended in 1822, when Fiume was returned to Hungarian hands, and for the next quarter-century Fiume resumed a regular rhythm of growth and commercial development.

The year 1848, which was a major turning point for much of Western Europe, had great significance for Fiume as well, for it marked the beginning of the city's one long period of Croatian domination, which lasted until 1867. Hungarian rule had been unusually benevolent; the closest

Hungarian city lay more than two hundred miles away, and so the Hungarians were content to exploit the financial growth of the city without attempting to transform its basic character. The Croatians were a different breed and, having more ambitious programs for Fiume than the Hungarians ever had, represented a far greater menace to the traditions of the city. The Croatians wished to change Fiume into a Croatian post, impose the Croatian language on the town, change the educational system, and transform the city's literary and cultural activities into Slavic ones. The period from 1848 to 1867 was one of intense rivalry and conflict between two groups: Fiumans and those Croatians who wished to retain a previous heritage, and the Croatians who wished to annex Fiume to the Croatian nation.

The resolution of the conflict over Fiume was achieved in 1868 by one of the most fascinating documents in modern history: the *Kriptic*. This document, ostensibly a compromise between the Hungarian and Croatian governments, was drafted in two versions: one, in Hungarian, was presented to the Hungarian Parliament; the other, in Croatian, was submitted to the Croatian Diet. Surprisingly enough, the two versions differed in one fundamental detail: in the Croatian version the question of the control of Fiume was left unresolved (pending future negotiations), while in the Hungarian version Fiume was declared a "special body connected to the Hungarian Crown." Understandably, each parliament signed its respective treaty, being well satisfied with the arrangements as they appeared in the text. However, when the two versions went to Emperor Franz Joseph for his signature, a piece of paper (the *Kriptic*) containing a Croatian translation of the Hungarian claim to Fiume had been pasted over the Croatian version. The superiority of Hungarian arms and wealth guaranteed that their control of Fiume would endure.

In order to maintain their sway over Fiume, the Hungarians needed to provide for the likelihood of conflict with the Croats, for the Magyars could hardly hope to supply the city from a distance of over two hundred miles through hostile territory. They had to find some way to supply the city by sea, and to this end they embarked upon a campaign of luring Italian businessmen into the city. This served a dual function: in addition to giving the Hungarians Western allies, the influx of fairly well-to-do Italians created a solid anti-Croatian middle class committed to the defense of the city against its Slavic neighbors. The result of this policy was to add a new dimension to the conflict between Fiume and Croatia, since a class antagonism was added to the traditional political, economic, and ethnic tensions. Fatally, the ethnic conflict was mirrored in the class structure of the city—the working class of Fiume was largely composed of Croats, while the Italians tended to be part of the active bourgeoisie. The separation between Italian-speakers and Croats was physical as well, for the majority of the city's workers lived in the Croatian burgh of Sussak and commuted daily to their jobs in Fiume.

These various aspects of the struggle for control of the city came to a head in the area of culture and education. Whereas the Hungarians had tended to let the citizens of Fiume choose the language of their schools, the Croats were much more chauvinistic. Furthermore, from the Italian point of view, the matter took on a religious dimension. The Italian language had been introduced into the city's schools by the Jesuits, who retained control over the religious education of the Italian-speaking population. Croatian attempts to eliminate Italian schools from Fiume thus represented an attack against a religious tradition.

THE ECONOMY OF FIUME

The easiest yardstick against which to measure the economic development of Fiume is that of the growth of her sister-city on the Adriatic, Trieste. Both were major ports of the Austro-Hungarian Empire, and both depended on commerce as their major source of income. Yet Trieste quickly became highly successful, constantly expanding its industry and commerce, while Fiume went through long periods of stagnation. The difference between the two cities was fundamental: whereas Trieste was blessed with a local community capable of financing and carrying through programs of change and modernization, Fiume lacked the local initiative and the necessary capital for such undertakings. As a result, fundamental operations such as the modernization of the harbor and the expansion of industry depended almost exclusively on foreign investment. This meant that, in practice, the development of Fiume as a modern port depended upon Hungarian initiative.

Hungarian aid was indeed forthcoming in the period following the *Kriptic*, and Fiume was quickly equipped to handle modern shipping. This was desperately needed, as the city had fallen far behind in the modernization of her port, the capacity of her docks, and the development of modern machinery to load the newer, bigger ships; indeed, as of 1869 Fiume had not registered a single steamship.[2] The change in regime was highly propitious for Fiuman fortunes. Between 1869 and 1881 the tonnage of steamship traffic in the harbor increased seven times over and the number of ships using the port tripled. The successful expansion of Fiuman commerce was largely due to two factors: the modernization of the port facilities themselves, and the city's free port status. Further, starting in 1880, the Hungarian government launched a program to increase sea traffic in Fiume by creating a new international shipping company called the Adria, which was composed of English, Scottish, and Viennese companies that undertook to guarantee an increased tempo of steamship traffic in and out of Fiume in return for a substantial cash reward from the Hungarian government. The Adria was the first step in the creation of the Hungarian merchant marine, and it produced significant benefits for the city.[3]

With the exception of the port activities, the entire Fiuman economy was given a much-needed transfusion of money and energy, and the city began to take on aspects of a significant industrial center. By the early twentieth century it had become the site of the most important torpedo works in the empire, as well as of a major chemical plant, a refinery for mineral oils, a tobacco factory, a rice company, and other industrial installations. Shipbuilding continued apace, and in the booming years that preceded the First World War, over two thousand workers were employed in the shipyards. Unemployment was virtually nonexistent, and the life of Fiuman workers was greatly to be envied, thanks to the remarkably humane tradition of social security administered from Budapest. Not only were the workers of Fiume provided with health insurance, old-age pensions, and medical care, but this amazing Hungarian bureaucracy undertook to give its citizens the benefit of its own mistakes. There is an account, guaranteed to warm the heart of even the most cynical observer of the modern world, of a Fiuman worker who was erroneously awarded a pension substantially greater than he deserved. This happy soul continued to collect payments for a number of years, after which time the error was discovered. To his great delight, the Hungarian authorities decided to continue the payments at their previous level, because the pensioner "had already based the tenor of his life on the higher income, and to give him a dramatically lower sum as a result of an error he had not made would be considered an unjust and anti-social treatment . . . ."[4]

The shipyard owners provided housing for many of their workers, building modern apartments on the hillsides overlooking the port and offering them to employees at reasonable rents. In addition, the city's sanitary and hygienic facilities were unusually well developed for the period; virtually every house contained a toilet by the time of the Great War and some forty percent of the houses had baths. By law, all apartments constructed after 1912 were required to have either a bath or a shower,[5] a requirement that was only instituted in Italy well after the Second World War. One of the major results of the quality of life in Fiume was a low level of social violence.

In addition to serving as a major Hungarian commercial port, Fiume was also used as an exit for Hungarian emigrants, primarily those headed for North America. By 1910, some twenty to thirty thousand persons passed through Fiume each year on their way to the New World. In order to facilitate this massive exodus, the government built an "Emigrants' House" in the city, capable of housing two thousand people. This constant passage of emigrants heightened the Magyar flavor of the city and emphasized the growing presence of the Hungarians in Fiume. What had once been a relatively distant and benevolent force in Fiuman affairs was taking on a new, often oppressive, aspect for the Italian-speaking population.

THE CONFLICT OVER FIUME

The success of the Hungarian initiatives and the separation of Fiume from her Croatian neighbors ironically produced a situation of heightened tension between Italians and Hungarians and led to a struggle over the "character" of the city. Since Fiume's growth was primarily due to the policies of her distant rulers, Fiuman claims to independence became increasingly less convincing. Further, the flourishing trade of the city increased Hungarian activity and inevitably enhanced Magyar control. As the city grew, the government in Budapest took a greater interest in its affairs and attempted to integrate it more completely into the Hungarian world. The extent of this attempted assimilation was evident in the city's educational system, which revealed a dramatic bias in favor of a Hungarian-speaking elite.[6]

In 1910 there were fourteen elementary schools in Fiume, of which two were solely Hungarian-speaking and the remainder were Italian. There was not a single school in which classes were conducted in Croatian, and indeed, even when the fifteen-thousand-odd Croats who resided in Fiume requested a school (to be paid for out of their own funds), the governors of the city rejected the plea. At the secondary school level, the true nature of Fiuman society became evident: of the seven secondary schools, six were conducted in Hungarian, and the seventh was Italian. The implications of this distribution are only too clear: while the Italians were permitted to educate their children in their native language, the members of the city's ruling class had to speak Hungarian. Further, no weight was to be given to the substantial Croatian population of Fiume, which was presented with the simple choice of assimilating into a Hungarian- and Italian-speaking society or being effectively excluded from the possibilities of social advancement.

The Croatians had good reason to feel outraged by these policies, since they had constituted a majority of the city's population for a long period and were a minority group only because of the separation of Fiume from Sussak. In 1851, nearly the entire population of Fiume (roughly 12,600 persons) was Croatian, while the census of 1910 showed that of the nearly fifty thousand residents of the city some twenty-four thousand were Italians, fifteen thousand were Croats, and the remainder were members of other nationalities. If Sussak had been counted as part of Fiume, the Croats would have made up a majority of the population.[7]

The bias in favor of Hungarian-speaking members in Fiume's ruling class was, however, clearly justified by the city's economic activities, which were almost exclusively directed toward the wealth and enterprise of Budapest. Although a majority of the population of Fiume spoke Italian, they maintained very few ties with the "mother country." In 1913, for example, of the nearly eight thousand ships that passed through the harbor of the city, just over two hundred flew the Italian flag. In the same year, of the nearly three million tons of merchandise handled in port, only about one hundred fifty thousand came from Italy.[8] As time passed Hungarian forces replaced indigenous elements within the city's political and legal structures, and by the early twentieth century both policemen and governors came largely from Budapest or were closely tied to the Magyars.

The government of Fiume was entrusted to a Magyar governor, assisted by a Municipal Council composed of many of the city's most influential and wealthy citizens. As in the city's schools, Fiuman government accurately reflected the successful Hungarian-Italian alliance that had led to the wave of prosperity and success on which the city was happily riding. In the words of an English observer, "the elections to [the Municipal Council] were manipulated in such a way that it became nothing more or less than a coalition of Magyar bureaucrats and small Italian capitalists."[9] This coalition, however, barely covered the internal conflict, for the Italian businessmen involved in Fiume's thriving commerce were frequently resentful of the Hungarians who passed the city's laws and administered the city's policies. There had already been a certain Italian chauvinism during the period when Fiuman autonomy had been threatened only by the Croats, and this hyperpatriotism grew stronger when the Magyars came to be viewed in the same light as their Slavic neighbors.

The introduction of this Hungarian "presence" in Fiume was a relatively late development, and it was viewed by the Italians in the city as the intrusion of a "foreign" body into their midst. During the early years of the century, there were numerous patriotic demonstrations emphasizing Fiuman ties with Italy. In the fall of 1908, for example, a large deputation left Fiume for Ravenna for a celebration in honor of Dante, and only three years earlier a group of patriots had created the *Giovine Fiume* ("Young Fiume") association, which would subsequently play a major role in the D'Annunzian coup of 1919.[10]

Understandably, the Italophiles in Fiume attempted to enhance the cultural life of the Italian community. To this end they founded libraries, literary circles, and theater groups dedicated to keeping Italian culture alive in the newly hostile atmosphere of Hungarian Fiume, and they began to talk about a project that had theretofore been unthinkable: the annexation of Fiume by Italy. As a counterforce to the virtual Hungarian monopoly on higher education in the city, they organized a popular university in which Italian was the official language, as well as numerous theatrical performances that became occasions for demonstrations of loyalty to Italy. So intensely patriotic were these dramatic presentations that, in the words of one historian of the city's theater, in the twentieth century theatrical activities became "an arm of defense. The voice of Italy reached Fiume through the theatre."[11]

It was, then, quite appropriate that the great Italian dramatist and irredentist Gabriele D'Annunzio should come to Fiume in 1907 to read from his highly nationalistic work, *La Nave*. The symbolism of his visit to Fiume was clear: the Italian citizens of Fiume were determined to maintain their own identity among an alien culture, and they were delighted that one of the most outspoken representatives of Italian culture was willing to lend his active collaboration to this enterprise.

By the eve of the Great War the relations between Hungarians and Italians in Fiume were very poor, producing a situation akin to those in many European colonies on the verge of demanding liberation from their former masters. In 1913 Italian patriots exploded a bomb outside the Municipal Palace, shattering the windows and blasting chunks of stone out of the walls. Unable to find the perpetrators of this gesture, the Hungarians hired their own "conspirators" to explode another bomb outside the palace and to leave "evidence" connecting the incident to the Italian patriotic groups in the city. This was preparatory to a series of repressive actions against the Italians, including the nullification of the results of municipal elections and the elimination of patriotic elements the Hungarian authorities considered undesirable. The sordid enterprise was fortunately exposed before the Hungarians had time to fully enforce their plans for the repression of the Italian forces, but many Fiumans were forced to seek refuge in Italy.[12]

Not surprisingly, the political parties in Fiume became increasingly preoccupied with the issue of the sovereignty of the city, and in the years before the war both of the major political organizations—the Autonomist Party and the Workers' Socialist Party—grew increasingly pro-Italian in their orientation. In the last elections held before the onset of hostilities, Riccardo Zanella, the leader of the Autonomist Party, was elected mayor. This was clearly not acceptable to the Magyar governors in the hostile climate of the first years of the war, and in 1915, soon after the elections, the emperor nullified the results and substitued a figure more sympathetic to Budapest: Francesco Gilberto Corossacz, whose name accurately reflects his political alignment.

The Fiumans protested against this arbitrary treatment of their political desires, only to find the Hungarians prepared to escalate the conflict. With the onset of war, Zanella was among the first men drafted into the Hungarian army, and he had the good fortune to be captured by the Russians. He was eventually transferred to Italy, where he continued his agitation on behalf of Fiuman autonomy.[13] While Zanella was blessed with extraordinarily good luck, his fellow citizens were not so fortunate. In the summer of 1915 the Municipal Council was dissolved by imperial decree, and a new governing body was elected along with a new mayor, Antonio Vio. This body was remarkably representative of the political forces of the city, but it was under terrible pressure from the Hungarians and Croats to keep the local population under control. At the same time that the Hungarians were manipulating the political leadership of the city, they were threatening to starve it to death if anti-Hungarian activities continued.[14] As one might have expected, the Croats in the surrounding area (Sussak, Grobniko, and Castua) were only too happy to join in this grim enterprise, and enforced an economic and food boycott on Fiume.

Thus the new Municipal Council, effectively installed from above, had to deal with an alarming series of political, economic, and alimentary problems that threatened the existence of the city. Under the circumstances, it is remarkable that the ruling group not only managed to navigate the treacherous waters in which they found themselves but also succeeded in putting together a council that was fairly representative of the diverse elements that formed political life in Fiume. Socialists and autonomists joined with pro-Hungarian representatives to keep a steady hand on Fiume's rudder, and the city eventually emerged from the conflict headed by a group of politicians who were intimately familiar with the problems and personalities of the city.

The war, then, served to catalyze the Italian revolt that had been brewing for several decades. While the conduct of hostilities brought the commercial activities of Fiume to a virtual standstill, the outcome of the struggle seemed a blessing to the Italophiles. With the destruction of the Hapsburg Empire and the triumph of Italian forces in the Veneto, the prospects for Fiume seemed excellent. Yet, as had been true so often before, the elimination of one of the traditional enemies of Fiuman autonomy simply brought the other into stark relief. With the dissolution of Hungarian control of Fiume, the Croatians—now part of a new Yugoslavian nation and aided by French allies—moved to assert their "historic" claims to the city.

THE POSTWAR CRISIS

The war brought an end to the Hapsburg Empire, and a new coterie of nations emerged with its passing. Those Fiumans who had asserted their right to self-determination in the days before the dissolution of the empire might have expected their demands to fall on sympathetic ears among the victorious Allies, but in fact they did not, and Fiume found itself confronted by an ancient enemy, the Croats. The sequence of events that followed the collapse of the empire is hotly contested by pro-Italian and pro-Yugoslav writers,[15] but in its basic outlines, the story seems fairly clear.

On the evening of the 28 October, Zoltan Jekelfalussy, the Hungarian governor of Fiume, called Mayor Antonio Vio to his office to give him the news that the president of the council of ministers in Budapest had decided that Fiume was to be abandoned both militarily and politically. Jekelfalussy therefore advised the mayor of the situation and prepared to leave. Vio immediately met with the other members of the municipal government, who took the interesting step of declaring Vio the mayor of Fiume by "will of the people." The reasoning behind this move was important in future debates over the sovereignty of Fiume. It was felt by several members of the Municipal Council that Vio, having been appointed by the Hungarians, could no longer base his right to authority on his appointment by a power that no longer existed in its previous form. Given the vogue of the doctrine of self-determination of peoples, the Municipal Council, as the incarnation of the general will of Fiume, reappointed Vio and at the same time confirmed its own members in office. The following day the Municipal Council was expanded to some sixty members.

The same day that the Municipal Council of Fiume was expanding its ranks, representatives of the newly created Yugoslavian National Council arrived in the city and wrested command of the Governor's Palace from Jekelfalussy. By evening, the Croatian flag was flying from the palace, despite the claims of Vio and the Municipal Council to be the rightful governors of Fiume. The city now had two self-proclaimed governments, each basing its claim on the same principle.

The culmination of the maneuvers between the two groups came on the thirtieth. Early in the morning, a substantial body of Croatian troops entered Fiume, and Dr. Rojvecvic, the Croatian commissioner, forbade all public meetings in the interest of order and the safety of the citizenry. Notwithstanding this attempt to suppress any possible show of strength by the Italians, the Municipal Council met that same morning, transformed itself into the Italian National Council of Fiume and declared its intention to resist the Croatians. Finally, basing its action on the right of self-determination of peoples, the National Council announced that Fiume was henceforth united with its "mother country, Italy." Early in the afternoon a mass rally was held in the streets just off the central piazza of the town, where the representatives of the National Council read proclamations declaring Fiume part of Italy. At the same time these public demonstrations were taking place, representatives of the council were on their way to Rome and to the headquarters of the Third Army, seeking support for their actions.

The Italian National Council was not the only new group organized in Fiume in the hours immediately following the dissolution of the Hapsburg Empire. While the National Council was arrogating to itself the right to formulate the will of the people of Fiume, a multinational workers' council was being created.[16] This group called for a plebiscite to determine the future of Fiume and urged that every adult who had lived in the city for at least a year be permitted to participate in this historic decision. Such a process, in the eyes of the workers' council, would not only ensure the right of the citizens of Fiume to choose their own destinies but would also provide for a much-needed democratization of the political life of Fiume. The National Council was drawn almost exclusively from the wealthier strata of the city's society. For this reason, despite the presence of many figures of undoubted quality and honesty, the self-proclaimed governing body of the city was, and would remain, a class-bound institution, unpopular with the Italian workers because it refused to deal reasonably with their demands, and opposed by the non-Italian population because of its explicit opposition to granting the Croats an active role in the city's affairs. The workers' council, which had recognized the necessity of facing the "ethnic problem" by creating a multinational governing body, was quickly driven into the background of Fiuman politics by the far more powerful competing Italian and Croatian groups. Even at the outset, the force of numbers was against the workers' council: no more than thirty-odd citizens participated in the group at its inception. The National Council, with twice that number and a more influential membership, carried the day.

The character of the men who composed the National Council of Fiume is extremely difficult to determine at a distance of over half a century. To some observers,[17] these men were dedicated patriots actively involved in an attempt to save Fiume from her Slavic enemies. To others, they were a clique of wealthy citizens who were simply looking for the best financial settlement of the city's affairs and who chose to ally themselves with Italy rather than with the new Yugoslavia because the former position looked more attractive economically. To still others, they were "well known Croatian renegades who made no scruple of turning their coats to suit the times."[18] The truth is rather more complicated, for while there is no doubt that the majority of the members of the National Council had very few scruples about the company they kept, it is also clear that the identification most of them made with Italy represented considerably more than an opportunistic desire to side with their stronger neighbor. The decades of struggle with Hungary and Croatia had produced a genuine pro-Italian sentiment in the city, and even men with names like Grossich and Corosac considered themselves linked to the destiny of Italy by ties of blood and tradition. The decision to proclaim Fiume part of Italy could hardly have been one of cold calculation, for there were far more lucrative alternatives available to the National Council in the fall of 1918. They explicitly opposed the most attractive of these: to proclaim Fiume a Free City and demand that the League of Nations give the necessary guarantees and aid to establish a viable commercial center that could draw on the wealth of Fiume's immediate neighbors and the wealthy and powerful nations who would dictate the policies of the league. Instead, the National Council sent representatives to Paris, Rome, and Budapest to advise all and sundry that Fiume wished to be part of Italy and would exert all her energies to that end.[19]

Following the events of 28, 29, and 30 October, it was clear that while the Italian National Council might well be able to proclaim its allegiance to Italy, in the end the matter was likely to be resolved militarily. On the twenty-ninth, the council constituted a National Guard for the city, which was armed with a hoard of rifles and pistols that had been collected (mostly from Austrian deserters) during the course of the war.[20] The pro-Italian elements had collected some eight or nine hundred rifles for such an eventuality, and even after supplying the National Guard there were enough arms left over to equip a "Red Guard,"[21] which the National Council created in early November. This body, which had been called for by the socialists and the workers' council, was given the job of supervising the public warehouses, with their substantial food supplies, and maintaining public order. The Red Guard lasted only a couple of weeks; the Inter-Allied Command dissolved it on 18 October, when the Allies assumed responsibility for the tranquillity of the city.

With each passing day, more Serbian and Croatian troops entered Fiume, and the National Council sought to obtain the help of the Italian Army to defend its interests. This was no easy matter, for communications with Italy were difficult. The council set up a radio transmitter on top of the highest hill in the city but received no answer to its frantic appeals for Italian military intervention. Since the roads were blocked by a variety of troops, it decided to send out two groups of men (later, in the lore of Fiume, known as the Argonauts) in small boats toward Venice in an effort to enlist the support of the Italian Navy.[22]

The Argonauts succeeded in their mission. Upon hearing the Fiuman request, Admiral Thaon de Revel wired to Rome for instructions, citing two good reasons for proceeding to the defense of the Italian elements in Fiume: citizens of undoubted Italian origin felt themselves threatened by hostile elements, and there were several excellent ships in the harbor that might become war prizes if Italy took control of the area.[23] Orlando's response has unfortunately been lost, but whatever his reasoning, an Italian warship, accompanied by four torpedo-boat destroyers steamed into the harbor on 4 November, to the jubilant welcome of the Italian citizens of Fiume.

The arrival of the *Emanuele Filiberto* under the command of Admiral Rainer gave the Fiumans reason to believe that Italy had decided to support the demand for annexation, but this was not the case. As events would demonstrate, the Italian government was indeed interested in control of Fiume, but it was not prepared to risk direct conflict with Italy's wartime allies in order to achieve it. Rainer entered the harbor and announced that he had come to protect the Italian nationals in the city and to ensure that Italy's interests would be safe. Beyond that, no substantive action was taken or, evidently, contemplated by the admiral. The sailors remained on board, no challenge was made to the Croatian authorities, and no formal support was given to the Italian National Council. Further, when the French torpedo-boat destroyer *Touareg* arrived in port the following day, Rainer welcomed it as part of the Allied Army, despite the obvious pro-Croatian intentions of the French. For the next two weeks Rainer remained in the city, with his troops garrisoned in their ships, waiting for orders from Rome. During this period Fiume became an international armed camp, as soldiers under French command poured into the city and its environs to protect the Yugoslav interests against the Italians, and American and British ships entered the harbor to make sure that events did not escape their control. Daily life in Fiume was characterized by a series of hostilities between the conflicting factions, and hardly a day passed without some encounter between pro-Slavic and pro-Italian elements.

The two weeks between 4 November and 17 November were highly revealing to those who were looking for the pattern of the postwar world, for during this period the conflict over Fiume was transformed from a struggle between local elements into an international conflict between the victorious powers of the Great War. What had begun as a fight between Italian and Croatian forces, who had traditionally contested the sovereignty of the city, soon became a conflict between France and Italy. The French, as "protectors" of a newly emerging Yugoslavia, proclaimed the justice of the demand for a Yugoslav Fiume, while Italy insisted that tradition and the national make-up of the city logically made it part of the "new" Italy. Since conflicts of this sort could only be resolved by the Peace Conference of the Allies at Versailles, the matter was finally put in a tense limbo by the decision to place the city under the control of *all* the Allies. Accordingly, on 17 November, Italian and American troops entered Fiume, and General Di Marzano assumed control of the city on behalf of the Allies. The Croatian governor was asked to leave, as were the Croatian troops that had been garrisoned there. In short order the city was effectively under Italian command, with a token force from the other Allied powers. This situation lasted only a couple of days, however, as the French asked General Tranie to establish a base in Fiume for the Franco-Serbian Army of the Orient. When the Italians heard of this plan, they countered by sending General Francesco Saverio Grazioli, one of the heroes of the battle of Vittorio Veneto, to Fiume, as commander in chief of the Italian and Allied forces. Grazioli could claim his command by dint of seniority. Indeed, one cynical observer has claimed that the Italians had a trump up their sleeve in the event that one of the other Allies attempted to send a general with higher seniority than Grazioli to Fiume. "So determined were they to retain supremacy in this area of Fiume that they even went so far as to quarter a very senior General, *viz.*, Caneva, in the background of the palace, whose sole *raison d'être* was to step forward in the event of any Allied General senior to General Grazioli being posted to the town. His presence was a source of constant amusement to the Allies, who referred to him as 'the man in the cellar.'"[24]

There is no trace of General Caneva in the Italian documents of the Allied occupation of Fiume, and while Italian preoccupations with seniority were very real, it is likely that "the man in the cellar" was the creation of the overactive imaginations of non-Italian participants in the affair. Nonetheless, the ability of the other Allied officers to believe in the hypothesis provides an accurate insight into the state of mind of many of the Allies. For the most part they were convinced that since Orlando and Sonnino were so passionately committed to the Fiuman cause, the Italian government was firmly in control of events in Fiume. Once this notion had been accepted, it followed that the actions of the Italian National Council were orchestrated from Rome and that the various maneuvers of the Italians in Fiume to achieve the annexation of the city were carried out in concert with the moves of Italy's foreign diplomats. In fact this was not true. Not only was the Italian National Council not acting in concert with the Italian government, but General Grazioli was given explicit orders not to recognize its authority in any way. Furthermore, there was considerable trepidation in Rome that the Italians in Fiume might seize too much initiative and precipitate a crisis too grave to be successfully manipulated by Italian diplomacy. For this reason, Grazioli was told to watch the National Council very carefully in order to prevent any act that "did not conform to the interests of the Italian State."[25]

While the Italian government correctly believed the National Council to be a volatile group, it also recognized the advantages its existence gave to Italy in the conduct of her negotiations with the other Allies. Grazioli was accordingly advised to keep in mind that "the formal existence of an elected authority of secure Italian faith may become of great utility should it become necessary to demonstrate to foreign powers that Fiume, by free choice, wishes to become Italian."[26]

THE "COLD WAR" OVER FIUME

Between November 1918 and September of the following year, a well-financed conspiracy to seize Fiume was organized by nationalistic elements in Italy in collaboration with Fiuman leaders. The growth of this movement was due to the failure to resolve the Fiume question satisfactorily in the intervening months. Consequently, the citizens of Fiume found themselves living under intense pressure and in an increasingly desperate economic condition. These factors themselves derived from the maneuvers of the major powers, each seeking to gain some sort of leverage over Fiume.

The story of the struggle for control over Fiume among the four major powers is essential to an understanding of later events and thus must be explored briefly. All the Allies were aware of the importance of the port of Fiume. One need not even look into the archives of these nations to find a sensitivity to Fiume's strategic importance; the British *Shipbuilding and Shipping Record* of 1 May 1919 asserted that "British shipbuilders cannot ignore the Italian crisis. The question of the Italianness of Fiume is an international one. As an ocean port for the Balkans . . . inhabited by populations which tend to grow more rapidly than their merchant marines, that port offers a promising traffic for British shipping. . . . Already before the War it was not easy to deal with the Italian authorities; now that their ambition to have a national navy has been awakened, foreign competition will certainly not be welcomed. . . ."[27]

For all their interest in getting a share of Fiume trade, British shippers were not particularly interested in obtaining political control of Fiume; it was sufficient for them that Italy be prevented from achieving a monopoly over commerce in the port. Consequently, the British were amenable to a variety of solutions to the problem. The same was true for the Americans; many solutions were possible, but not that of turning control of Fiume over to the Italians. The situation was more complicated for the French.[28] They were not so much interested in dominating the commerce of a single city on the Adriatic coast as they were in establishing their own position as the most zealous "protectors" of the new nations emerging from the ruins of the old Hapsburg Empire. French foreign policy was actively directed toward the manipulation of the Balkan states, and Fiume was consequently of two-fold importance to Paris. In the first place, it served as a base for supplying the Franco-Serbian Army of the Orient. Secondly, the French hoped that Fiume would become the most important Adriatic port of a nation that France could influence to her own advantage. From the beginning, France was committed to the struggle with Italy for control of Fiume, and on several occasions the conflict became an armed one. The dispatches from Fiume to Rome leave no doubt about Italian fears of open conflict with France and her Yugoslav allies,[29] and throughout the period from the end of 1918 to the D'Annunzian march on the city the following September, the conflict between Italians and Frenchmen continued unabated.

By December, the essential nature of the Franco-Italian conflict in Fiume, which is contained in its broad outlines in the dispatches sent by General Grazioli to Rome, was clear. Grazioli's most telling observation toward the end of the month was purely numerical: the French were making certain that they would have the same number of troops in and around Fiume as the Italians had. This was not only alarming from a purely strategic point of view, but it also posed enormous problems for Grazioli as supervisor of public order. He did not know where to garrison all the newly arrived Frenchmen and Vietnamese (who constituted a large part of the Army of the Orient), and the constant influx threatened to produce outbursts in the streets. In addition, several thousand Serbian troops had been transported through the city from an English ship, when high seas and bad weather had made it impossible for them to reach Belgrade by other routes. Furthermore, Grazioli was convinced that the French were determined to replace the Italians as the occupying force in the city, possibly by bringing in one of their own generals with greater seniority than he had. His comment in a letter of 20 December that General "Franchet d'Esperey . . . is about to arrive in Fiume on the pretext of an inspection tour" reflects that conviction.[30]

These stratagems by the French led Grazioli to believe that there was a serious chance of an outbreak of hostilities, "given the hostile attitude of the newly created Yugoslav Army." Grazioli did not think that a new war would be touched off by the French or Yugoslav leaders, but he feared the former Austrian officers who were now in command positions in the Yugoslav Army. Grazioli had accordingly prepared plans for the defense of Fiume, and he was greatly alarmed at the steadily increasing number of French troops who would become allies of the Slavs in the event of war.

But quite apart from the possibility of open conflict, there was a more subtle battle going on between Frenchmen and Italians. Grazioli complained of finding himself in a position unworthy of Italy's dignity and contrary to Italian desires to maintain high prestige among the Fiuman population. "With all the honor of the Inter-Allied command, we are reduced to using an Italian general as the policeman to maintain public order, while the Allies have full freedom to do whatever they wish at our expense . . . it is clear that their action is hostile to us, since in recent days there has been proletarian and socialist agitation here, which never existed before. This was created by the provocation of certain agents who were very probably put up to the action by those who wish to disturb the splendid disposition of the local population. . . ."[31]

No foreign agents were needed to produce socialist and proletarian agitation in Fiume, where a workers' council and a proletarian army had been organized long before Grazioli's arrival. However, his fundamental complaint, that he was powerless to act against anti-Italian agitation, was indeed justified, for he was explicitly forbidden to take any political action. Further, he quickly found himself effectively cut off from the Slavic hinterland, since the French monopolized the telegraph and telephone lines from Fiume to Belgrade and Budapest.[32] Grazioli was convinced that these lines were being used by the Slavs to "pass orders from the Yugoslav government to the local Croatian population and authorities."

On 21 December, Grazioli implored his government to authorize him to launch a pro-Italian campaign among the local citizenry in order to combat the French propaganda and the Yugoslav plots. Grazioli's commanding officer, the Duke of Aosta, was quick to endorse his request.[33]

There was considerable justice to Grazioli's observations, and there is little to be said for the morality of the French troops and *agents provocateurs* who attempted to provoke conflicts in Fiume. At the same time, such complaints, and the tone of righteous indignation that so often accompanied them, were ill-suited to a member of an occupying army that was itself attempting to exploit the conflict between Italy and Yugoslavia for its own ends. In Fiume, as throughout Dalmatia, Italian troops ruthlessly and violently imposed Italian rule and Italian culture on native populations that were often opposed to them. The tactics that Grazioli found so vile when employed by the French in Fiume were the same tactics used by Italians in Zara, Split, and other coastal towns and islands along the Adriatic, at the expense of the Slavs. By the summer of 1919, of thirty-three communities in Dalmatia under Italian occupation, thirty of the traditional governing bodies had been eliminated, and Italian groups substituted for them.[34] While Grazioli piously objected to French attempts to undermine a representative Italian governing body in Fiume, his comrades in the army had no scruples about doing precisely the same thing elsewhere.

Under the circumstances it is hardly surprising to find outbursts of that socialistic and proletarian activity of which Grazioli spoke at the end of December. What is surprising is that so little came of it, and that it vanished so quickly. Conditions were not good in Fiume, and the economy of the city had ground to an almost complete halt under the Allied occupation.[35] There was very little commercial activity, the port was inactive, the factories, when they functioned at all, worked very little, the shipyards were closed, and supplies of such vital elements as oil and coal were running low. The population was anxious for a resolution of their problems, and they grew increasingly restive with the passage of time.

The inability of the conflicting powers to resolve the crisis produced a significant explosion in Fiume in the summer of 1919,[36] when hostilities between pro-French and pro-Italian forces reached a level that forced the Allied powers to take a more active interest in the internal affairs of the city. The tiny war between France and Italy in the streets of Fiume was sparked by a series of apparently trivial incidents, each of which led to the armed skirmishes of the summer battle. On one evening early in July, for example, some French sailors, joking with some Fiuman girls, dislodged a patriotic ribbon one of the girls was wearing on her blouse. News of the incident spread rapidly through the streets (subsequently provoking charges that the scene had been staged), and the local citizenry descended upon every Frenchman in sight, sending several of them to the infirmary. A couple of nights later there was a mock battle between some French troops and local youths, during which a live bomb was thrown into an Italian crowd. Fortunately no one was injured, but the incident prepared the way for the tragedy of the following morning, the sixth of July. An Italian patrol opened fire on three French sailors, killing one of them, wounding another, and arresting the third. By evening the city was in an ugly mood, and the climax came toward sunset, when an Italian company from one of the warships in the harbor opened fire on a French barracks. At the end of the encounter, nine Frenchmen were dead and scores of others wounded; the Italians counted only a handful of injuries. The French command protested the matter to the Inter-Allied occupying force, and a committee of admirals was appointed to investigate the matter and recommend actions for the security of the city. This, of course, was all of a temporary nature, for the final disposition of the question awaited the decisions of the Paris Peace Conference.

The Peace Conference was busy with other matters, and the activist elements in Fiume were hardly in a mood to await the pontifications of a collection of foreign ministers and presidents who seemed increasingly hostile to Italian demands. Just as the National Council had succeeded in turning the crisis of the previous October to their own advantage, many Fiumans felt that a similar initiative was necessary to break the impasse in the summer of 1919. Indeed, preparations for a dramatic march on the city by Italian nationalist forces had already been under way for some time, and the hostilities of the summer served to accelerate the pace of these efforts.

3
Setting the Stage

D'Annunzio's seizure of Fiume was a spectacular event, in keeping with the personality of the poet-warrior. Yet such an enterprise needed more than the charisma of its leader, whose triumphal entry into Fiume on the morning of 12 September 1919 was in large part due to a powerful combination of forces in the Italian political world. This dramatic tour de force was, in fact, simply one piece in the intricate crazy-quilt of maneuvers and conspiracies that characterized the postwar scene. Some of these forces sought to topple the precarious Italian government and substitute a strong-arm regime for the constitutional monarchy; others were limited to attempts to guarantee the annexation of Fiume to Italy; still others wanted an anarchist or communist revolution. Without the support of his powerful allies, D'Annunzio would have been just another dreamer and a great war hero; with their aid, he became one of the pivotal figures in the twentieth century.

D'Annunzio himself was not always aware of the groups and interests that swirled about him, for his own world and his own activities were utterly and totally fascinating to him. He evidently intended his gesture as a tactical stroke to force the diplomats at Paris to recognize the Italian claim to Fiume and Dalmatia. In addition, he hoped to topple the Nitti government in Rome and replace it with a government composed of war heroes and interventionist leaders. Such a government would, he thought, be able to defend Italian "honor" and prevent the triumphant conclusion of the Great War from becoming the "mutilated victory" he saw emerging from the conference tables at Versailles. For D'Annunzio, Fiume was more than a political and military coup. Had it been conceived in such terms alone, the feverish poet would never have risen from his sick-bed to lead the assault on the city. The "March of Ronchi" was, rather, the setting for the last, triumphant act of the drama of the Great War, and D'Annunzio assigned to himself the lead-

36

ing role and the directorship. Nonetheless, the drama that finally unfolded on the shores of the Carnaro was staged by many men, and while D'Annunzio played a decisive role, he was but one of several actors.

As the negotiations in Paris wore on, it became increasingly clear that Italy was becoming involved in a new struggle for the spoils of victory, this time with her former allies. The months following the armistice produced intense frustrations within Italy, frustrations that weighed heavily upon those who had been most directly involved in the war: the armed forces. These veterans played a very important part in the Fiume enterprise.

The most significant collaboration with D'Annunzio—both before and after the march—came from the military. Italy has had a long history of attempts by the military to take command of the country, and enterprising generals and Caesars have been potent figures in the political arena for millennia. As far back as Machiavelli, Italian statesmen and theoreticians have feared a dissident military, and such concerns have continued down to the present age. Oddly enough, despite the heritage of the Roman period and the Renaissance (when mercenary forces often determined the destinies of kings and popes), modern Italian politics have not been kind to military figures. Even the great Giuseppe Garibaldi never achieved a durable political base, and most Italian generals never became involved in the major parties in the age of electoral politics. Furthermore, in modern times there has been a distinct separation of military and civil administrations, and the generals have tended to stay out of formal political activities—though they have not stayed away from covert politics.

Italian politics are very much like a staged performance: the producers and directors are hidden from public view, while the actors play on the desires and fantasies of the audience. In the period following the Great War, much energy was directed toward the overthrow of the government and the installation of a new political regime. Yet most of this activity was carefully concealed from the public. The various plots and conspiracies that characterized the immediate postwar period were of a piece with D'Annunzio's march on Fiume: they partook of the wildly theatrical mood of the moment, having more in common with fantasies of a new world than with traditional political ideas. Before examining the conspiratorial themes, we must first meet the "chorus" of our Adriatic drama: the soldiers who made up the indispensable nucleus of the Fiuman Legionnaires.

THE CHORUS: THE VETERANS OF THE GREAT WAR

From the very beginning, peace created major problems. The Italian press clamored for the rapid return of the war veterans to their families and jobs—only to discover that the transformation of soldiers into citizens was a formidable undertaking, in some ways more difficult than the mobilization of the armed forces had been. The general staff, taken by surprise by the sudden "explosion" of peace, was largely unprepared for the task, and the problems of peacetime were serious. The sheer numbers of bodies involved posed considerable logistic difficulties. The situation was particularly bad in the Veneto, where there had been heavy bombing of bridges, roads and railroad lines. The area was full of soldiers who were no longer needed for fighting yet were unable to return to their homes and families.

There were other problems as well. Fears were widespread that the strained national economy might not be able to absorb the heavy influx of veterans into the labor force, and there was considerable opposition to massive demobilization by the general staff. This desire to keep large numbers of Italians in uniform was not, of course, solely (or even primarily) due to concerns about the labor market. Bureaucracies always seek to increase their numbers, and Italian bureaucracies are among the most highly developed (they would say "Byzantine") in the world. The entire period following the armistice was characterized by a monumental bureaucratic chaos—a chaos that has since become a trademark of Italian governments—that provided the daily press with an endless supply of fascinating copy for a frustrated public. Aside from this institutional momentum, there were other motives that led the generals to fight for a large army; for example, there were many who wished to use the army against Italy's *internal* enemies once the foreign fronts were secure. Finally, a striking change had taken place among the ranks of the officers' corps during the course of hostilities. Rapid battlefield promotions had been widespread, and an army that had entered the war with 142 generals now contained no fewer than 1,246 persons holding this rank. These men, anxious to retain their status (and their income), fought hard to maintain a large standing army and were alarmed to find a government in Rome that seemed determined to reduce the armed forces to their prewar levels. In the modern period, governments that have attempted to reduce the number of men under arms and that have severely cut military expenditures have invariably been considered somewhat subversive, if not downright treacherous, by the generals and their friends, and the government of Francesco Saverio Nitti was no exception to that rule. Few passions are stronger than that which combines concern for one's own personal status with an inflated sense of patriotism, and this passion was dangerously widespread among the military leadership of Italy at the end of the Great War.[1]

The very fact of peace, then, posed numerous problems to a government and a people that desperately wished to savor the joys of victory. In addition to the logistic problems and the growing menace of a dissident body of officers, there were other problems of a political nature that grew larger with the passage of time. These derived from the war's having created something entirely new in Italian politics: a large mass of men motivated by democratic ideals. During the last stages of the war, particularly following the catastrophic rout of the army at Caporetto, the government had embarked upon a campaign of indoctrination, convincing the soldiers that they had a deep personal stake in the outcome of the war and promising them all kinds of rewards for victory. The soldiers who returned from the front were not, politically speaking, those who had been recruited. They were convinced that they would play a major role in the postwar era, having been promised not only a share in the political future of the country but also a real economic windfall. Each veteran had been guaranteed his own plot of land if he desired it. Having won the war, the veterans now looked forward to a truly new world, and they felt increasingly betrayed by a government that had no hope of being able to deliver the anticipated rewards.

It soon became clear that the promises made by the government were not going to be fulfilled and that whatever rewards were available would go to those who least needed them. Non-officers were discharged with hardly a lira in their pockets, while the officers received substantial payments. Even when an outburst of public disgust at this deplorable state of affairs had led to some token financial aid being given to returning veterans in February 1919, the inequities remained great and widespread. A noncommissioned officer who had fought during the entire war received less upon discharge from active service than a newly commissioned second lieutenant earned in a single month. There were also privileged categories outside the officers corps who received unbelievably good treatment. A member of a profession could be transferred to his native city, where he drew his full salary from the army at the same time that he pursued his own affairs (dressed in civilian clothes). These professionals also had the option of delaying their discharge and continuing to earn double salaries long after the other, poorer members of their fighting groups had been returned to a society struggling with massive financial difficulties.

"Students" also received preferential treatment. They were permitted to attend special classes at the universities, while still retaining military privileges and drawing salaries. No attendance was taken at their classes, enabling these happy few to lead an almost idyllic existence, enjoying all the diversions of university life, while having none of the responsibilities. There were some twenty-three thousand of these lucky souls by the summer of 1919.

While such gross examples of favoritism produced considerable discontent in the army, and also some harsh criticism from the political opponents of the regime, by and large these were not issues that reached the passions of the Italian public. Above all else, the people craved a restoration of prewar conditions, so that all could return to their traditional concerns. Had this miracle occurred, D'Annunzio's March on Fiume most likely would not have taken place. But Italy did not return to "normalcy." The devaluation of the lira that took place largely between 1919 and 1920 is the most spectacular index of the economic catastrophe that swept the nation. By the end of 1920, the lira was worth only one-quarter of its 1914 value, and this devastated not only those who were living on fixed incomes and savings but also those who had supported the government's war efforts by subscribing to the "victory loans." It has been estimated that nearly thirty percent of the national income between 1916 and 1918 went back to the treasury in the form of such loans—and the value of the loans depreciated by seventy-five percent by the end of 1920.

The mass reaction to inflated prices after the war was fascinating, especially in the light of modern conditions; in the first months of 1919, consumers refused to buy in the hopes that prices would fall. This was only logical, given the lack of understanding of economic processes. Since high prices were believed to have been caused by the war, many people reasoned that once the war had ended, prices would drop—and when they didn't, despair turned to anger. In July 1919 an enraged populace began to sack warehouses, and the government imposed a compulsory reduction of fifty percent on some prices. But this massive price-cutting only slowed down the avalanche. In the first half of 1921, the cost of living for an average working-class family was 560 percent higher than it had been in 1914.[2]

The irony of this situation was that the veterans were in perhaps the most difficult economic plight. They found themselves without resources and without employment, and their anger was heightened by the realization that many who had avoided military service and remained at home had made fortunes on the war. It is consequently not surprising to find the official veterans' organization, the Associazione Nazionale Combattenti, expounding a fairly radical set of demands at its first national convention, in January 1919. They called for the convocation of a Constituent Assembly to draft a new constitution, the abolition of the Senate and the creation of a series of councils elected by the various categories of workers and management, and the reduction of military service to three months. They further demanded that unused land be distributed among returning veterans—the government's wartime promise.

The manifesto placed the veterans surprisingly close to the position of their ancient enemy, the Socialist Party, both in its proposal for a new governmental structure and in its demand for land distribution. The judg-ment of Emilio Lussu, one of the most thoughtful Italian leftists, was close to the mark when he wrote that much of the veterans' program seemed to have been written in order to encourage collaboration with the Socialists: "The veterans were, in essence . . . philosocialists, not be-cause they were familiar with the classics of socialism, but because of their profound sense of internationalism, achieved in the reality of war, and because of their desire for land."[3] Active collaboration between veterans and Socialists was out of the question, for the Socialists' opposi-tion to the war itself made it impossible for them to gain the veterans' formal support. Yet the veterans' social aspirations often coincided with those of the Socialists. This overlapping of desires made it hard to decipher the political future of Italy in the months following the armistice; coali-tions could come together over some important issues, only to be rup-tured the next week on some other question. In the meantime, the government sought to guarantee its security by turning to the army.

THE ARMY AS PRAETORIAN GUARD

By the summer of 1919, there were 1,575,000 men still under arms (excluding officers) in the Italian Army. Slightly more than half of these men were under the supreme command, and of these, some 740,000 were in the war zone, deployed against the risk of a new outbreak of hostilities—a distinct possibility at a time when the Italian delegation had temporarily withdrawn from the peace talks in Paris.

This left somewhat more than 600,000 men in the army. Of this figure, roughly half were deployed domestically, and were used to guaran-tee "public order" or "national domestic security." They constituted a modern praetorian guard, used to safeguard the government against potential internal enemies.

A government that maintains a personal police force of 300,000 thousand men is highly insecure about its stability and popularity, and indeed, fears of domestic insurgency were widespread in the Orlando government. Furthermore, the groups that were held to be dangerous were not only the left-wing political organizations; the government was equally concerned about the potential menace of the returning veterans. Ironically, the most feared veterans were those who had been the most heralded soldiers: the *Arditi*, or shock troops.

The Arditi were the most celebrated Italian troops of the Great War. In contrast to the foot soldiers who waited to die in a muddy trench, the Arditi died a "beautiful death," participating in desperate assaults on enemy positions, leading charges up exposed hillsides, singing (accord-ing to the legend) their own songs. These assault units lived apart, con-

Arditi

serving their energies for those moments of intense struggle and derring-do for which they were reserved. Their lives contrasted vividly with the lives of the regular troops and also with those of their countrymen far from the battle lines. This contrast became even more significant after the war, for many of them found that adjusting to peacetime existence was harder than facing Austrian rifles. Even before the formal declaration of peace, the Arditi were engaging in melancholy musings on the life that awaited them outside active service. Happily, there is a substantial literature written by Arditi, many of whom were extremely well educated, often resembling the young Ernest Hemingway in their attitudes. Ferruccio Vecchi, an eloquent *Ardito*, put it this way in the fall of 1918: "With the end of the war, *we* are precisely those who have no direction any more, those surrounded by the abyss, those without bread. Every one of us . . . is obliged to exclude the possibility of picking up our lives at the point at which they were interrupted in 1915. . . . The war has by now become our second nature . . . Where shall I go? What shall I do? I don't know. . . ."[4] For such personalities, peacetime pursuits could not possibly offer the drama and glory of war.

The Arditi were confronted with what we would now call an existential crisis—a crisis over the meaningfulness of life—and the "solution" they attempted was typical of their mentality—they transformed Italy into a battlefield. As early as December 1918, one of their members, the noted Futurist Mario Carli, called upon his comrades to continue their ardent labors for Italy outside of the armed forces. "There is much to be done down here," he told the readers of his newspaper (*Roma Futurista*) in September, and a couple of months later he spelled out the glorious future that awaited his fellow Arditi after the war: "For you, the future can only be a continuation of the glory conquered on bloody fields and a recognition by the nation of your immense *human* value, which must be used and channeled in the best possible way in the works of peace."[5] Carli was saying that the Arditi possessed qualities that set them apart from the great mass of the populace. Just as they had been the elite of the armed forces, they must now become the elite of the political forces of Italy. Having proven their value on the battlefield, they could not assume their rightful role as society's natural leaders.

This was not an idea restricted to a handful of shock troops; many Italians of varied political hues shared this view. In particular, Italian political leaders, regardless of their position along the political spectrum, believed that the Arditi would play a major role in Italy's future. While some welcomed the impending return of the Arditi, the transformation of elite fighting men into a domestic force was viewed ominously by many who had been among the Arditi's greatest supporters during the struggle, including General Enrico Caviglia, who became minister of war in February 1919:

> As Commander of the Army, I had expressed my opinion in favor of dissolv-
> ing the Arditi. . . . But as minister of war, I saw the necessity of maintaining
> them. . . . In moments of political disorder, such as was sweeping Italy, [the
> Arditi] constituted a useful force in the hands of the government, because
> they were greatly feared for their inclination for swift and violent action. If
> they were dissolved, they would pass to the reinforcement of the revolution-
> ary parties.[6]

Caviglia, like other members of the Italian "Establishment," feared
that the Arditi might become the private army of one or another of the
organized groups on the Italian political Left. Yet it would have been
extremely difficult for this to have taken place, as there really was no
political organization capable of "capturing" them for its own purposes.
Not surprisingly, the Arditi sought to keep themselves apart from other
groups, and while they waited for their destiny to unfold they created
a national organization, stressing the development of men with great
physical prowess and heroic wills. Heroism also meant—as it always has
in Italy—domination of Italy's women, and early Arditi proclamations
left no doubt about this important element in their program: "We will
love, with frenzy, both speed and beautiful women. Given the choice
we will speedily love beautiful women. But at the opportune moment,
speedily flee from beautiful women."[7]

Furthermore, the Arditi increasingly came to sound like anarchists,
striking out at the excesses of the modern state and suggesting that one
day their fury might be unleashed to destroy Italy itself. In their pictur-
esque language, typically the Arditi warned that they might "take
apart, clean, lubricate, and modernize all the parts of the complicated
political-bureaucratic-judicial Italian machine or, finding it out of
service, hurl it into the melting pot of revolution."[8]

This rhetoric seemed to confirm the worst fears of General Caviglia,
but the actions of the Arditi were far from revolutionary. Indeed, their
most notable incursion into Italian politics in the first half of 1919 was
on the side of the Fascists. On 15 April they staged a devastating assault
on the offices of the Socialist Party newspaper in Milan. The sack of the
Avanti offices was conducted with the same meticulous ruthlessness as
assaults on enemy positions during the war, and both the attack and the
subsequent official reaction tell a great deal about the attitudes of the
leaders of the Italian government.

There was a notable lack of intervention on behalf of the forces of
"law and order" during the assault, and when General Caviglia was asked
to investigate the matter, his attitude was highly sympathetic—toward
the aggressors. According to the testimony of Ferruccio Vecchi, one of

those involved in the assault, the general confided to the Arditi that he was pleased to see that the Socialists had been given a severe "lesson." Further, far from being shocked by this outbreak of paramilitary political violence, Caviglia seemed pleased to announce that the Arditi had won a significant victory against their Socialist enemy, and he warned the Left that they were engaged in a losing battle: "I warned the Socialists not to resort to violence, because they would undoubtedly get the worst of it. I said, 'Don't delude yourselves. . . . You are up against men who for four years risked their lives every day, a thousand times a day. . . . Stay within the framework of the law, and behave moderately.'"[9]

Violence was quite all right, as long as it was directed against those forces that opposed the government. Caviglia counselled moderation and prudence for the Left, whereas the Arditi, at least for the moment, served a useful purpose and received no lectures from the distinguished general.

While deployment of 300,000 troops for domestic purposes represented a new and ominous introduction of the military in the Italian political world, the actions of the Arditi transformed that world at its foundations. Renzo De Felice, the great historian of Italian Fascism, has characterized the uniqueness of this moment: "Political conflict in Italy had always been a 'family affair,' of orators, manifestos, newspapers, demonstrations, and mass meetings, which, while often raucous, were also peaceful. . . . But now the Arditi put political conflict on a new plane, organizing it according to military criteria."[10]

Italian politics had indeed been transformed into an armed conflict. In the end, the winner of this conflict—three years later—would be the movement with the strongest private army: Mussolini's Fascists. But for the moment, the Arditi, and indeed all veterans of the war, became suddenly indispensable to *all* the political forces of the nation, as the various groups began to organize their own troops for the coming struggle. Arditi were wooed by both Left and Right, and we find them participating in the most diverse organizations imaginable from 1919 to 1922. Yet, throughout the various struggles, there were many among them who firmly believed that the Arditi could not properly serve as a private army for any group, that the Arditi should determine Italy's destiny—by themselves.

It is extremely difficult to classify the Arditi in terms of the traditional Left-Right categories of modern politics, for much of their rhetoric seemed radical (if not downright revolutionary), at the same time that many of their actions were highly reactionary. The Italian "Establishment" didn't quite know what to make of them, either. Leading Socialists, like Filippo Turati and Giuseppe Emanuel Modigliani, denounced the Arditi as mercenaries at the disposal of the forces of reaction, whereas the army leaders were so convinced of the radical nature of their shock troops that in the middle of May the soldiers were forbidden to buy or read the "Bolshevik journal" *L'Ardito*.[11] In a sense, both the Socialists and the government were right; the Arditi were anti-Socialist revolutionaries, potentially a menace to all existing political organizations.

Even before D'Annunzio's march on Fiume, some among the Arditi had attempted to bring down the government in Rome. In the summer of 1919 a group of anarchists and Arditi had planned to seize power in Rome and proclaim a Constituent Assembly. Around midnight on the night of 6 July the Roman Police arrested a group of conspirators in a restaurant and then seized some twenty other revolutionaries who had gathered outside the Pietralata fortress, urging the soldiers garrisoned there to join in the revolt. The conspiracy was crushed routinely, and its members duly incarcerated. Although the group was small (only forty-eight members, who were charged with activities against the state), virtually every Ardito knew of the maneuvers underway, and there is evidence that they all would have joined the movement had it achieved some initial success. In addition, members of the Republican Party were ready to join in a general insurrection and there is even some suggestion—from a government agent—that D'Annunzio himself was involved in the conspiracy.[12]

Despite the failure of the Pietralata plot, the notion that the Arditi could serve as the fighting arm of a revolutionary movement endured. Perhaps the most interesting example of the potential radicalism of the shock troops (aside from their role in the Fiume enterprise) was the so-called Arditi del Popolo, the anti-Fascist "people's army" that appeared briefly in the summer of 1921.[13]

The Arditi del Popolo represented the culmination of two years of intensive underground organizational efforts by Argo Secondari, the man who had masterminded the Pietralata fiasco two years earlier. The Arditi del Popolo was explicitly anti-Fascist: "Until the Fascists stop assassinating our brother workers," Secondari bravely announced, "the Arditi of Italy can have nothing in common with them." The Arditi del Popolo was a group organized for the defense of the working class, and it promised to respond to the Fascist squads with equal violence. Furthermore, as Secondari made clear on several occasions, the ultimate goal of the organization was revolution.

Argo Secondari's career ended in a typically bizarre manner: in the summer of 1924, in the throes of violent mental disorders, he entered a mental institution, where he remained until his death in 1942. Yet this obsessed Ardito and conspirator managed to attract a remarkable following for the Arditi del Popolo. On 6 July 1921, Secondari led some two thousand followers through the Roman Botanical Gardens, to the enthusiastic applause of a large crowd of supporters. The rest of the country was similarly aroused, and reports from police spies and informers flooded into the offices of the Minister of the Interior, announcing the presence of Arditi del Popolo throughout the country. The Arditi del Popolo numbered several thousand, and their headquarters in Rome were in the same section of the Palazzo Venezia as the National Veterans' Association. There were ominous signs that the long-feared radical movement had finally moved from the trenches to the streets of Italy. Indeed, the Communist International urged the Italian Communists to join Secondari's ranks.

Like most efforts of this sort, that of the Arditi failed, but political failures are often as instructive as successes, and this case supplies several important lessons. First and foremost, the sudden eruption of a national organization shows the almost ubiquitous nature of underground veterans' groups in postwar Italy. That such a marginal figure as Argo Secondari was able to generate a nationwide following of thousands shows that resentment against Italian "business as usual" was deepseated in the hearts of those who had fought for a "greater" nation in the war, and it confirms the accuracy of governmental fears of a subversive movement organized by the war heroes. Further, Secondari's activities during the period from the summer of 1919 to the summer of 1921 illustrate the continuity of such efforts and help us to understand the phenomenon of D'Annunzio's Fiume. Among the many places that one finds Argo Secondari during the late summer and early fall of 1919 is Fiume, and the agents of the Ministry of the Interior reported his presence there over a three-month period from August to October of that eventful year.[14] Many of those who were sympathetic to the Arditi del Popolo were strongly attracted by D'Annunzio's adventures on the Adriatic, and it is significant that the Arditi del Popolo emerged *after* the end of D'Annunzian Fiume.

The City of the Holocaust was not a momentary aberration in the otherwise smooth flow of Italian history, nor was it an event that only took place because of the singular charisma and imagination of the *Comandante*. Indeed, the seizure of Fiume was of a piece with the entire period. Attempts by frustrated and highly idealistic veterans to reshape the world in the image of the heroism of the war both preceded and followed the Fiuman adventure, and D'Annunzio's was simply one in a series of such efforts. The wave of public support for the Arditi del Popolo, like that which rushed toward D'Annunzio at Fiume, demonstrates the deep wellsprings of public sentiment upon which such theatrical enterprises were able to draw. In the long run, this strong undercurrent of public sentiment, so easily tapped by the great choreographers

of the masses, proved fatal to Italian democracy; the other great political
dramatist of the period, Benito Mussolini, was able to capture this sentiment and make it the accomplice of his own march to power. Profound
disgust with the Italian "Establishment," disillusionment with the epi-
logue to a victorious war effort, and alarm at the state of national affairs
all combined to drive Italy into a fevered search for leaders who could
inspire the newly mobilized masses and for a government that could
give meaning to the lives of the Italian people. These were the powerful
emotions that were ultimately channeled into the successful Fascist
movement. The reasons for Mussolini's success are beyond our present
concern, but the world from which Fascism emerged is very much at
the center of the D'Annunzian melodrama.

The officials of Fiume had already expressed their desire to be
united with Italy, their "mother country." As their economic and political conditions became more desperate, the leaders of the annexationist program turned for help to those who seemed best able to act on
their behalf. In the spring and summer of 1919 the friends of Fiume
appeared to be primarily among the ranks of the Right (or so they have
been traditionally classified): men who had supported intervention in
the Great War, who had reveled in the struggle, and who had seen the
humiliation of the rout at Caporetto give way to the final, triumphant
days of the battle of Vittorio Veneto. These were men who spoke the
language of the Arditi. They consequently desired, as the all-too-familiar
rhetoric went, a "greater Italy," an "Italy redeemed" by its suffering
and its struggles on the battlefield. When it began to appear that Italy
would be deprived of its "rightful" booty at the peace table, these patriots and activist chauvinists decided to take matters into their own
hands. There was a remarkable number of these people, all dedicated to
"vindicating" Italian honor, even if they had to destroy the country in
order to save its good name.

The idea of an armed action to "liberate" Fiume from its Allied
occupiers evidently arose first in the late winter and early spring of 1919,
on the occasion of the passage of the First *Divisione d'Assalto* to Libya
by way of Venice. This division, commanded by General Ottavio Zoppi,
was the very same in which Captain Nino Host-Venturi, a passionate
Fiuman, had served, and he wrote to his former comrades to announce
that Fiume had decided upon its own destiny: "Italy or death." The
Arditis' reaction was exactly what one might have expected: they were
quite prepared to lend their support to the undertaking. At the same
time, it seems that Zoppi was involved in two other plots: one to capture Split, the other to create a republic—under the direction of D'Annunzio and Duke Emanuel Filiberto of Aosta—including Fiume and Venice.
The scheme to capture Split, well documented by the correspondence

between D'Annunzio and Zoppi, developed in February and March. Zoppi had agreed to commit his troops to the action, but at the last moment the plan had to be abandoned when it encountered strong resistance on the part of General Badoglio.[15]

Such contacts between the leaders of the annexationist cause in Fiume and military units—Arditi and others—were frequent in the following months, and every time the question was raised the response was the same: the military was in favor of decisive action. They were prepared to drive out the Allied soldiers (French, English, and American) who served in the Occupation Forces at Fiume and proclaim the annexation of the city to Italy. Nothing came of these early discussions—the conspiracy lacked leadership and a specific plan of action. But these attempts convinced the Fiuman patriots that powerful support was readily available among the elitist troops of the armed forces and, significantly, among their commanding officers.

There is dramatic evidence that the notion of an armed expedition to capture Fiume had the tacit approval of the Italian government as well. On 11 May, Oscar Sinigaglia met with Orlando in Paris to discuss the Fiuman question. Sinigaglia was a leading industrialist from Trieste and was to become a major financier of the Fiuman expedition the following September. Called "the impresario of Fiumanism" by Filippo Turati,[16] Sinigaglia had served with Nitti in the ministry of the treasury in the summer of 1918 and had easy access to governmental leaders.

In his talk with Orlando, Sinigaglia explicitly raised the question of an armed coup in Fiume: "Who could stop thirty or forty thousand free Italian citizens from undertaking an expedition in the old style, and going to occupy Fiume . . . ? When 40 million Italians want Fiume to be an Italian city, when the entire population of Fiume wants to be united with Italy, who will be able to oppose this union from taking place? Will America launch a military expedition to give Fiume back to the Yugoslavs?"[17]

Orlando had nothing to say against the scheme, and the absence of any opposition from the leader of the Italian government could only encourage those who were, with increased energy, planning to take matters into their own hands.

Later in the summer and fall, Host-Venturi and other Fiuman leaders (including Edoardo Susmel, who later wrote the "official" history of the enterprise) established contacts with several Arditi units, the most notable of which were those commanded by Ferruccio Vecchi and by Captain Francesco Argentino.[18] Ultimately, many Arditi joined D'Annunzio at the gates of the city, arriving there well in advance of the poet; but then, just as numerous military units in the past had failed to seize the city because they lacked the proper leadership, the Arditi significantly awaited the arrival of their leader before entering the city itself.

The idea of an armed advance on Fiume was quite widespread in the late spring and early summer of 1919. While the name of Gabriele D'Annunzio figured in many of the plots to capture the city, the poet was by no means the only candidate to lead the expedition.[19] Indeed, for many Fiumans, he was not the first choice for the job, and even some of his most fervent supporters were somewhat ambivalent. Host-Venturi, for example, believed that the occupation of Fiume must be accomplished by Fiumans, and while he was quite willing to collaborate with outside elements, he was adamant that the coup originate within the city. To use a metaphor that became the symbol of D'Annunzian Fiume, the heroism of the city of Fiume would become a purifying fire for the entire world, but it was important that the spark come from within and not be brought from without the city gates. In the end, the matter was settled by compromise: D'Annunzio led the troops, but the entire operation was closely supervised by Fiumans.

For a while, the National Council attempted to organize the coup by negotiating with various potential leaders of the sortie: the poet Sem Benelli, the Duke of Aosta, D'Annunzio himself, and various military figures, including General Peppino Garibaldi. Benelli was the council's prime candidate, and his plan for the operation was calculated to warm the hearts of the good burghers who served on the council. Benelli offered to head an army of mercenaries, which surely served the interests of the council more than the alternative of a dedicated and highly motivated group of rag-tag patriotic fanatics. The members of the National Council were not interested in revolution, and when, in June, Host-Venturi suggested that D'Annunzio would be a more effective leader than Benelli (and advised Antonio Grossich, the council president, that negotiations with the poet had already begun), Grossich flew into a rage. Evidently it was quite a historic anger, for Susmel, generally not given to such excesses, records that Grossich looked like the great god Thor, with his beard aflame from his rage.[20]

The conflict between Grossich and Host-Venturi was more than a debate over the relative leadership abilities of Sem Benelli and Gabriele D'Annunzio. The struggle was really over the future of Fiume and who would control the postcoup regime. Benelli, the agent of the council with his salaried troops, would obviously be easier to deal with than would the unpredictable comandante. Yet, significantly, Host-Venturi's proposal carried the day. Evidently he had succeeded in mastering the political arena of the city, for within a very few days he had installed himself as the effective cornerstone of the entire conspiratorial edifice. On the evening of 13 June the National Council appropriated a sizable sum of money for the creation of a Fiuman Army, naming Benelli to head the new troops. But Benelli refused the job: he had seen the handwriting on the wall (or perhaps the situation had been explained to him). That very evening, a telegram arrived from D'Annunzio himself: "Await me with faith and discipline. I will fail neither you nor destiny. Long live Italian Fiume."[21] The pieces were beginning to come together. Two days later, on 16 June, a group of veterans protested the exclusion of their forces from the National Council, accusing the city fathers of attempting to create an army without those most qualified to organize and lead it, the veterans of the city. Their protest was quickly respected, and five of their members, led by Host-Venturi, were admitted to the council. From that moment, the conspiracy was in the hands of those who, as Caviglia had so presciently feared in the last days of the war, were most menacing to the forces of "business as usual" in Rome.

The conspirators were greatly aided by developments in Paris. The conflict at the Versailles Peace Conference was actually over two distinct issues: what would happen to the city of Fiume, and what part of the acquisitions promised Italy in the Treaty of London would actually pass into its hands? The menace to the ultranationalists was that neither the one nor the other would become part of the much-desired "greater Italy," and their counterdemand was the virtually impossible one of the "Treaty of London plus Fiume." The territory at issue (promised by the Treaty of London) was the Adriatic coast of Yugoslavia in the region known as Dalmatia, and along with the schemes to annex Fiume went a number of plans to acquire the entire package: Zara, Split, and all the rest of the Dalmatian territory. D'Annunzio was completely in accord with this grandiose plan, and on at least two separate occasions following the occupation of Fiume he threatened to launch a general expedition for the annexation of Dalmatia. Furthermore, until the very last moment, there was a serious question as to which city should be taken first. Fiume eventually prevailed, but many felt that Split was the more desirable objective, since its capture would force the government to face the Treaty of London issue and resolve, with a single stroke, the question of the destiny of Dalmatia.

News of these various plans began to filter to the surface of the Italian cauldron in the spring of 1919, when Orlando and Sonnino abruptly left the Peace Conference and returned to Italy to mobilize public support for the maximum Italian demand: "Treaty of London plus Fiume." They thereby performed an invaluable service for those who favored a dramatic coup because they produced a state of virtual mass hysteria in the country. The artificial unity that followed greatly resembled the mob enthusiasm that had accompanied Italy's entry into the war some four years before. But the expectations they raised could not possibly have been fulfilled at Versailles: Wilson had made it altogether clear that, whatever the resolution of the Dalmatia issue, he would never grant Italian sovereignty over Fiume. Hence, "Treaty of London plus Fiume" was an impossible goal at Paris and could only be realized by other forces within the country. These forces, capitalizing on the enthusiasm created by the government, then turned these energies against the Orlando government. Rarely has the metaphor of Doctor Frankenstein's monster been so apt in illustrating historical reality: having created the chauvinist beast, Sonnino and Orlando now had to endure its violence.

Even before the return of the peace delegation from Paris in late April, the activist forces had begun to consider a coup in the Adriatic. Early in April, according to the Office of Special Investigations, a group had met in Milan to discuss the possibility of a coup at Split. The conspirators included Garibaldi, D'Annunzio, representatives of the Milanese interventionists, and the Futurists.[22] By June, the government was being advised of various plots and conspiracies, including one that their spy intriguingly entitled the "madness of General Giardino; conspiracy for a coup d'état."[23] Evidently, people other than the spies of the minister of the interior had heard rumors of Giardino's involvement in a planned coup, for in mid-June the *Giornale d'Italia* printed a public denial by the general, who announced that he was *not* involved in a plot with D'Annunzio, Mussolini, or Federzoni on behalf of the Duke of Aosta. Further, Giardino declared, he had not planned to have the duke installed as the leader of a republic consisting of Venice, Dalmatia, and Fiume.[24] The details of this presumed plot are not known, nor can anyone be absolutely certain that there actually was such a plan. Yet no less an authority than General Enrico Caviglia believed the reports.[25] The Duke of Aosta was the commander of the Third Army (which was in charge of the Eastern frontier) at the end of the war. The duke was very close to the Nationalists and, Caviglia wrote, was deeply involved in the revolutionary schemes revolving around Dalmatia and the Adriatic towns and islands under discussion at the Peace Conference. "In the preparation of all revolutions," Caviglia sagely observed, "there is always some prince who deludes himself into believing that the revolutionaries work for *him*." Such may have been the case with the illustrious Duke of Aosta. Further, the troops under the duke's command were completely committed to such an undertaking, so he had no need to resort to intensive proselytizing of the soldiers. If anything, he would be acting in concert with their desires.

Besides the Duke of Aosta, the general staff of the Third Army included Generals Gandolfo and Sailer, each of whom had emerged from the war with somewhat tarnished reputations and who therefore might have been disposed to embark upon a spectacular adventure to add luster to their names.

Thus, according to Caviglia, at least two distinct plots emerged: the first, which we have already discussed, involved the use of General Zoppi's Arditi in a coup against Fiume and/or Split and the surrounding region. The second, referred to in the *Giornale d'Italia*, was a far more ambitious project, designed to create a revolutionary "Republic of the Three Venices," embracing Dalmatia, Fiume, and Venice.

Caviglia confirmed that the atmosphere was heavy with intrigue, and the government feared sedition among the armed forces. Not surprisingly, the Third Army was dissolved on 22 July, and the territory that had been under its command passed into the hands of the undoubtedly loyal General di Robilant (whose hostility to the Fiuman cause was amply demonstrated the following month, when he served as a member of the Inter-Allied Commission of Inquiry into disturbances in the city).

One final note on these plotting generals is in order: Caviglia wrote that General Zoppi had posed one condition for his participating in any coup: that General Badoglio be informed and that he not actively oppose the project. Badoglio *was* informed (by D'Annunzio, as we have seen), and his objections to the plan resulted in its cancellation. According to Caviglia, Badoglio felt that such an act would ruin all hopes for a settlement in Paris. While Caviglia claimed that Badoglio did not actively oppose the plans, the bulk of the evidence documents Badoglio's hostility to the conspirators.

It is impossible to accept all Caviglia's testimony without a good measure of skepticism, especially his analysis of the motives of the "tarnished" generals. Yet the significant part of his testimony, which is confirmed by all the other sources, concerns the widespread willingness among the highest levels of the military to engage in seditious conspiracies. Political groups interested in subverting the government could count on a high degree of either active participation or benevolent indifference from the generals. In particular, the political forces that arranged the march on Fiume were in frequent contact with various military groups, and the final plans entailed close collaboration between the two elements.

The groups that successfully organized the Fiume expedition formed a sort of ad hoc committee called Il Comitato per le Rivendicazioni Nazionali, the Committee for National Claims, which included the leaders of the Dante Alighieri Association (nominally dedicated to the expansion of Italian cultural activities abroad), the Trento-Trieste Association (which, as its name suggests, was an irredentist group), the Veterans' Association, and several other smaller groups of similar mind. In addition, the Committee for National Claims was in close contact with the Fascists, the Futurists, the Nationalists, and the Arditi. In short, in some way all the ultra nationalist elements of Italian society were in touch with one another, and all wanted a decisive action in the Adriatic. The Republicans and some elements of other political groups in the country participated from time to time in these plans.

The president of the Comitato was Giovanni Giuriati, who simultaneously held the post of president of the Trento-Trieste Association (he later became D'Annunzio's first head of cabinet). By the end of June, with the advent of Nitti to power, Giuriati had spoken with representatives from Fiume and with D'Annunzio about the urgency for an armed "defense" of Fiume against the likely decision of the Peace Conference. Giuriati was an ideal intermediary for all the participating groups, for he had the confidence of the Nationalists (such as Preziosi and Sinigaglia), of the more "radical" elements (such as the Fascists and the Arditi), of the Fiumans (Grossich and Host-Venturi), and of pivotal military figures like General Badoglio and Admirals Enrico Millo and Umberto Cagni. Despite Giuriati's apparent respectability, his subversive intentions were well known to those who watched the Italian political scene with care. The irredentists had more than one string to their bow, and while they were plotting the seizure of Fiume and the various Adriatic expeditions, they were also attempting to arrange some way to topple the Nitti government in Rome. One such attempt was apparently scheduled for the evening of 29 June, on the occasion of a speech by the poet in the Augusteo. At the last minute the plan collapsed, and D'Annunzio did not appear to give his speech on behalf of an Italian Fiume.[26] The speakers on that summer evening were clearly indicative of the assembled forces: Corradini, Host-Venturi, Eugenio Coselschi (one of D'Annunzio's closest collaborators), and Oscar Sinigaglia.

At the end of his speech on the twenty-ninth, Sinigaglia called upon the assembled crowd (mostly veterans) to march to Piazza Barberini, where Nitti's hotel was located. But the government, having been advised of the plan, barred the way with armed troops. There was to be no insurrection that night.

The Committee for National Claims, thwarted in its attempt to overthrow Nitti in Rome, turned its attentions to the problem of creating a volunteer force for the "defense" of the Adriatic. Host-Venturi had already organized a handful of men into a makeshift unit in Fiume, but a more systematic effort was to be undertaken. To this end, Giuriati obtained the promise of the Fiume National Council to put the considerable resources of its members and the wealth of the city (in addition to a guarantee to launch a city loan if it proved necessary) at the disposal of the new forces; and he then turned to the creation of the Fiuman Volunteer Army. For his part, Giuriati pledged the active participation of the Trento-Trieste Association, which he turned into a national recruiting office. In the first week in July, the Trento-Trieste was distributing circulars throughout the country, calling for volunteers. The documents these potential soldiers signed left no doubt about the intentions of the organization: "I declare that I wish to participate as a volunteer in the National Fiuman Army, and that I will, from today onward, place myself at the disposal of the National Trento-Trieste Association, swearing upon my honor to reach, at the time and by the means that will be indicated to me, the place that will be selected for the gathering of these forces. I further declare that I will accept without protest the rank and the arms that will be assigned to me, according to my previous service."[27]

Meanwhile, the Fasci di Combattimento were carrying out a similar recruitment campaign for the same army. By the middle of the month, Giuriati went to Fiume to discuss problems of logistics: Where were the troops to be housed? When would they be deployed? The funds at his disposition were more than adequate, men were reaching their recruiting centers in Trieste, D'Annunzio was kept advised of the progress, and all seemed in readiness.

The conspiracy was nearing fruition and needed only a go-ahead from the military. Giuriati sent a note to Badoglio announcing their intentions, and his expectations of the general's response were typical of those we have already seen: "We wanted to prepare a potent defense for which the government, if it really had the intention to resist and a will to win, should have thanked us. Therefore, when we sent [Oscar] Sinigaglia to discuss the matter with Badoglio, we had, if not the certainty, at least an excellent expectation that . . . his response would be positive."[28]

But, for once, the military leadership did not embrace a Nationalist scheme. On 27 July, Sinigaglia brought the unexpected news that Badoglio was absolutely opposed to the creation of a private army for Fiume, and on the thirty-first, Badoglio gave orders to increase surveillance of the Fiuman frontier and to prevent the passage of anybody "capable of sustaining or participating in movements contrary to the government's order." This was explicitly directed against "noted politicians, members of patriotic organizations with action programs."[29]

Without at least Badoglio's tacit approval, the scheme could not go forward, and Giuriati and his allies had to regroup their forces. Men, recruited by the various organizations, continued to pour into the city, and by 8 August the Fiuman legion was fully staffed. Yet they were unwilling to chance all on one dramatic attempt, and the summer weeks dragged on without any resolution of the tension.

As the forces of sedition attempted to figure out their best strategy in the Adriatic, D'Annunzio toyed with a variety of lofty projects. Should he join with these men and "liberate" Fiume and/or Dalmatia? Or should he embark upon a long-discussed and highly dramatic exploit

—a plane trip to Tokyo? This project was highly congenial to the poet; it would have enabled him finally to visit the Orient, with all of its exotic mysteries. (Years later, D'Annunzio turned to the Orient for inspiration, at a time when he believed that the West had become sterile and that only the East possessed the wisdom and profundity capable of restoring European creativity.) The governors of Italy leaped at the chance to dispatch the poet outside Italian borders, and they actively encouraged him in these dreams, sending a parade of generals and admirals to his home in Venice, urging him to fly to Japan.

The events that finally precipitated the march on Fiume came from the city itself and catalyzed all the elements into action. After the disturbances in Fiume during June, the Allied powers appointed a Four Power Commission to investigate the disorders, empowering this body to make recommendations concerning the disposition of the city. They finished their hearings early in August, and toward the end of the month the first rumors about the contents of their report began to leak out. The news was highly alarming to the annexationists, for the commission had recommended a series of actions designed to deprive Fiume of any effective Italian leadership. The commission proposed to dissolve the Fiume legion and the National Council, to remove General Grazioli from command (replacing him with the more obedient and less mercurial Pittaluga), and to replace the government of the city with an Inter-Allied body and a new council elected by a system of proportional representation, one that included the Slavic quarters of the city's suburbs. They called for the removal of the Sardinian Grenadiers, the group that had "liberated" Fiume the previous November. Finally, the commission called for the removal of French troops from the city, since there had been considerable conflict between them and the local citizenry.

These proposals struck at the heart of all the schemes to seize Fiume; it was one thing to capture a city under the command of a sympathetic Italian general, but quite another to fight American and British troops. Further, replacement of the National Council with a new body would not only mean depriving the conspirators a sound political base in Fiume; it would also mean a significant loss of funding for the project. Procrastination was no longer possible.

The problems facing the conspirators were enormous, and it was not immediately clear how they were to be overcome. In the first place, they would have to confront the military representatives of the Allied powers in Fiume, and they could hardly expect the British and American forces to collaborate in an attempt to subvert the efforts of the Peace Conference in Paris. In addition, the position of Badoglio himself was hardly calculated to calm the nerves of the plotters, who did not want to find themselves in armed conflict with regular Italian troops. Nitti was clearly opposed to any adventures, and while it was hoped that his government would collapse at the first sign of trouble, such an outcome was far from certain. Finally, there was the question of D'Annunzio himself. Would he appear at the moment he was needed? Or would he prefer some other adventure? This was the delicate situation faced by the conspiracy to take Fiume in the early autumn of 1919.

.

4

The Sacred Entrance

We live at a time when myths are debunked, and enterprises undertaken in the name of great ideals are often revealed to have been motivated by more common and baser desires. Confronted with an event that appears highly idealistic, our tendency is to look for the "real" motivation, believing that men generally act out of personal interest, and very rarely for a more abstract good.

D'Annunzio's seizure of Fiume is a difficult phenomenon to evaluate in this framework, for while there were many self-serving people involved in the conspiracy to take the city, the poet's motivation was highly idealistic. D'Annunzio's personality was in many ways a throwback to an earlier period, and his search for glory is difficult to understand for those who no longer believe in its existence. Yet, in the end, D'Annunzio's constant search for grandiose gestures and heroic undertakings frustrated many of the plans of his more cynical and "realistic" allies, and the interplay between the cynical and the D'Annunzian elements gives the Fiume enterprise much of its peculiar fascination.

The march of the poet-warrior into Fiume on 12 September 1919 was very much in keeping with his love for melodrama. Rising from a sickbed, weakened by a fever, poorly supplied, guiding only a handful of troops, D'Annunzio threw the calculations of the diplomats into chaos and placed himself for a brief period at the center of the political stage.

The success of the enterprise serves to demonstrate the strength of the many forces that converged to aid the expedition. The sequence of events leading up to the march on the city was entirely worthy of the poet's imagination; had he been permitted to provide the scenario, it is doubtful he could have done better.

The first scene began with the announcement of the decision of the Inter-Allied Commission to have the Sardinian Grenadiers, the National Council, and General Grazioli removed from authority in Fiume. This threatened to erode the base of action from within the city, and those conspirators concerned about the destiny of Fiume itself (as opposed to those who saw it primarily as a stepping-stone to grander actions) were forced to accelerate their preparations. These were the Fiuman patriots, whose actions were based upon Wilson's vaunted principle of self-determination of peoples. It is symptomatic of the populist nature of the Fiuman enterprise that the first action of the conspirators was to mobilize the population of the city in a grandiose demonstration in behalf of the departing grenadiers. To this end, on the evening of 24 August, the Giovine Italia held a mass meeting in the main theater of town, in order to plan the events of the following morning—the scheduled departure date of the Second Regiment of the Sardinian Grenadiers.

The grenadiers had become the symbol of the "liberation" of Fiume, having arrived on 17 November of the preceding year, the first Italian troops to take command of the city. There they had remained, and for nine months these soldiers had been "Fiumanized," participating in the life of the city and identifying with the Italian commitment to free Fiume from limbo. The grenadiers' lives in Fiume were exceedingly pleasant, and if the reaction of the young Giovanni Comisso was typical, their sojourn bordered on the idyllic:

> The city abounded with beautiful girls; the pastry shops were bursting with extraordinary sweets, the vast cafes with their many illustrated journals, delicious zabaglionis, obsequious waiters, stores with perfumes from every corner of the the world. . . . The Fiumans invited the Italian officers to their homes every night for parties that lasted until the following day. One ate, one danced, one drank; indeed, it truly seemed that this city, with its life overflowing with gifts, was the reward for all our exertions during the war.[1]

It is easy to understand why the soldiers were reluctant to leave this earthly paradise and why the Fiumans, for their part, were deeply dismayed at their departure. One can well sympathize with the troops' declarations of support for Fiume, and their promises to return.

At three o'clock on the morning of 25 September, in the predawn blackness, the bell of the town hall began to chime, alerting the citizenry that the demonstration was about to begin. Young patriots raced through the streets, shouting "Awake, awake!" and ringing little hand bells. This effectively ended the city's repose, and the populace descended into the streets, finding their way by torchlight to their appointed posts. With trumpets sounding fanfares, thousands of Fiumans, wrapped in Italian flags and other patriotic costumes, advanced to block the path of the marching grenadiers as they reached the edge of the public gardens.

The two groups met at the gardens, each in full costume: the citizens in red, white, and green, the soldiers in full battle gear (but with their helmets decorated with miniature flags of the city). The Fiumans hurled flowers at the troops, crying "Brothers, do not leave us! Do not leave us in Croatian hands! " The soldiers shouted "Long live Italian Fiume! " The Fiumans blocked the road by spreading their flags and banners across the path, and the troops briefly halted. At this moment, women dropped to their knees in front of the grenadiers, imploring them to remain, and little children raced forward to grab the hands and legs of the officers. As the scene threatened to degenerate into complete chaos, General Anfossi of the grenadiers arrived at the head of the column, greeted by cries to give the order to remain in Fiume. But the general was not about to lose his head in the abundant hysteria, and the liberators of Fiume marched north along the coast.

The scene was not yet over. As the grenadiers departed, General Grazioli walked into the middle of the crowd, and the emotions of the people immediately focused on the Italian commander of the city. New demonstrations burst out, and at the height of the celebration the replacements for the grenadiers—the first platoons of the Regina brigade—paraded into the public gardens. The new troops were immediately deluged with kisses, applause, cheers, patriotic songs and hymns, and a veritable torrent of flowers. The citizens of Fiume, having lost their Sardinian protectors, immediately undertook to win over the new Italian troops.

The impression this ceremony made upon the new arrivals can easily be imagined. They must have been astonished to discover that the city— even though it was at the center of a serious diplomatic storm—was frequently the scene of an ongoing celebration of the most frenetic sort. This bacchic atmosphere was characteristic of Fiume, noted by all who went there. It is particularly fascinating to speculate about the reaction of the redoubtable General Vittorio E. Pittaluga, the commander of the new troops, who arrived several days later. Pittaluga had accepted his new command with considerable diffidence, for he frankly doubted his political talents and was anxious about being sent to such a delicate post. He had expressed his concern to Prime Minister Nitti, only to be reassured that strict orders had been given to maintain control at the armistice line, that potential agitators were known and would be arrested, and that it remained to Pittaluga to maintain tight reins on public order. The general, with his usual tact, recorded his impressions of the city some years later: "Not a few of the officers . . . worked very little, and even those . . . not employed along the armistice line were given to a certain comfortableness of existence. It appeared to me that the 'city of passion,' in its tense anticipation, had become a place of the happy life for all."[2]

In its style of life and exuberance of celebration, Fiume was a D'Annunzian city long before the arrival of the poet-warrior. While many have claimed that D'Annunzio transformed Fiume into a beehive of degenerate activity, the city had already achieved a considerable notoriety for its *dolce vita* before the poet took command. D'Annunzio did not create a new world overnight in Fiume, but rather arrived upon a scene highly congenial to his particular tastes and talents.

On the morning of 27 September, the First Regiment of the Sardinian Grenadiers departed, and again the scene of mass hysteria at four in the morning was repeated, this time at the bridge crossing the Fiuman river. The First Regiment became the nucleus of the troops that marched on Fiume slightly more than two weeks later, and their seriousness was immediately manifest. The day after they had left the city, they found themselves temporarily housed in the little town of Ronchi, four kilometers from Monfalcone, in the province of Trieste. From their new barracks, the grenadiers immediately contacted the hypernationalist leaders of Italy in an attempt to enlist support for an expedition to Fiume. They tried Enrico Corradini, Luigi Federzoni, Benito Mussolini, and Peppino Garibaldi, but without success.[3] It seems that they did not immediately turn to D'Annunzio as a potential leader, despite the frequent linkage of his name with the Fiuman cause.

At the end of August, D'Annunzio was engaged in plans for his long-discussed airplane flight to the Orient, and his energies seemed to be directly solely toward that end. One heard great things about his preparations for the journey to Tokyo, and the grenadiers, like many others at this time, doubted that the poet would be available for patriotic enterprises on the Adriatic coast. Some of D'Annunzio's biographers have argued that the projected Tokyo flight was a brilliant ruse, serving as a cover for his subversive plans and effectively removing him from the intense governmental surveillance that had followed his every move. This view was supported by the U.S. representative to Rome, immediately following D'Annunzio's march on Fiume. Citing a "well-informed source," Peter Jay sent a telegram to Paris saying that, according to his informant, "D'Annunzio's project long known to Government which had him followed by police until D'Annunzio proposed he should make air flight to Tokyo. Nitty [*sic*] believed him, made all preparations for flight even sending to Orient two ships laden with supplies, when police surveillance was relaxed and D'Annunzio was able to carry out Fiume plan. . . ."[4]

On the other hand, the conspiracy to take Fiume was one of the worst-kept secrets of all time, and had D'Annunzio been actively involved in preparations for an Adriatic or Fiuman expedition in late August, the grenadiers would have known about it. As later events demonstrated, D'Annunzio was not convinced that the moment for a march on Fiume was at hand, and the lure of the Orient undoubtedly played a large part in producing his monumental indecision in the weeks following the departure of the grenadiers.

When the grenadiers did approach D'Annunzio, they did so in that overwrought style that characterized virtually all exchanges with the poet:

> The Great Mother does not know Fiume; she is not permitted to know the finest of her daughters, the purest, the most holy Italian woman. When . . . the Grenadiers left Fiume . . . you cannot imagine the convulsion of patriotic enthusiasm that seized the hearts of the people of Fiume.
>
> We have sworn upon the memory of all who died for the unity of Italy: Fiume or death!
>
> And you do nothing for Fiume? You who have all Italy in your hands, great, noble, generous Italy, will you not break the lethargy into which she has fallen for so long?[5]

This plea was signed by seven officers of the First Regiment, who subsequently passed into the lore of Fiume under the name of *i giurati di Ronchi*, "the oath-swearers of Ronchi." The message was carried personally by one of the seven, Second Lieutenant Claudio Grandjacquet, to the poet in Venice.

D'Annunzio's Red House in Venice had become a clearing-house for a great variety of causes. Messengers, politicians, generals, and volunteers brought information and proposals from Fiume, Milan, Rome, Split, and Zara and carried answers and counterproposals back across the Italian peninsula and Dalmatia. D'Annunzio had long been involved in this network, but now that the moment for action appeared imminent, his nerve began to weaken, and he doubted himself and his allies. Quite aside from being tempted by the tantalizing possibility of flying to Japan, his health was not good, there was an entire army between him and Fiume, and he was, in any event, not convinced that Fiume was the proper target for an action. Perhaps it would be better to move on Split, and from there, having claimed all of Dalmatia, sail to Fiume. Even if the time was right for action, which action was the right one? And so he pondered, and days passed.

On the other hand, the appeal from the Ronchi Seven was one he could not very well ignore. Just two months before, D'Annunzio had written a celebrated article entitled "The Command Passes to the People," in which he had declared himself the logical leader of the irredentist forces and the spokesman for all who believed that the war experience must be vindicated in the postwar world. There must be, he wrote, "a lyric order, in the impetuous and vigorous sense of the word. . . . Thus it is good and just that an armed poet is today its spokesman."[6] Command may have passed to the people, but its inspiration would come from the poet.

It was not an easy decision for D'Annunzio; indeed, with the exception of his amorous activities, there were no easy decisions for him. Time and time again he would masterfully orchestrate the world around him, building up to an epic climax that never arrived, his decision faltering at the critical moment. To help himself surmount such psychological barriers, D'Annunzio embraced superstitions, and he often preferred flipping a coin to making a rational choice of his own volition. At other times, he would await a "sign of destiny" to decide his actions.

It is not known precisely who (or what) finally convinced D'Annunzio to join with the grenadiers to march on Fiume; nor, after all, is such knowledge a vital piece in the jigsaw puzzle. Any one of a number of people might have tipped the balance: General Grazioli; Lieutenant Grandjacquet; the great lyrical aviator and "action secretary" of the poet, Guido Keller; Captain Nino Host-Venturi; Major Carlo Reina (who ultimately commanded the group of grenadiers who left Ronchi for Fiume); or others unnamed and perhaps unknown. More likely, several people combined to sway D'Annunzio's will. Although many have claimed this distinction, the most colorful claimant was Attilio Prodam, a friend of Host-Venturi, a member of the National Council of Fiume, and president of the Giovine Fiume organization that had arranged the spectacular demonstrations on the nights of the departures of the grenadiers.

Some twenty years later, having fallen upon evil days and in need of money from the Italian government, Prodam wrote Mussolini a summary of his actions during the days between the departure of the grenadiers and the arrival of D'Annunzio, and his version of this period is confirmed in large part by a diary of the same days written by another Fiuman patriot, Captain Ugo Gnata. These stories are difficult to confirm, but they are of such a piece with the rest of the D'Annunzian enterprise that they carry a certain ring of truth (and, as the Italians say, if they are not true, they are at least beautifully constructed).

On or about the evening of the second of September, we are told, Prodam and Gnata, along with another officer, Captain Carlo Cocco, were walking along via XVII Novembre (named after the day the grenadiers had arrived in Fiume) in front of the Hotel Wilson (formerly the Hotel Deak), when they encountered the distraught Host-Venturi. "What can we do?" he lamented, showing them a letter from D'Annunzio. The note was full of objections to the projected march, calling attention to military and political obstacles, observing that only one-half (or one-third, depending upon which version one believes) of the grenadiers were absolutely dependable, that they would be grossly outnumbered, and so forth. Worse still, the letter contained a phrase that was highly offensive to Captain Host-Venturi, who had worked so hard to organize the Fiuman Legion. "*Ardito, perchè non ardisti?*" This pun demanded of Host-Venturi why he had not had the courage to launch the undertaking himself.

The four conspirators discussed the question, agreeing that D'Annunzio alone was capable of leading the armed expedition. At this juncture, Prodam announced that he would leave Fiume the following morning for the Red House to convince the poet of his proper course of action. "If the poet does not accept the task of liberating us," he told his friends, "I will not return to Fiume alive." [7]

During the next several days, Prodam met with D'Annunzio four or five times, for several hours at each session. D'Annunzio was finally convinced to lead an expedition on Fiume only after Prodam had managed to stage yet another of those operatic episodes that were such an integral part of the adventure. Prodam had learned that General Diaz, the commander of the army, had come to Venice to participate in a ceremony in which he would receive the sword of honor from the people of the city. By imposing on several of his pro-Fiuman friends, Prodam was able to arrange for his little daughter (who had come from Fiume to Venice with him) to give a bouquet of flowers to the general. The girl appeared, wearing a ribbon with the colors of Fiume around her throat, with the phrase "Fiume or death!" written upon it. Handing the bouquet to Diaz, she asked his permission to add to the honors of the day "the flower of the passion of my city." She delivered an eloquent address, concluding with an impassioned plea: "As you have saved the mother (Venice), save also the daughter . . . Fiume, ready to immolate herself in an heroic holocaust upon the altar of the Motherland, salutes you, oh hero, and hopes always in your immaculate faith." [8]

The next day, Prodam went to his meeting with D'Annunzio accompanied by his beautiful daughter, and the poet agreed to lead the march. His agreement, however, hinged on various conditions. Above all, D'Annunzio demanded the most complete possible expression of the will of the city. He required that the entire population meet him upon his arrival, so as to demonstrate that this was not merely a military coup, but a response to the desires of the citizenry. Prodam promised that this would be done, and on 6 September the poet gave him a letter addressed to the editors of the irredentist newspaper of Fiume, *La Vedetta d'Italia*. D'Annunzio announced that he was "ready for anything," but at the same time he indicated some further hesitation about the precise date of the operation. "The words I am sending to you," he wrote, "which will be followed by other, even cruder ones—announce nothing if not violence. But what—according to your enlightened ones—will be the means and the hour to take up arms? It is difficult to write of these ruinous things. Our Prodam will tell you about them."[9]

Had D'Annunzio arranged the time and place of the operation with Prodam? More likely, as some other participants have suggested, that was finally decided two days later, in conversations with General Grazioli, Lieutenant Frassetto (another of the Ronchi Seven), and Captain Host-Venturi. Once again, we may never know the full story. But there is a further tale to be told in connection with the selection of the date of the operation. In the intense discussions in the Red House in Venice, various dates were proposed for the assault on the city. Host-Venturi, Reina, and Frassetto were inclined toward September the tenth, but this was not acceptable to the poet. Deeply superstitious about the significance of numbers, he pondered the problem and emerged with a mystical solution. "The eleventh is a lucky day for me,"[10] he told his collaborators. It was the date of the famous *beffa*, or joke, of Buccari during the Great War. On this day in February 1918, D'Annunzio had led a group of torpedo boats into the Bay of Buccari (just a few miles from Fiume) and had sunk an Austrian ship, leaving behind floating glass containers with excerpts from his war propaganda within them. What better date for an undertaking of equal bravura? And so the date was set.

If it was characteristic of D'Annunzio to use superstition in his selection of the date for the enterprise, it was equally characteristic for him to reconsider his decision, and the days between the "decision" and the event were filled with frenetic activity around the poet. The Fiumans, in order to keep their part of the bargain, had to make sure of the total mobilization of the populace. Their troops had to be armed and drilled for the operation. Frassetto, the messenger for the group, shuttled back and forth between Ronchi, Venice, and Fiume, making sure everyone was in agreement about the timing of the operation and that D'Annunzio would indeed appear at the appointed moment. The matter was thrown into question at the last moment once again, as D'Annunzio was forced to bed with a high fever. On the tenth, Frassetto came to the poet's bedside to tell him that the key elements of the troops at Ronchi had officially abandoned their units and would be exposed to courts-martial if D'Annunzio did not fulfill his obligation. Frassetto found the poet resolute. "Do not worry about me," he told the young lieutenant, "tomorrow I shall be at my post."

THE MARCH FROM RONCHI

D'Annunzio left Venice on the eleventh of September for Ronchi, where he arrived without incident. There he rested on a makeshift bed composed of four small tables and gathered strength for the expedition, which was scheduled to being around midnight. The coup began with only a small band of men: 186 Sardinian Grenadiers, plus whatever forces would join them at the gates of Fiume (several Arditi were expected, along with Host-Venturi's "legion"). As midnight approached, Major Reina gravely announced that they had apparently been betrayed: the transport trucks, desperately needed if the troops were to move with speed through the night, had not arrived.

Yet before noon on the morning of the twelfth, D'Annunzio entered Fiume at the head of a massive armored column, composed of trucks, automobiles, armored cars and tanks—and between two thousand and twenty-five hundred men: grenadiers, artillery, Arditi, and foot soldiers.

The trucks were obtained by D'Annunzio's "action secretary," Guido Keller. Here, as on many other occasions in the future, Keller's unique ability to generate action at moments of inertia proved invaluable and inspirational to the poet. Upon hearing of the lack of transportation, Keller and a handful of others vanished into the night, returning a few hours later with twenty-six vehicles, stolen from a motor pool a few kilometers away.

The swelling of the poet's ranks was another matter, less pictur-esque than Keller's escape, but of fundamental importance, both in the expedition to Fiume and in the reaction of the government that followed. The major part of the forces that D'Annunzio led on the morning of 12 September either joined the column en route to Fiume or marched of their own accord to the city and met D'Annunzio there. This occurred despite rigorous governmental instructions to all commanding officers in the zone to stop any attempt to seize Fiume. Yet during the long night and early morning, not a single shot was fired in an attempt to arrest D'Annunzio or to stop his advance. Just outside the city gates a few empty words were spoken, calling the poet's attention to what he already knew full well—that the march was an act of sedition.

The most famous of the defections to D'Annunzio was that of a large body of Arditi under the command of General Ottavio Zoppi. These vaunted heroes of the Great War had been told to fire on the poet if he refused to turn back from Fiume. Yet they chose to obey, not their commanding general, but their spiritual ally, Captain Host-Venturi, who had asked them to meet the advancing troops and escort them to Fiume. The officer in charge, Colonel Raffaele Repetto, even had the effrontery to disobey a direct order given to him on the morning of the expedition by General Pittaluga himself. Pittaluga, encountering the advancing column (led at that moment by Repetto and the Arditi, in order to re-move any hostile forces from the route), told Repetto that if he did not shoot D'Annunzio, Pittaluga would have the Colonel executed on the spot. Repetto saluted the general but made no move to obey the order. This forced Pittaluga himself into a confrontation that was subsequently immortalized in the Fiuman literature. The general drove down the road in a final attempt to convince the poet to turn back (or perhaps to make one grand gesture that would prevent him from being sacked himself, should his role be called into question). Invoking obedience to duty and Italy's overriding interests, Pittaluga called upon D'Annunzio to turn back. D'Annunzio reenacted Napoleon's gesture at the lake of Laffrey over a century earlier, when Bonaparte exposed his chest to the French troops who had come to arrest him. "All you have to do is order the troops to shoot me, General," D'Annunzio exclaimed, and he lifted his coat, exposing his uniform and the gold medal he wore over his heart. It is difficult to conceive of any Italian general giving the order to fire on D'Annunzio's medals in such a setting (few Italians would wish to be recorded as the man who had had D'Annunzio shot), and Pittaluga, noting that he was himself a descendant of Garibaldian soldiers, decided to spill no Italian blood, and he accompanied the poet into the city. The troops under the command of the poet-warrior entered Fiume around eleven o'clock to the sound of bells and sirens. Laurel leaves cascaded from rooftops, the city seemed a forest of banner and ribbons, and songs and cheers echoed through all the piazzas. "Long live D'Annunzio! Long live Italian Fiume!" The entering Arditi chanted their famous song, "Giovinezza."

This civic explosion had been building for nearly twenty-four hours. Few citizens of Fiume had slept the night before the "sacred entrance," for few of them were certain when D'Annunzio would arrive. There is excellent evidence from members of the Fiuman legion that the troops themselves were not certain that the poet was coming to Fiume until around eleven o'clock the evening before his arrival. It was Host-Venturi who told them of the final preparations and led them in a repetition of the oath they had already sworn, to defend Fiume at all costs from the decisions of the Inter-Allied Commission.[11] The plans for the seizure of the city were two-fold: from within, the legion would capture the command post of the city, urging the Allied forces to leave without violence. If they refused to do so, they were to be driven out of Fiume by the volunteers. From without, the grenadiers and other troops under D'Annunzio's command would enter the city at dawn. Everything hinged on perfect timing: the command post had to be taken prior to the entry of the troops from Ronchi, but not so early that the alarm would spread outside the city, thus jeopardizing the poet's advance.

The rest of the night was given over to frantic preparations and drills. Arms were distributed, and the program for the early morning was discussed and reviewed. At three in the morning, "under the pretext of doing calisthenics,"[12] a group of Fiuman legionnaires left the city to meet D'Annunzio's troops on the road outside the walls. By five, the conspirators were beginning to get nervous. They did not know that the poet had begun his slow advance on the city only an hour or so earlier, and they feared that something had gone wrong. Host-Venturi, beside himself with anxiety, began to take measures to call off the plot within the city, in the event that D'Annunzio did not come. By six o'clock Host-Venturi, virtually certain that the plot had failed, gave orders to his followers to call off the operation; the command post was to be left untouched. But just as the troops on the road to Fiume had failed to obey governmental orders, many of those under Host-Venturi's command refused to abandon hope, and carried on despite the order to demobilize. Captain Gaglioni, who had been ordered to seize the command post, decided to leave the city and find out what had happened. (Eventually he met D'Annunzio and reentered the city alongside the poet's automobile.)

Another element of the conspiracy, the women of the city, also refused to disband, and as Gaglioni drove from Fiume around half-past seven, he saw the streets leading into Piàzza Dante (the main square of the city) filled with women, dressed in their finest clothes, brandishing rifles, clubs, and knives, ready for all eventualities.[13] The Fiuman women had taken a very active part in the proceedings (and would continue to do so after Fiume came under D'Annunzio's control). Already in early September, they had prevailed upon the National Council to hold a referendum that would give them the vote in all civic elections (this was passed by a huge majority on 9 September). They figured prominently in the demonstrations organized by the Giovine Fiume, and on the night of the march from Ronchi they had a crucial role to play (in addition to their preparations for armed conflict). The Giovine Fiume believed it imperative to keep the maximum possible number of Italian soldiers and sailors in the city and hence felt that something must be done to prevent the scheduled departure of the *Dante Alighieri*. The *Dante* was supposed to sail on the night of 11 September, but the Giovine Fiume produced a double-barreled scheme to keep the vessel in port: the women of the city entertained the sailors throughout the night, preventing them from hearing the ship's siren calls by "sealing their ears with the wax of their kisses,"[14] while other members of the group removed pieces of the *Dante*'s machinery and stored them at the Giovine Fiume headquarters. The ship thus stayed in the harbor and eventually became part of D'Annunzio's rather substantial naval forces.

Once the troops entered the city, Fiume erupted into festivities that lasted the entire day. The poet, exhausted by the journey, was shepherded by a group of Arditi to the Hotel Europa for some rest, while other soldiers took up positions throughout the city. The afternoon passed quickly. While D'Annunzio attempted to recover his energies,

Guido Keller met with the president of the National Council, Antonio Grossich, to discuss the future government of Fiume. D'Annunzio had not come with any clear notion of taking command himself; he was more concerned with the great gesture he had made and with future actions in Dalmatia and beyond. Keller managed to convince Grossich that it was in the best interests of Fiume to have D'Annunzio in formal command of the city, for as the sphere of the poet's actions increased, Fiume would eventually hold sway over a sort of Adriatic empire, including Croatians, Italians, and the various inhabitants of Dalmatia.[15] Thus, D'Annunzio was awakened by Keller with the news that he had become the comandante of Fiume. His first words upon learning of his new post were in stark contrast to the orations that had preceded the event: "Who, me? Governor?"

At six o'clock that evening D'Annunzio appeared on the balcony of the palace to accept the applause of the citizens and to announce the fulfillment of their dream: the annexation of Fiume to Italy. The ensuing scene was to be repeated hundreds of times in the months that followed, and it never lost its magic for the people of the city. Much of the ritual of modern politics was born in Fiume under the leadership of D'Annunzio, and the first balcony address made by the new comandante was a paradigm for the harangues that followed in the months ahead.

D'Annunzio's first words were those the Fiumans had fought so hard to hear: "Italians of Fiume"! He continued, creating an image of the city that became the essence of the propaganda emanating from Fiume: "In the mad and cowardly world, Fiume today is the symbol of liberty. In the mad and cowardly world there is a single pure element: Fiume. There is a single truth: and this is Fiume. There is a single love: and this is Fiume! Fiume is like a blazing searchlight that radiates in the midst of an ocean of abjection."[16]

The poet reviewed the great events of the day, giving full tribute to his supporting troops, naming them unit by unit and leader by leader. He then presented the crowd with the dramatic symbol of the expedition, a bright red, white, and green flag, the banner that had covered the body of his close friend and comrade in arms, Giovanni Randaccio, after he had fallen in the war. This banner was well known to Italian patriots, for the poet had unveiled it in the Campidoglio in Rome during a speech in May and had placed a black band around it as a sign of mourning for Dalmatia and Fiume.

"Today," he told the Fiumans, "I show you this flag which, by the will of the soldier himself, I had to give to Trieste. But before carrying it to Trieste it had to come to Fiume, to be reconsecrated by your faith."

The banner of Randaccio was transformed into a sacred relic in the hands of the comandante, and its quasi-religious significance was made

D'Annunzio Unfurls the Banner of Randaccio upon His Entry into Fiume

explicit by the gesture that followed: D'Annunzio asked the Fiumans to swear their fealty to the city on Randaccio's flag. "Do you confirm your vote of October thirtieth in front of the banner of the Timavo?" The crowd shouted its Yes! Yes! at the poet on the balcony. As the echoes died down, D'Annunzio presented himself as the embodiment of the Italian will and the prophet of Italy's destiny: "After this renewed act of will, I proclaim: I, a soldier, a volunteer, a wounded veteran of the war, believe that I interpret the will of all the people of Italy, proclaiming the annexation of Fiume." The piazza exploded into another tumultuous celebration, which lasted throughout the night.

There is a traditional theatricality to all Italian politics, and much of it is dictated by the architecture of Italian cities. Built as they are around great public areas, the cities of Italy seem almost to have been created for outdoor celebrations and civic festivals. To anyone who has been in Piazza Navona in Rome for a political rally or the *Befana*, in Piazza della Signoria in Florence to witness the *calcio in costume*, or in the great *campo* of Siena for the *palio*, this will seem obvious. But for those who live in countries whose cities were designed around interior space, it is a point that needs to be stressed. D'Annunzio's political style was uniquely suited to Italy, where outdoor rallies, whether under the sun or beneath the stars, were part of the civic tradition.

D'Annunzio's innovative genius went far beyond the traditional sphere of politics, however, and his appearance as an actor on the European stage heralded widespread changes in the organization of political celebration. The major elements of the new style were clear in his opening speech to the Fiumans: politics had become something greater, something transcendental. In his dialogue with the crowd, D'Annunzio manipulated the mass of his listeners into a single personality, which spoke to him with a single voice. When he asked for its act of faith, it spoke to him with a single *si*, and he expected this unanimity.

In the contrast D'Annunzio drew between Fiume and the rest of the world, there was an elitist element that had long characterized his writing and his public statements. For D'Annunzio, the world was divided into two realms—one might even say into two levels of moral reality. The symbols for these two realms were Fiume and Rome: Fiume, where the will of the oppressed people had expressed itself in a single act of heroic virility; and Rome, which muddled through its daily ordeal of business as usual, politics conducted by old men in closed rooms, and the banalities of the postwar world. In making this contrast between *his* world and the rest of the world, D'Annunzio evolved a coherent and powerful set of myths and symbols that graphically illustrated the distinction. The use of the "sacred" flag of Giovanni Randaccio is simply one of many symbols the poet used to stress the sanctity of Fiume. The symbols were drawn from all areas of life, and they soon became part of the language of the city. The most important of these was the symbolic flame.[17]

Flames are an old religious symbol, and they were used, appropriately enough, by the Arditi during the war. These storm troopers wore arm patches with black flames on them, symbolizing both the intensity of their passion and the steellike strength they were believed to possess. D'Annunzio, as an honorary Ardito, used the flame as the symbol of Fiume. Indeed, the concept of Fiume as a city ablaze, consumed by its own passion, had been one of D'Annunzio's theses for some time. It was he who coined the phrase by which the city became widely known: the City of the Holocaust. This image typified much of D'Annunzio's oratory about Fiume, for it embodied the central theme of his belief about the city. For him, Fiume was the beginning of a spiritual blaze that would consume all of the rotting and decrepit Western world and that would purify the West, eventually transforming it into something finer and holier. It took some time for this image to develop in his rhetoric, but to understand D'Annunzio's actions at Fiume one must attempt to understand this quasi-mystical frame of mind. His conception of the Fiume enterprise was not limited to traditional political categories, and as time passed it became clear that the mere annexation of Fiume to Italy was not a sufficiently grandiose goal to induce the poet to risk his life and reputation. While many of those who were involved in the seizure of Fiume viewed it as an action designed to further Italy's territorial and political goals, from the very beginning D'Annunzio had a more "poetic," and consequently more exalted, view of the undertaking.

Such considerations help to explain many otherwise surprising aspects of his first hours in the city: D'Annunzio had not provided for the transfer of power, nor was he quick to take command of Fiume. He had hoped that his action, in and of itself, would provoke a dramatic response from Rome and Paris. He was looking for a "sign" that he had altered the course of history. Typically, the poet waited through the night for a response from the government in Rome (hoping for both the collapse of Nitti's cabinet and the annexation proclamation from the government itself). When no news came, he sent a brief message to General Pittaluga (at five o'clock in the morning) that it was "absolutely necessary that [he] assume the military command of Italian Fiume."[18] Pittaluga, hardly in a mood to argue the point, told D'Annunzio he did not feel that he could arrogate the right to contest the command with the poet, who had, after all, assured the security of the borders.

Pittaluga left the next day, and D'Annunzio was faced with a series of problems: the city had to be governed and supplied, contact had to be established with other forces in Italy, and the diplomatic reaction to the coup had to be gauged. This last point was of the greatest immediate importance, for if the Allies could be convinced to cede Fiume to Italy, D'Annunzio's military adventure could quickly end in triumph.

THE DIPLOMATIC REACTION

Francesco Saverio Nitti had long known that D'Annunzio was involved in a conspiracy to capture Fiume.[19] He was further aware of the various preparations that had gone forward within the city and had given orders for the troops along the border to arrest the volunteers who tried to enter the city. In late August and early September, Nitti had checked and rechecked with the generals around Fiume, Trieste, and the Venezia Giulia region to make sure that they all understood the government's desire to avoid a Fiuman coup. He knew that he had to undo the effects of the propaganda of the Orlando regime, and he gave orders that refractory elements be removed from the scene. The treatment of the Duke of Aosta was symptomatic of Nitti's determination to replace officers of dubious loyalty with more secure elements, and by the end of August he had heard from Diaz that "the high sense of discipline that reigns among officers and troops gives full confidence that, whatever decisions the government may make, the necessary orders . . . will be obeyed in perfect obedience."[20]

When news of the seizure of the city reached Nitti in Rome, he exploded in rage, pounding his hand on the table and giving signs of profound shock and disbelief. It is clear that he could not possibly have been surprised by D'Annunzio's actions; why did he put on such an act? The answer is that Nitti *was* amazed, not at D'Annunzio's attempt to take Fiume, but rather at the success of the venture. Nitti had not believed that his troops would refuse to obey their orders, and the success of the march on Fiume demonstrated the extent to which Italy had fallen victim to a thoroughly disloyal army. One must not be too harsh in judging Nitti in such circumstances, for he was not alone in being misinformed about the state of affairs at the Italian frontier. "I am sure," Nitti wrote years later, "that General Diaz and the Minister of War, Albricci, were as deceived as I."[21]

The success of the coup thus revealed the actual situation in alarming detail: the ground beneath his feet, as Nitti himself observed, had been mined. If the army had not defended Italian interests at the border, what reason was there to believe they would defend them in Rome? The march on Fiume was rightly interpreted as a serious menace to the government itself, and the panic D'Annunzio produced in Rome was not restricted to Italian circles; some foreign observers, with access to the best sources of information, shared Nitti's pessimistic appraisal and placed the Fiume coup in a European perspective.

The American diplomats in Italy did not at first know exactly what to make of events on the Adriatic coast. Early speculation (aided by cynical analyses coming from Belgrade) hinged on Nitti's possible connivance with D'Annunzio in the enterprise. Indeed, it was not until 20 September that the U.S. chargé d'affaires in Belgrade, Mr. H. Percival Dodge, was able to wire his delegation at the Paris Peace Conference that the Yugoslavs had figured out that "the present apparently rebellious movement of the Italian forces was not encouraged by the Italian cabinet."[22] The Yugoslavs might have been permitted to be suspicious of the coup, and they were not alone in harboring such thoughts. None other than General De Robilant had delayed in taking any sort of action against D'Annunzio for several crucial hours, because he strongly suspected that the march on Fiume had been undertaken with the tacit consent of the Nitti government. De Robilant's reasoning was hardly far-fetched. D'Annunzio was not being followed by government agents in the days before the march; the demonstrations of the grenadiers at Fiume were not hindered in any way by General Grazioli and were duly reported in the national press (if the government had been truly concerned, De Robilant reasoned, they would have censored the dispatches); when the Grenadiers left the city, they were conveniently housed nearby, in order to facilitate a possible return, and so forth. "The sum total of these facts . . . created in me the grave suspicion that something, unknown to me and for reasons that had eluded me, had been organized by the government for ends which I could not imagine by myself and which I did not wish to hinder."[23]

If an Italian general at the scene could harbor such suspicions of the Nitti regime (and suspicions of this sort would continue for many months within the Italian armed forces), it was even easier for Italy's suspicious allies to harbor serious doubts about Nitti's role in the seizure of Fiume. For the first few days, the American diplomats viewed D'Annunzio's position as completely untenable and awaited some melodramatic termination of the adventure. On 16 September the U.S. ambassador in Rome wired Paris that it had been suggested that D'Annunzio would "choose some sensational way out of situation, such as a melodramatic attempt at suicide."[24] The situation was clearer, however, to some other observers. On the fourteenth, a message from Admiral Andrews (by then a veteran of Fiuman politics) was relayed via London to Paris: "Italian general commanding definitely states he has lost control. He stated this morning had graver matter than defense of Fiume which may refer to revolution in Italy of which I hear rumors."[25]

The significance of the march on Fiume was growing clearer to the U.S. diplomatic corps in Italy, and as time passed it became even more evident. Once the original suspicion—that the whole enterprise was a plot by the government in league with D'Annunzio—had been dispelled, it became clear that Nitti had been confronted with an act of sedition within the armed forces, and no one knew from one day to the next whether the infection was going to spread throughout the entire country or whether it could be isolated in the Bay of the Carnaro. By the end of the month, the tone of the messages from Italy to the U.S. delegation at Paris had changed drastically. On 23 September Jay sent a coded cable marked *very urgent* to Polk in Paris, and it is worth quoting at length from this dispatch:

> [Nitti] feels it is not a question of men but of saving the country. It is in the fighting forces the Government sees the greatest peril; it fears it cannot hold the army any longer, while already the navy has practically gone over to D'Annunzio and it is feared that perhaps one half the population would rise in favor of Italian claims and the liberation of Italian brothers in the Adriatic.
> . . . There are still two million soldiers under arms who would follow it is said their officers. Against this militarist movement would be the Socialists and labor organizations, which represent roughly the other half of the population . . .
> The result it is feared by the Government would be civil disruption if not civil war. . . . This disaster . . . the Government believes may be precipitated at any moment. . . . The Government fears the situation may be brought to a crisis at any moment and if civil disruption breaks out in Italy, and law and order go by the board, fears anarchy will spread within a week to France and later to England.[26]

This is one of those developments that permit historians to sagely observe that truth is often stranger than fiction. A major European power, emerging victorious from the First World War, fears the outbreak of revolution from its own army. If there were signs of an approaching military *Putsch*, the Socialists and their allies might fight against the armed forces, thus precipitating a civil war in Italy. Indeed, Nitti himself had done his best to foster precisely this mentality, for in his speech to the Chamber of Deputies on the Fiume question, he had called upon the workers to defend the country against the seditious menace that threatened it.[27] Having lost confidence in the standing army, Nitti turned to the alternative forces of Italy to defend himself. The irony could hardly be more perfect: Orlando had set aside a substantial number of troops to defend his government against "revolutionary" forces. Only a year later the head of the government was forced to turn to these same forces to defend his regime against the troops.

However, this scenario was not entirely accurate. There were still many in the armed forces who (like General Enrico Caviglia) had a strong sense of duty and who resented the damage that D'Annunzio's coup had done to the reputation of the army. There were also many Socialists who were enthusiastic supporters of D'Annunzio's expedition and who saw in it a chance for the spread of a revolutionary movement within Italy. If civil war broke out in Italy, it would most likely pit those who saw something meaningful in the Great War against those who did not. This was the contrast that D'Annunzio had already drawn in his opening speech in Fiume. Those who believed that the war must vindicate Italian heroism and valor tended to support the coup in Fiume, while those who were anxious to put the war experience behind them and return to "normalcy" tended to oppose it. Not surprisingly, the division within the armed forces was frequently a generational one: the younger officers tended to be pro-Fiume, whereas the older officers were more likely to support the government.

Finally, there was the purported menace to "law and order" that D'Annunzio represented. The people of Fiume challenged that description of their activities, for they felt that they had sound legal precedents for annexing their city to Italy. Indeed, just a few days before the march, the National Council had sent a message to Senator Lodge, imploring him to muster support for the self-determination of their city.[28] Why, they asked, did America not remain true to its own principles? If self-determination was really the basis for the new order, then why had Fiume not been granted this right? For many, both in Fiume and Italy, the annexation was based upon the announced principles of the postwar world, and thus D'Annunzio's supporters accused the Allies of gross hypocrisy in refusing to back the action. In this context, the *moral* quality of the enterprise must be stressed. The question at issue was not whether "law and order" would "go by the board," but simply *whose* law and *whose* order would be preserved. Would it be the orders passed on down from the Peace Conference, or would it be a truly new order, based on the rights of peoples to freely determine their own destinies?

President Wilson did not view the question in this light. For Wilson, there seemed to be a direct challenge to his own integrity, a testing of his will. He did not trust the Italians, and he remained convinced that the entire operation had been carried out with the knowledge (and probably the support) of Nitti. His position could hardly have been clearer, as is demonstrated by a telegram he sent to Jay on 28 September:

> Do not allow yourself to be or even seem to be impressed with what is being said to you by members of the Italian Government with regard to the present crisis. It is all part of a desperate endeavor to get me to yield to claims which, if allowed, would destroy the peace of Europe. You cannot make the impression too definite and final that I will not yield. . . . With a little decision and courage they could have stopped this agitation long ago, but they fomented it rather than checked it . . . the only course to be pursued is *one of absolute firmness*, in which the whole responsibility is put upon the Italian Government and they are given no possible excuse for unloading it on anybody else.[29]

Wilson believed that the matter was one of punishing a disobedient child, and he was not about to let the D'Annunzian infant have its own way (especially, to continue the metaphor, since he suspected that its parents had put him up to it in the first place). Under the circumstances, there was precious little room for Nitti to maneuver in, and while his original reaction to the coup had been that it might help Italy negotiate with Wilson,[30] he soon recognized that the American president was not going to make the slightest concession to the Italians. Furthermore, Wilson quickly alerted the U.S. naval forces in the Adriatic to the possibility of the spread of the D'Annunzian madness, asking that every possible precaution be taken to prevent this from taking place.

The impact of all these developments upon Nitti, as well as upon several leaders of the Italian army, was profoundly embarrassing. Sedition was something that characterized tiny Balkan countries, not one of the major continental powers. If Wilson viewed the coup as a challenge to *his* will, Nitti had much more reason to do so. Yet the Italian prime minister was a far more subtle man than the American president, and Nitti had learned an important political lesson, one that Wilson would only recognize too late: it is folly to let personal emotions sway political judgment. No matter how offensive the Fiume enterprise was to Nitti personally (and it would become far worse when D'Annunzio began to direct harsh invectives and vulgar puns against Nitti himself), Nitti's conduct of Italian policy had to be based on objective considerations.

Even so, in the middle of September Nitti was not certain about the best course of action, and he felt his way in the weeks that followed, awaiting a clarification of the nature of the D'Annunzian enterprise. Would the comandante pursue his intention of "redeeming" all of Dalmatia, or would he become fascinated with Fiume, like a child with a shiny new toy? As Nitti waited for the answers to these and other questions, he ordered a strict embargo placed on the city. But after a few days, he permitted food and supplies to enter Fiume, keeping his ships and troops in place in the event they were needed. Fiume breathed, but it had a noose around its throat, and the cord could be tightened at an order from Rome.

5
Searching for Definition

The seizure of Fiume produced great drama, but it did not resolve the problems at hand. To use D'Annunzio's own metaphor, the fire that had been ignited in Fiume did not spread. Nitti did not fall, the Italian population of Dalmatia did not rise to proclaim its allegiance to the mother country, the forces of the Great War did not take power in Rome, and despite the eloquent proclamation of the new comandante and the National Council, Fiume was not yet part of Italy. Clearly, other measures were needed to bring about the widespread transformation for which D'Annunzio and his allies had hoped. However, these new measures had to be defined, and while decisions were being reached, it was necessary to govern the city.

The city government was in the hands of the Italian National Council, and D'Annunzio's first impulse was to leave the council's powers intact. D'Annunzio had no great desire to take an active role in the interior affairs of Fiume—as his words to Keller had amply demonstrated—but preferred to devote his energies to military and external matters. Nonetheless, after a few days Keller had convinced him that it was impossible to permit a total separation of powers and that he must be able to exercise some control over the actions of the National Council. On 20 September D'Annunzio confirmed the members of the council in office but stipulated that he would assume veto power; all decisions of the council would have to be ratified by the comandante, who thereby became the ultimate arbiter of all decisions affecting the city.

The passage of powers from the National Council to D'Annunzio was not done with great attention to parliamentary detail, and issues regarding the administration of Fiume were left undefined.[1] D'Annunzio's veto power was purely political in nature and left the administrative powers of the council intact. In practice, this ambiguity laid the basis for a serious long-term conflict between the command and the

78

council, a conflict that became increasingly intense with the passage of time and the failure of the command to achieve the annexation of Fiume. For the moment, however, no challenge to D'Annunzio's authority emerged from the National Council. It was obviously impossible for anyone to effectively challenge his rule, and almost everyone believed that the crisis would be resolved in short order. Questions of control of the city could be resolved later on, once annexation had been achieved and D'Annunzio and the legionnaires had left the city, leaving the National Council as the only governing institution.

Potential problems with the Allied forces in Fiume were quickly avoided, as both the U.S. and English contingents left the city on the fourteenth. Given implicit guarantees by the Italians that the matter would be resolved (by force, if necessary) within days (weeks at the most),[2] Lieutenant Colonel Peck for the English and Admiral Andrews for the United States ordered their troops to depart immediately, leaving behind substantial stores and supplies. The French were rather more recalcitrant, perhaps because of the greater material investment they had made in Fiume. No less than sixty days' supply of food for a force of two thousand men was in the French deposits in port, and Commander Gaillard and General Savy were loath to abandon them. In time, however, this obstacle was also overcome, and by the twentieth the French had departed. Military surveillance of the city was left in the hands of the Italian troops, under the command of General Pietro Badoglio, sent expressly to the scene by Nitti.[3]

The Italian government was well aware of the dimensions of the Fiume crisis, and the information that arrived in Rome was strikingly unanimous in one particular: it was impossible to depend upon the loyalty of the armed forces in the event of a battle with D'Annunzio. Badoglio, arriving on the scene immediately after the march on Fiume, reinforced these impressions. On 15 September he reported his convictions to Rome: "I am compelled to say that the words spoken by Your Excellency in the Chamber, to the effect of classifying D'Annunzio's act as folly or sport, have not found the soldiers and the officers in agreement; on the contrary they are infatuated. . . . These magnificent troops, which would move at the first whisper against Yugoslavs or against Allies, will they move against Fiume? . . . I doubt it. . . ."[4]

The day before, Admiral Casanuova had gone to the city under orders from Nitti, to sail the Italian warships out of the harbor. The admiral's description of the emotional state of both the sailors and their officers was virtually the same as Badoglio's account of the army. "The crews (of the four ships in question) not only would refuse to obey orders relative to a repressive action against the troops occupying Fiume," the admiral reported, "but they would be most unwilling to leave the harbor."[5] Further, he found the ships closely guarded by sentinels and bands of Arditi, ready to open fire at the first sign of trouble. Casanuova found himself in a terrible dilemma: he was convinced that it was impossible to sail the ships out of the harbor, but he was under orders to do so. He thus had a choice of precipitating an armed conflict or of disobeying orders. The matter was resolved when the admiral was "arrested" by D'Annunzio. Casanuova remained under an injunction not to leave Fiume until the twenty-second, when Nitti removed him from the obligation to sail the Italian vessels out of Fiume.

Perhaps the most succinct analysis of the military situation was given by Badoglio on the fifteenth, when, having listed the troops in Fiume under D'Annunzio's command, he added, "there are no others, because D'Annunzio didn't want any more. He sent back a battalion of the Seventy-third. . . ."[6]

The fever that spread through the troops on the borders of Yugoslavia infected many of those deep within the territory of Italy, as well as those abroad. In a report to the director of public safety written in the middle of October, an observer who had spent several weeks in the Romagna reported an extremely widespread sympathy for the Fiume enterprise. A few lines from his report suffice to summarize the situation: [An officers' mess in Forlì] "is a hotbed of lovers of Fiume and admirers of D'Annunzio. . . . The young officials of the mess . . . have already tried to reach Fiume . . . they are avid readers of the *Popolo d'Italia* [Mussolini's newspaper]. In Faenza it appears that [the officers of] the entire regiment take D'Annunzio's side. . . . In Verona and the surrounding region . . . there is a committee[including officers] . . . that gathers funds and volunteers for Fiume. . . . [In Libya] the king is greatly beloved by the army, and the name of Fiume is equally dear to the troops. . . ."[7]

Under the circumstances, the Italian government could hardly expect to resolve the crisis by armed intervention. Italian troops would simply defect to D'Annunzio, aggravating the international embarrassment that had already been caused by the march on Fiume and also the chance of a military uprising within Italy. The only strategy possible for Nitti was the one he actually adopted: to play a waiting game, hoping that D'Annunzian Fiume would fall of its own weight. There were various ploys available to Nitti within this context: to gradually foment discontent within the Fiuman populace by limiting food and heating supplies; to send *agents provocateurs* to the city; and to attempt to split off the National Council from D'Annunzio by negotiating separately with the two groups. All these ploys were used, with very limited success. Each of them offered D'Annunzio the opportunity of a colorful response "in kind," which was duly seized. To the embargo, Fiume replied with a

series of sorties (the famous *colpi di mano*) across Italian lines and
among Italian shipping, capturing food and equipment seemingly at
will from Italian and Allied forces. The presence of *agents provocateurs* in Fiume justified the comandante's sending his own men into
Trieste and other areas to stir up anti-Nitti sentiment. According to the
U.S. vice-consul in Trieste, Mr. V. Winthrop O'Hara, this was often done
by women: "The Press Bureau [of Fiume] is more a propaganda office,
which has at its services a large number of girls. Every day the girls are
taken in trucks to Abbazia where they mix with officers and soldiers
still faithful to the Italian government and make propaganda for the
D'Annunzio's [*sic*] cause. The Italian soldiers, whose sentimentality is
well known, desert the regular army as soon as they hear from these
girls the stories of the suffering of the population. . . ."[8]

The attempt to wean the National Council away from the comandante was rather more successful, for the council was not interested
in grandiose projects. For the most part, its members wanted Fiume
annexed, the various economic questions of the city resolved, and peace,
at long last, guaranteed. To this end Mayor Vio and other leading members of the National Council met with Badoglio as early as 21 September
and advised him that they would be satisfied with the simple annexation
of Fiume to Italy, leaving aside the issue of sovereignty over the port and
the territory adjacent to Fiume to the north and east.[9]

In late September and early October, members of the National
Council met with Badoglio in Abbazia to discuss various compromises
but D'Annunzio's resolute opposition to any arrangement that would
produce less than the complete annexation of the city and its port made
all such discussions purely academic and led to considerable embarrassment for council members when word of the negotiations spread. To
make matters worse, no one was quite sure of the comandante's intentions, and rumors about his immediate plans were extremely threatening, both to the Italian government and to many of the men who had
financed and organized the seizure of the city.

THE VISIONS OF D'ANNUNZIO

D'Annunzio's plans were unknown, and the poet himself was probably unsure of his future course. Traditional notions of strategy were
foreign to him, and his actions were often based on aesthetic, rather
than practical, considerations. Furthermore, as we shall see later, he was
under a variety of pressures from conflicting forces within Fiume. One
solid basis for his thinking was his attitude toward the Italian government. The contrast between him and Nitti was profound, and the complete disgust the poet felt for the consummate politician in Rome led

him to invent a new word: *Cagoia.** D'Annunzio's intense feelings about Nitti were at the center of his thinking about the future and were elaborated in a series of speeches to the legionnaires and to the people during his first three weeks in Fiume.

From the first moments of his arrival, D'Annunzio had attempted to characterize himself and his supporters as the representatives of the *real* Italy, the incarnation of a spiritual force superior to that in the Italian peninsula. This notion was, as we have seen, common in the nationalist rhetoric of the early twentieth century, and it led the poet to define his troops as the genuine representatives of the Italian Army. On the morning of 13 September a plane had dropped leaflets signed by Badoglio, urging the troops that had defected to D'Annunzio to return to their units. The comandante replied with an angry speech, proclaiming that the real deserters were the troops that had abandoned Fiume and that ignored its plight. These, he said, were of the same character as those who had run from the battle of Caporetto and who were now the recipients of a general amnesty from the Nitti regime.[10]

These statements were only to be expected from a man who claimed to represent a higher national interest than the one perceived by the government, but they hardly suggested the total rupture that was to come soon afterwards. By the end of the month, D'Annunzio was speaking in quite different terms, using his newly minted epithet:

> *Cagoia* is the name of a low, crapulous creature without a country. . . . Led before the court, interrogated by the judge, he denied all faiths . . . denied himself, denied to have yelled "down with Italy," . . . stating that he did not even know if Italy existed; swore that he knew nothing about anything . . . aside from eating and swilling, down to the last mouthful and the last drop; and he concluded with this immortal definition of his congenital cowardice: "I only think of my stomach."[11]

This was, for D'Annunzio, the figure who headed the Italian government, and he called on the people of Fiume to give Nitti a blasphemous "baptism." "How do we baptize such a creature?" he called to the crowd, and a voice replied, "by spitting on him." As the people burst into laughter, the comandante gave his own followers a nickname: *Teste-diferro*, "the Ironheads." He closed his oration with a sardonic salute to Nitti and a fervent tribute to his legionnaires, invoking as always the participation of the crowd in his closing lines:

> Citizens, soldiers, Arditi of Fiume, Arditi of Italy, to the pillory with Cagoia and his slaves and accomplices. Alala! [shouted first by D'Annunzio, then in

---

* *"Cagoia"* is virtually untranslatable, even into Italian. It invokes the image of Nitti as a fetid, excremental creature.

unison by all] Health and glory to the ironheads!
Alala!
To the day, soon, when Victor Emanuel III will want to enter Italian Fiume,
to be crowned king twice over.
Eia, eia, eia! Alala!

These last words were a signal for the recitation of the chant in unison by the crowd, followed by a spontaneous chanting of the oath to resist "against all and everything" and then a general eruption of songs, laughter, and festivities.

In the development of Fiume under D'Annunzio, both the form and the content of the comandante's speeches were of fundamental importance. The speeches and civic celebrations were dramatic creations of the poet, who was a master at controlling crowds and manipulating the people around him. While he loved his own voice and his own language, D'Annunzio did not give speeches for purely theatrical or exhibitionist motives. His characterization of Nitti as *Cagoia* accurately expressed his contempt for an official Italy that refused to embrace D'Annunzian Fiume as a heroic gesture and a rightful conquest. When he told the people of Fiume that "the *patria* is *here*," he was certainly using a carefully studied rhetorical flourish calculated to heighten the passions of the Fiumans for their leader, but he was also expressing his own genuine belief. For D'Annunzio the Fiuman adventure had an almost religious significance. He not only wanted Fiume annexed to Italy; he also insisted that the Italian people recognize the righteousness and meaningfulness of his gesture. His thinking about the future was consequently two-fold: he wished to see both the purification of Italy and the annexation of Fiume. Both were necessary for the redemption of the nation and the vindication of the war experience. The two events were ineluctably tied together in D'Annunzio's mind, for only a government worthy of the war victory would be willing to proclaim the annexation, and the addition of Fiume to Italy would help to "complete" a triumphant nation. The ultimate success of his Adriatic adventure thus hinged on the elimination of *Cagoia* and the triumph of D'Annunzio's world view in Rome.

The entire Fiuman adventure represented an attempt by the poet-warrior to create a morally purified and territorially amplified Italy—an Italy, in other words, worthy of his exploit. D'Annunzio had not projected a detailed plan for the future, for it was of the very essence of his worldview that tactics and strategy were always secondary to the fundamental vision. To be sure, D'Annunzio was committed in principle to the "Italianization" of Dalmatia, but as we shall see, his plans in this regard were far from clear. Had Nitti fallen at once and had a new government annexed Fiume, D'Annunzio would not have known what to do any more than he had a clear idea of action when Nitti remained in

power. The best description of D'Annunzio's "political philosophy"
has been given by Emilio Mariano. For the poet, Mariano has explained,[12]
the forces in Fiume, along with those that supported the enterprise, constituted a kind of "superworld," a higher level of reality. Those, in contrast, that opposed them were an "underworld." On this poetic vision of
the postwar world rested D'Annunzio's analysis of his own role.

Many of the other leaders of Fiume had a far narrower and more
modest view of the significance of the enterprise. The National Council,
with few exceptions, was simply interested in the annexation of the city
and was not committed to changing the character of the Italian government. The "command" of Fiume was rather conservative: aside from
Keller, the other members of the poet's staff were hardly revolutionary
figures. Eugenio Coselschi, who later played a role in the creation of the
Fascist International,[13] was D'Annunzio's private secretary. Giuriati was
the head of the cabinet, Major Carlo Reina took charge of the army, and
Orazio Pedrazzi directed the press office. Pedrazzi was a correspondent
for the right-wing L'Idea Nazionale and had been one of the most vitupera-
tive opponents of Allied policies in Fiume. He had been in the city long
before the poet's march, and in May the English General Gordon had
protested his speeches against Wilson's programs.[14]

D'Annunzio's staff, then, represented the activist element of the
Italian "Establishment"; men who were anxious to redeem Italy's honor
and who wished to see Fiume annexed, but not men who were interested
in a fundamental change in the nature of Italian society or in the institutional structure of the Italian government. Immediately following the
capture of the city, however, several figures of a more radical tinge
arrived in Fiume, giving rise to widespread fears of a new, revolutionary direction to D'Annunzio's actions.

The first clearly radical elements to arrive in Fiume were two leading Futurists. Filippo Tommaso Marinetti, the author of the famous
document that had proclaimed war to be the "only hygiene" for the
modern world,[15] and Ferruccio Vecchi, one of the most literate of the
Arditi, had long advocated the complete dismemberment of the political institutions of Italy. Aside from their more dramatic calls for the
"devaticanization" of the country, Marinetti and Vecchi, dedicated as
they were to the eradication of all traditional elements, had demanded
the abolition of the Senate and its substitution with a body of young
and brilliant thinkers. These men were not content to function as isolated intellectuals; they were involved in the creation of the first Fasci
di combattimento, they had been volunteers in the war, and they continued their bellicose activities in the streets at the end of the conflict.
On 16 September these two firebrands, along with D'Annunzio, Giuriati,
the military leaders of Fiume (Host-Venturi, Rizzo, and Reina), and

several other activists (Susmel, Miani, and Mazzuccato), met to discuss the possibility of taking action within Italy itself. The plan under discussion, which involved an action in Trieste, was rejected when Miani and Mazzuccato advised the group that there was no chance of success in a city with such a large Socialist Party.[16] Further, while the Futurists were anxious for such exploits to take place, the likes of Giuriati and Rizzo were steadfastly opposed to any similar adventures, and they eventually carried the day.

Vecchi and Marinetti stayed in Fiume until the end of the month, holding rallies in the streets, addressing Arditi, and on the evening of the twenty-fifth, participating in a wild party with the comandante and numerous Arditi. Marinetti hailed D'Annunzio as the "first truly potent and decisive appearance of Italian pride,"[17] pointing to the wide range of exploits successfully undertaken by the poet and to the example he held out to young Italians.

However, by the end of the month the two Futurists had been asked to leave Fiume. There were undoubtedly many reasons for their expulsions, and this matter must be viewed in the larger context of the contacts between the comandante and the Fascists. Relations between D'Annunzio and Mussolini were strained, and in addition, the two Futurist-Fascist leaders wanted to do some proselytizing of their own in the streets and barracks of Fiume. Carlo Guglielmino, a Genovese legionnaire, wrote in his diary that the notion of a mass meeting of Arditi conducted by Marinetti was not at all attractive to the comandante. "I would have been pleased to listen to a recitation of 'the Battle of Adrianapolis' if he had read to me alone," D'Annunzio reportedly told Guglielmino, "but it's a good idea not to give the Arditi swelled heads. *I* talk too much as it is. . . ."[18]

Aside from this somewhat facetious explanation, D'Annunzio was not enthusiastic about having another fiery orator in the streets of Fiume, and Marinetti recognized that there were political motives for his expulsion. The situation becomes clearer when one looks at the letter to D'Annunzio, signed by both Marinetti and Vecchi on the thirtieth of September: "The rumors that are running through Fiume about our propaganda are completely false . . . we carefully avoided any discussions of politics, a feat which was not easy, given that your gesture is undoubtedly more political than military. . . . We completely agree with you about everything . . . we are, however, convinced that our mere presence in Fiume is sufficient to alarm the timid and the foolish to the point of nervous collapse. . . . We are leaving to continue the campaign . . . which will lead us to victory. . . ."[19]

D'Annunzio replied cooly, thanking them for their help and observing that he had heard that their activities were being requested "in the cities of Italy, especially in Milan." He closed by asking them to guide the "ready" and to strike out against the "sated."[20] There was no hint of sadness at their departure, nor any indication that the comandante wished to collaborate with them in the future. Further evidence of the intention of the Futurists and Fascists to recruit some of D'Annunzio's forces for their own purposes is found in a second, undated letter from Marinetti, evidently written the following month. "I beg you," he said, "to send us in Milan, as soon as possible, all the select Milanese elements . . . it is a matter of defending and consolidating Fascism with a decisive action, which, as you know, means Vittorio Veneto and Italian Fiume."[21] D'Annunzio's reply, if he made one, is not known. But there was no great flow of legionnaires from Fiume to Milan to aid the Fascists in their street battles. And there was no alliance between Marinetti and D'Annunzio, the two great activist poets of the early twentieth century.

In addition to Marinetti and Vecchi, D'Annunzio discussed the possibility of wider actions with the leader of the young Fascist movement. D'Annunzio and Mussolini had been in contact since before the march on Fiume. On the night of 11 September, D'Annunzio had sent the now-famous "die is cast" letter to Mussolini, advising him of the enterprise, asking him to reprint an article D'Annunzio had written for another newspaper, and urging him to support "the cause."[22] The next letter from the comandante was a blistering tirade, beginning "I am stupefied by you and the Italian people." D'Annunzio had risked everything, he said; he had taken the city, he and only he could command the armed forces, "and you tremble with fear. You let the most abject faker of all time put his piggish foot on your neck. . . ."[23]

The letter suggests that the two men had agreed that if D'Annunzio succeeded in taking Fiume, Mussolini would immediately come to his aid with men and funds. "Where are the veterans, the Arditi, the volunteers, the Futurists?" Later on, he became even more explicit: "And your promises? Punch a hole in that stomach that weighs you down, and deflate it. Otherwise, when I have consolidated my power here, I will come."

Mussolini reacted, as is well known, by launching a drive to raise funds for Fiume, and in the first week of October he went to Fiume to deliver some money and talk to D'Annunzio about joint projects for the future. Two weeks earlier he had sent the comandante a short letter,[24] in which he proposed a series of actions: march on Trieste; declare the monarchy defunct; organize a directorate for a new government, to be composed of the comandante, and Generals Caviglia and Giardino and Commander Rizzo; announce elections for a Constituent Assembly; proclaim the annexation of Fiume; and launch a series of attacks, on

Ravenna, on Ancona, and in the Abruzzi. On 7 October, Mussolini flew to
Fiume and discussed the question with D'Annunzio for an hour and a
half. There are diverse versions of the discussion between the two men.[25]
By and large, those who were close to D'Annunzio claimed that Mussolini was in favor of an action in Italy but was uncertain about the best
timing for the coup. Mussolini subsequently claimed that he had dissuaded the comandante from the adventure, but the circumstances of
this claim are such as to throw its veracity into serious question. For our
purposes, it is not crucial whether Mussolini counseled an attempted seizure of power in Italy; the basic relationship between the two men and
the existence of a general agreement that, sooner or later, events might
lead them to attempt the coup is what matters.

The relationship between Mussolini and D'Annunzio in the fall of
1919 was that of an aspiring politician to an established national hero.
Mussolini hitched on to the blazing D'Annunzian star, lent the pages of
the *Popolo d'Italia* to the support of the Fiuman enterprise, and collected money for D'Annunzio (although many later claimed that much
of it went into fascist pockets). This linking of fascism with the
D'Annunzian occupation of Fiume produced the first great wave of
support for the fledgling fascist movement, and it is worth noting that
the two men drew their strength from similar bases: veterans, Arditi,
and intellectuals who wished to see the redemption of Italy's victory in
the Great War.

Mussolini was wary of D'Annunzio for several reasons. The future
dictator was committed to an electoral strategy to swell the fascist ranks,
and he certainly could not expect to lead a campaign within Italy at the
head of D'Annunzio's army. If such an enterprise were to take place, it
could only be led by the poet. Given Mussolini's personality and grandiose ambitions, this scheme was not among those closest to his heart.
While we do not know what transpired during their discussion, it is clear
that Mussolini could not afford to separate himself from the poet if the
latter chose to act. Nearly a year later, when the relationship between
the two was very different, this question would be raised again.[26]

The mere presence of such figures as Vecchi, Marinetti, and Mussolini in Fiume helped to enhance the credibility of rumors that were circulating widely about D'Annunzio's plans. On 18 September, for example, Ambassador Jay wired to Paris: "It is said that Fiume is only
part of his proposed action, and [he is] awaiting invitation to take Spalato
Zara Seb Glamour, Coahiula, and Dalmatia region. . . ."[27] Five days
later the U.S. consul in Berne wired to Polk to tell him of an impending
coup in all of Dalmatia and warning of the restoration of the monarchy
in Montenegro, all engineered by D'Annunzio.[28]

Similar rumors were circulating within Italian circles. One of the more spectacular stories was carried to Nitti by Riccardo Zanella, the former head of the Autonomist Party, who had gone to offer D'Annunzio his support. Zanella had no interest in the grandiose schemes being discussed in Fiume, wishing only to guarantee the independence of the city from the Yugoslavs. On the nineteenth, according to his version of the encounter, Zanella spoke with D'Annunzio and was alarmed to hear the comandante tell him that "the Fiume enterprise was only the point of departure for a vast national-military movement, headed by the Duke of Aosta . . . a movement aimed at the military occupation of Rome, the dissolution of the Parliament, the destitution of King Victor Emmanuel III and his replacement by the duke himself, along with the suppression of the *Statuto* and the installation of a military dictatorship."[29]

This "information" was the basic theme of a report given by Zanella to Nitti a few days later, and variations were to be found from other sources. U. S. Vice-Consul O'Hara wired from Trieste on the twenty-sixth that D'Annunzio was threatening to "proceed from Fiume to Pola, Trieste and Venice, and [to bring about] the complete downfall of Italian monarchy and the establishment of a Republic not later than November. . . ."[30]

Both actual events and D'Annunzio's speeches in Fiume lent credence to these stories. While it is virtually impossible that Zanella's report was accurate (if Zanella ever heard such a story, it would more likely have come from some other source inside the palace), D'Annunzio was certainly committed to the "liberation" of Dalmatia. On the twenty-first he had issued a statement entitled "To My Dalmatian Brothers," in which he expressed his conviction that all Dalmatia had to become Italian. "We have not forgotten you," he wrote, "we can not forget you."[31]

The comandante was not alone. On the twenty-fifth, an Italian task force under the command of Count Nino De Fanfogna landed in Trau, attempting to duplicate D'Annunzio's Fiuman exploit. Unfortunately for the count, American troops had been advised to combat all such adventures, and a group of marines put ashore from a torpedo boat shortly thereafter and forced the Italians to evacuate the town.[32] As far as can be determined, Count De Fanfogna had no connection with D'Annunzio, but an observer could be permitted to believe in a link between the two.

Virtually all the forces around the comandante were dedicated to the eventual Italian control of Dalmatia, including those that had organized the Fiuman Legion and put the entire plan into action. The two major figures in this group were Giuriati and Oscar Sinigaglia, who was actively involved in behind-the-scenes maneuvers in Rome. For these men, the Fiuman adventure was solely a means to an end: to remove Nitti from power, install a new government, and realize the irredentist dreams of the Nationalists. D'Annunzio was only one piece on the complicated chessboard of the postwar world, and both men were preoccupied with the possibility that the comandante might decide to make some dramatic move on his own initiative.

Giuriati's early letters to Sinigaglia from Fiume were full of good news:[33] discipline was excellent, morale was high, the city was not suffering from any grave want of supplies or funds, and the general expectation was that the crisis would be resolved momentarily with the annexation of the city. It is worth noting that this expectation was widespread in Fiume; Badoglio reported the same sentiments in his reports of conversations with members of the National Council. Further, for Sinigaglia and Giuriati, D'Annunzio's position on the resolution of the crisis was in basic agreement with their own; while other matters might be negotiable, no alternative to annexation was acceptable for Fiume itself. No "cushion state" or buffer zone, of the sort sometimes discussed by the Americans,[34] would be considered by the comandante.

The annexation and the achievement of the more grandiose desires of the irredentists hinged on the elimination of Nitti. This was so fundamental that, as Sinigaglia wrote Giuriati on 25 September in a very important letter,[35] "one might permit, if absolutely necessary, some small temporary sacrifice of the territorial solutions." To be sure, he anticipated that these goals would be quickly realized under a new minister, but the emphasis was significant for its revelation of the political basis of Sinigaglia's thinking. Sinigaglia hoped to convince Tittoni to resign, thus precipitating a governmental crisis that could produce the kind of cabinet he desired (although he recognized that there was not a great chance of this maneuver succeeding). After analyzing the various political possibilities, Sinigaglia touched on a question which suggested that his view of the Fiume enterprise might be even more cynical than his previous statements suggested: "On the other hand, for all that I perfectly understand the desire of D'Annunzio and the Fiumans that Fiume be Italian, and that it be in contact with Italy (as we all firmly wish), I confess to you . . ."

The end of the letter is missing from the typescript conserved by Sinigaglia. Is it possible that he considered leaving Fiume in a state of limbo, pending the resolution of Italy's internal problems? Much of his correspondence with Giuriati suggests this possibility. Sinigaglia was certainly not willing to risk the entire game on the Fiume gambit, and in particular he was terrified at the prospect that D'Annunzio's actions might precipitate drastic actions in Italy. Above all, no "revolutionary" means to the end of removing Nitti were acceptable, and Sinigaglia listed three reasons for his position: "Primarily, because the vast organization that would be indispensable does not exist, even in principle; second

. . . because a large part of the population that is now with us . . . would turn against us. . . . Third, a movement of revolt on our part would certainly unleash a violent and probably better-organized movement from the Socialists. . . ."

From whom did Sinigaglia fear a revolutionary outburst? The Socialists were not a primary threat. Rather, Sinigaglia feared the same elements Nitti was so concerned about: those members of the armed forces that were intoxicated by D'Annunzio. "The country must be repacified and the grave agitation from all our supporters must be calmed, since it is now reinforced by the entire army and the entire navy, unanimously in favor of Fiume and D'Annunzio. . . ."[36]

Continuation of the kind of action D'Annunzio had launched in Fiume would open a Pandora's box for Italy. The coup Sinigaglia envisaged could best be achieved in a climate of order and tranquillity, and for that reason he wanted to contain D'Annunzio at Fiume: "the magnificent action of D'Annunzio must remain a glorious episode, but it must be closed as quickly as possible."

Such attitudes are typical of those who dislike or distrust the uncertainties of democratic politics, and men like Sinigaglia and Giuriati preferred behind-the-scenes maneuvering to the hazardous game of electoral campaigns. Their hope was that Fiume could be quickly annexed or, at the very least, that the situation could be "normalized" so as to remove the menace of mass action led by D'Annunzio. Giuriati's role in Fiume was thus one of observer and manipulator; he would sound the alarm at the first sign of action and at the same time he would attempt to dissuade the comandante and those around him from any effort to enlarge the scope of their activities. As events were soon to demonstrate, the success of this scheme depended on a speedy resolution of the crisis. The longer it took to "normalize" the situation in Fiume, the greater the danger of independent action by the comandante. As Giuriati and Sinigaglia knew only too well, representatives of very different political movements were working on D'Annunzio and received a much warmer reception at the palace than Marinetti and Vecchi had obtained.

Before turning to the failure of the attempts to resolve the crisis in September and early October, two other elements of the attitudes of Sinigaglia and Giuriati must be discussed, for they had an importance above and beyond the immediate context of early efforts to "contain" the Fiume adventure. The first is the evaluation of the figure of D'Annunzio himself. As we have seen, D'Annunzio had been and continued to be at the center of nationalist conspiracies, and he was widely considered to be the figure most likely to lead the forces of the war against their internal enemies. Sinigaglia and Giuriati did not share this appraisal, for while they recognized D'Annunzio's charisma, they maintained that he was incapable of heading a new national government. Giuriati expounded this view in early October,[37] when two of the leading Nationalists, Piero Foscari and Enrico Corradini, came to Fiume to attempt to convince D'Annunzio to lead an armed incursion into the Venezia Giulia region, and from there to Rome. Giuriati reached the two before they had talked to the comandante, and he implored them to abandon the scheme. After introducing a series of "practical" objections to the plan, he observed that it was not sufficient to have a leader for the revolution; it was necessary to find the future dictator, the figure who would constitute the new regime. When Corradini and Foscari told him that they believed D'Annunzio to be such a figure, Giuriati launched into a long discourse on D'Annunzio's shortcomings as a potential dictator of Italy. The poet had no sense of administration, Giuriati observed, and was notoriously bad at handling money. He was extremely superstitions, and important decisions often depended on chance events rather than on close reasoning. Finally, D'Annunzio was incapable of severity and rigor which, Giuriati believed, were absolutely indispensable for the government of the country. He was, in short, too much the poet and too little the comandante. He might be acceptable as the leader of a tiny "nation" of some fifty thousand men for a brief period, but he was totally inadequate for the more demanding role that Foscari and Corradini had in mind.

Giuriati justified his own participation in the seizure of Fiume by pointing to the small size of the city and to the existence of a stable governing body (the National Council). D'Annunzio did not have to worry about administration, but could limit his activities to giving speeches, attracting the attention of the world to the Italian cause, and eventually, negotiating face-to-face with Nitti. Giuriati hoped that D'Annunzio's formidable powers of persuasion would help to overcome governmental resistance to annexation.

The other reservation about a "revolutionary" development in Fiume was one that Giuriati and Sinigaglia shared with Nitti. As Sinigaglia wrote, it was absolutely impossible for Italy to obtain foreign credits unless peace was firmly established.[38] If D'Annunzio precipitated a military crisis or if his actions prolonged the peace negotiations, Italy would be cut off from desperately needed money. Foremost among those foreign powers that were certain to withhold funds until the Fiume matter was settled was the United States.

THE FIRST TURNING POINT:
LATE SEPTEMBER-EARLY OCTOBER

The occupation of Fiume, with the consequent revelation of the government's inability to resolve the crisis, threatened to bring down

Nitti's ministry. In practice, given the nature of the Italian parliamentary system, Nitti had only two options available: he could declare the annexation of Fiume or he could dissolve Parliament and call for new elections. The latter course was more attractive to him, but if he simply took this action it would appear too arbitrary, and he needed a broad base of support. To this end, he took the extraordinary step of asking the king to convoke a meeting of the Council of the Crown, consisting of the leading political figures of the country, along with ex-chairmen of the Council of Ministers, the military leaders, and Nitti and the king. This meeting, the only such reunion during the entire Fiume adventure, was held on 25 September, and the outcome of the session was thoroughly satisfying to Nitti: not a single voice was raised invoking annexation.[39] With this tacit support for his policies, Nitti turned to the Chamber for a vote of confidence in his policy of continuing to negotiate for the acquisition of Fiume, while not risking open conflict with the Allies to achieve it. On 28 September the Chamber gave him a substantial majority on this question, and the following day Nitti dissolved Parliament, scheduling new elections for 16 November. In the meantime, despite the intensity of D'Annunzio's *Cagoia* speech, Nitti attempted to reach an agreement with the comandante.

Prospects for reaching an accommodation with D'Annunzio were exceedingly poor. On the day the Council of the Crown met, Nitti attempted to exploit the potential division between the command and the National Council by sending Admiral Cagni to Fiume. Cagni was authorized to offer a compromise arrangement to D'Annunzio, promising that the Italian government would never abandon Fiume to the Yugoslavs, that Fiume would be either Italian or an independent city, and that at the very least the status of *corpus separatum* would be maintained. But D'Annunzio was not interested, and he issued an icy statement in which he announced his refusal to recognize the "anti-Italian government of Francesco Saverio Nitti."[40] All negotiations with its representatives were thus impossible.

D'Annunzio's ranks were growing rapidly, and he had been compelled to issue a general appeal to Italian soldiers to stop defecting to Fiume,[41] for he could not handle the numbers of men who were attempting to join him. There were some nine thousand troops under his command in the late fall, and he could have doubled that number had he so desired. In addition to the troops, the ranks of the Officers' Corps had grown as well. On 19 September Commander Luigi Rizzo, one of D'Annunzio's wartime comrades and one of Italy's most decorated men, arrived in Fiume. Less than a month later, on 6 October, two distinguished generals, Sante Ceccherini and Corrado Tamaio, arrived in the city. The

defections of such illustrious figures illustrates once again the extent to
which D'Annunzio's ideas had penetrated the Italian "Establishment"
and the threatening nature of the situation in which Nitti found himself.
Ceccherini came to Fiume out of a double motive: to join the poet and
to reunite himself with his son, who was already there. The general wrote
an open letter to the king and his soldiers explaining his defection,[42] a
letter which, as Ferdinando Gerra has rightly stated, "should be known
and thought about by all those who . . . study the period, because it
documents . . . how Gabriele D'Annunzio had become, for many Italians,
the highest symbol of love and dedication to the *patria*."[43] In his letter,
Ceccherini recounted having received a note from D'Annunzio, "the
greatest spirit in Italy," which evoked their wartime experiences together.
The comandante told the general what a pleasure it was to have his son
in Fiume and closed the brief epistle with a tantalizing question: "Shall
I tell you our wish? I will not say it. But I will say that my devotion is
total." Ceccherini was deeply moved, but he stayed at his post for several
days. In the end, however, he could not refuse the implicit invitation:
"Whoever joins the purest spokesman of the Great Italy, goes against
those who have betrayed you . . . Fiume today is something more than
the affirmation of a sacrosanct right of Italianness. Fiume is a beacon that
lights the world, and the world, today in anguished convulsions, must
recognize it as the source and the symbol of our beloved country. . . ."

As events had demonstrated, the enthusiasm D'Annunzio was able to
generate in those who heard his words was remarkable, and in the course
of the first weeks in Fiume he had developed his already notable oratorical
gifts to a new level of effectiveness. Ceccherini had already fallen under
D'Annunzio's spell years before and was reacting to the appeal of a man
he already admired; but for many others who lived in Fiume or who had
gone there out of curiosity or a pure sense of adventure, D'Annunzio's
public ceremonies served to rally them to the "cause" and give them a
sense of participating in the enterprise. One of the most famous of these
celebrations was held the day following the arrival of Ceccherini and
Tamaio, at the funerals of Aldo Bini and Giovanni Zeppegno.

Bini and Zeppegno were aviators, who had taken off on the morning of
the sixth on a reconnaissance flight over Fiume and Sussak. The engine failed,
and the two crashed. Zeppegno was thrown from the cockpit and impaled
on an iron stake. Bini was still alive when the first people reached the scene
of the crash, but he died soon afterwards in the hospital. These were the first
persons to die on behalf of the Fiuman cause since D'Annunzio had marched
on the city nearly a month before, and their deaths were peculiarly "D'Annunzian," for the comandante was closely linked to aerial adventures in a period
when the airplane had come to symbolize courage and derring-do. The city
went into mourning, and the following day the funerals were celebrated.

Funeral of Two Aviators at Fiume

According to the reports in the *Vedetta d'Italia*,[44] every person in the city participated in the ceremonies in one way or another, either in the processional or at the cemetery. The city was bedecked with flowers, and in the hours leading up to the ceremony there had been a frantic hunt for the few flowers left in town: having exhausted all the florists' supplies, the citizens sacked the public gardens and private yards. So it was that the long ("interminable," the newspaper said) funeral procession was a blaze of colors, composed of flowers, flags, and uniforms. The march began with two platoons of marksmen, followed by the city's orphans and an instrumental band. On the heels of the little children came the two funeral carriages, covered with wreaths and banners. On each side of the carriages were war wounded and decorated veterans, paying homage to their fallen comrades. Immediately following the biers came the comandante, surrounded by his general staff: Rizzo, Ceccherini, Casagrande (the head of the air force), Vadalà (for the Royal Guards), and other, lesser figures. After them came two large trucks filled with floral displays of all sorts, to be placed on and around the graves.

The parade continued, embracing all manner of citizens' groups: soldiers and railroad workers, firemen and musicians, workers and gymnasts, politicians and teachers, and finally thousands of citizens who simply wished to be part of the massive civic demonstration, what the *Vedetta* called "a plebiscite of love and pity."

The procession stopped in Piazza Dante, filled to overflowing, and D'Annunzio addressed the multitude:

> Glory to the winged pair that has offered the first holocaust of liberty to the City of Holocaust!
>
> Lieutenant Aldo Bini, Brigadier Giovanni Zeppegno, Italians of the new Italy . . . young winged and sworn couple, I order that the great banner . . . be spread over the double bier, the banner on which the unanimous oath was sworn and renewed. . . .
>
> My pilots, cloak the two coffins. Perform the rite of the sign of that cross that is made by the shadow of the winged machine, with its double wings. . . .
>
> People of Fiume, gentlemen of the council, we consign these first of our dead to the sacred earth, to the free earth. . . .
>
> And be certain that all, like these two burnt confessors of the faith, wish to die for faith.[45]

Today, nearly sixty years after these events, it is difficult to evoke the emotions and the passions of those moments. The physical feat D'Annunzio achieved in these civic festivals is almost unbelievable to a world accustomed to hearing electronically reproduced and amplified voices. D'Annunzio did not have the benefit of loudspeakers, yet he succeeded in speaking to tens of thousands of people in open piazzas and holding them spellbound. Those who were present at such ceremonies still recall the effect of the comandante's voice, even at a distance of several hundred yards, in all sorts of weather.

The description of Giuseppe Maranini helps to reconstruct the drama of the ceremony: "The words of the poet rang high and clear in the great piazza; and they were surrounded by a silence of the tomb. It seemed that those thousands and thousands of persons who listened, did not breath, did not live; it seemed that they were a people of mournful shades. The poet spoke under the full and clear moon . . . in the great immense silence that followed, one could only hear restrained crying. And truly the air was full of an immense and profound lament, the sorrowful passion of Italy."[46]

While such ceremonies as the funerals of the two aviators were quite extraordinary, Fiume under D'Annunzio was a kind of ongoing celebration, highlighted by speeches, marches, and parades. At the end of September, nearly three weeks after the "sacred entrance," Vice-Consul O'Hara wrote to Paris that "the city is completely beflagged. It looks like a town in which the people having nothing to do because of the continuous demonstrations. . . ."[47] And the *Chicago Tribune* correspondent, John Clayton, began his story a week later with the words, "everywhere is a blaze of light and color."[48]

Fiume was a political theater, and its citizens and legionnaires were both audience and chorus. This dual role was important, for D'Annunzio would not have been able to sustain the enthusiasm for his regime if he had depended on one role to the exclusion of the other. The people could not simply stand by and be enthralled by the comandante day after day without soon losing interest in the spectacle, and the festivals served to convince them that they were active participants in a great cause. On the other hand, they constantly needed to be reminded about the meaning of their activities, and the almost daily harangues from the balcony functioned as the litany of Fiume, a constant lesson in the significance of everything they did.

Years after the Fiuman adventure, Giovanni Comisso reflected that D'Annunzio was the first person to recognize that political problems could be solved by speeches to the people, "a dangerous method, although perhaps the only practicable one in Italy, where it is still not known if a responsible and conscientious citizenry can be created."[49] Comisso's attitude is typical of those of most Italian observers, but it misses the important element of D'Annunzio's dramaturgy. D'Annunzio was not so much a speech-giver as a festival-creator. He virtually never gave a speech that was not, at least in part, a dialogue with the crowd, and the people filled the piazzas for well over a year to participate. Without the activist element in these celebrations, the people would soon have tired even of D'Annunzio's melodic voice.

Yet the very nature of D'Annunzio's political drama was such that it imposed the need for action on the command. If, as the comandante told his followers, Fiume was to issue in a new era of grandeur, there must be some palpable sign that changes were taking place. As Sinigaglia and Giuriati recognized early on, it was psychologically impossible for the status quo to continue for long, and with the meeting of the Council of the Crown and the failure of the Italian Parliament to act on behalf of Fiume, the need for action became compelling. It is significant that Mussolini's letter to the comandante was dated the same day as the meeting of the Council of the Crown, which took place while Marinetti and Vecchi were in Fiume.

It was certainly not necessary to look outside Fiume for sources of adventurous ideas; the city was filled to overflowing with inventive people. D'Annunzio had to have two of the legionnaires arrested when he learned of their plan to travel to Rome and assassinate Nitti. There were many wild-eyed adventurers alongside the more sober military men, and a fair summary of the composition of the legionnaires was given to the government in October by Admiral Nunes Franco, who had been in and around Fiume since late the previous month: "Among [elements of undoubted patriotism and monarchical faith], taking advantage of the abnormality of the moment, one finds that, from the beginning, there have been other elements that . . . hope to find in the name of Fiume a . . . screen for the activation of their subversive ideas, even going so far as to think about a radical change of the present monarchical regime . . . the subversives believe that their task has been facilitated as well by the fact that in all of Dalmatia, and even more so in Fiume, the names of Minister Nitti and the Honorable Giolitti arouse the gravest hostility. . . ."[50]

This hatred for Italy's political leadership, as we have seen, was a fundamental element of D'Annunzio's rhetoric, and since the fall of Nitti was considered of paramount importance to virtually every leading figure involved in the seizure of Fiume, it was only natural for them to seek some way to hasten his collapse. While Sinigaglia, with his almost pathological fear of mass movements, might insist that behind-the-scenes maneuvering was the only secure method for toppling Nitti, many of those who surrounded the comandante were not fettered by such compunctions. Foremost among those who wished to initiate a series of actions against Nitti was Guido Keller, who, on several occasions, revealed himself to be one of the determinant elements in the Fiume adventure.

Keller was a man who could never sit still and for whom mortal risks were essential for a happy life. The war had been a splendid adventure for him, and he, like D'Annunzio, had found a home among the clouds.

Keller was one of the leading Italian aces during the conflict, and he continued to embark on spectacular flights long after he had left Fiume. Giuriati's description of Keller, whom he strongly opposed, is perhaps the most accurate: "Like all true heroes, he disdained . . . all poses. Like all great comedians, he never laughed. He considered life a game, both his and that of others, the only game that never lacked interest. Since he could never perceive, and still less evaluate, obstacles, he was convinced that nothing was impossible. He painted a rural scene with the same tranquillity with which he defied death."[51]

Keller's life-style had much in common with the German Youth Movement, the so-called *Wandervogel*,[52] in the late nineteenth and early twentieth centuries, although his activist ideology took quite a different form from theirs. He would often walk naked along the beach (even near Genoa, before the war, where he was arrested more than once for indecent exposure), and when he grew tired of city life in Fiume, he went to the countryside, where he slept in a huge haystack in the open air and ate fruit and nuts gathered from trees and bushes nearby. He had a pet eagle, which became something of a cause célèbre one day when D'Annunzio had it stolen and brought to the palace. Keller's love for practical jokes and acts of piracy found a kindred spirit in the comandante.

Given this restless spirit, Keller was constitutionally incapable of sitting idly by while diplomats debated the destiny of Fiume. He consequently established an office of armed coups (the famous *colpi di mano*), with himself in charge, in order to create an ongoing embarrassment for Nitti and a constant amusement for himself. These coups became a trademark of D'Annunzian Fiume, and as Giuriati has rightly observed, one could fill a volume with stories about them. The most famous of the episodes was carried out by the maritime section of the Office of Armed Coups, which became known as the *Uscocchi*, taking its name from that of the medieval pirates of the Adriatic who had terrorized Venetian shipping for several centuries. These friends of Keller became twentieth-century pirates, capturing ships loaded with food and arms and sailing them into port to the great delight of the comandante and the citizens of the city. Similar episodes were conducted by night across the armistice line, and a seemingly endless supply of food and supplies was procured for the city's warehouses in this manner. Indeed, these operations were so successful that Giuriati complained that D'Annunzio did not even think about providing for supplying Fiume by standard means, since the *colpi di mano* were quite sufficient.[53]

In addition to providing supplies for Fiume, Keller also provided entertainment and information. Under his leadership, and with the assistance of such kindred spirits as Comisso and Cabruna,[54] telegraph lines between Sussak and Abbazia were tapped, providing the command with accurate information about Italian military plans around the Fiuman border. When Keller grew bored, he would strike off on his own, sometimes by plane, sometimes by boat, sometimes on foot, in search of adventure. In October, for example, he took off on a surveillance flight over nearby Yugoslav territory. The engine of his plane failed, and as he floated slowly down over a broad plain, he saw a set of buildings beneath him with a spacious field in their midst. He landed his aircraft in the field, and discovered that he had set down in a monastery, and the monks leaned out of their cells to shout at him in a language he did not understand. In a few hours he managed to repair his plane, but in the meantime he had found a midget donkey in the field and had become quite fond of it. So it was that when Keller flew back to Fiume he had a tiny donkey lashed to the struts of his landing gear, and he gave the animal to the comandante.[55]

Giuriati has written that these coups constituted a veritable nightmare for the government,[56] and one can well believe it. The combination of D'Annunzio's *Cagoia* speeches and the coups ridiculed Nitti, demonstrated the impotence of the government, and added to the mystique of the Fiuman adventure. It appeared that D'Annunzio and his followers could do almost anything they chose. Consequently, while Keller might at first glance appear to be so bizarre a figure as to preclude giving him political significance, in practice his actions were of considerable political importance. And, as we shall see, Keller was also seriously involved in constructing political ideas. For our present purposes, the crucial significance of Keller—and those in Fiume who aided and sympathized with him—was his total rejection of the Giuriati-Sinigaglia model for Fiume. Keller could not accept stasis; he took D'Annunzio at his word when the comandante spoke of establishing a beacon for the world in Fiume, and he was determined to generate a never-ending series of activities until this vision was fulfilled.

It is now necessary to investigate the state of affairs within Fiume at the end of the first month of the occupation, because the direction the comandante gave to his actions was based in large part on the internal situation that confronted him.

Behind the Stage Door

The Fiumans were well-equipped for difficult and confusing circumstances, as the previous half-century of struggle for control of the city had demonstrated. They had mastered the delicate skill—indispensable in an area contested by various colonial powers—of maneuvering between different cultures and political forces. Nonetheless, D'Annunzio's occupation of the city presented unique problems. Much of the chaos of the first months of the comandante's rule stemmed from the very circumstances of Fiume's plight, and the forms life took were determined both by the traditions and ideas of the Fiumans and by the actions of the command.

The dilemmas regarding the legal system were symbolic of the situation. The traditional code was that of the defunct Dual Monarchy, and while it seemed logical to abolish the Hungarian laws, it was not clear what was to be substituted, nor by what authority such a transformation could be achieved. On more than one occasion the *Vedetta d'Italia* called for the installation of Italian laws, but there was no solid basis for an act of this nature (which would have been extremely provocative to the Allies and extremely hard for Nitti to digest). In the end, the command was left to pick and choose between Italian and Hungarian precedents. Several years after the event, Giuriati claimed that the command had acted as a sort of trustee for the Italian crown: "the power held by D'Annunzio was derived from that which was due to the king of Italy. Justice was consequently administered in the name of the king."[1]

This highly questionable principle worked well enough in most civil actions and enabled the command to take several humane measures on behalf of both citizens and legionnaires. Thus, for example, when an officer asked for permission to marry a Fiuman woman, Giuriati found himself in a curious position, since according to the military code of Italy the soldier required royal approval for the marriage. Since the

troops under D'Annunzio's command were considered traitors by the
Italian government, this permission was most unlikely to be granted.
Giuriati resolved the dilemma by having the comandante sign the royal
decree,[2] on the assumption that the permission would be confirmed as
soon as the Fiuman crisis was resolved. He was proven a good judge of
the situation, for the marriage and others like it were subsequently given
full legal status.

Giuriati's contention that D'Annunzio's powers were derived from
those of the monarchy found application in other spheres of activity,
and the comandante did not hesitate to grant pardons and amnesties
when he felt circumstances warranted such actions. Yet it would be a
mistake to accept Giuriati's explanation, because while it wraps many of
the command's actions in the mantle of Italian legality, it does not conform to the bulk of D'Annunzio's measures, nor, indeed, to Giuriati's
own account of the comandante's attitude toward the law. D'Annunzio
considered himself to be above all laws, and he exercised his own pre-
rogatives in Fiume as an absolute monarch, with no institutional or formal check of any sort on his actions, save his own "sense of justice."
Long before a new constitution was promulgated for the city (in the
late winter and the spring), it was clear that D'Annunzio defined justice
without being bound by Italian tradition or precedent. Giuriati spelled
this out in his memoirs: "D'Annunzio considered himself superior to
justice, both in theory and in practice. I was interrogated by him endlessly about legal matters, always with a lightly ironic tone . . . he considered the subject beneath the altitude at which nature had placed
him."[3]

While this "system" was extremely perilous in theory, it worked out
fairly well for the citizens of Fiume, for if the comandante erred in the
application of justice, he invariably sinned on the side of leniency. Giuriati was driven to despair by D'Annunzio's habit of pardoning criminals
and ignoring serious breaches of discipline. Even treason was treated
with surprising forbearance. Comisso tells of D'Annunzio's behavior
when a group of Nittian agents was discovered among the legionnaires.[4]
The comandante decided to expel them from the city, but he wanted
first to interrogate them in front of their former comrades. One by one
the men were questioned, each offering a variety of excuses for his behavior. After hearing the grandiose promises that had been made to the
agents, had they succeeded in undermining the command, D'Annunzio
laughingly said that the government had promised him a triumphal parade
along the Via Sacra in the ruins of the Forum if he left Fiume. Amid
the general hilarity, D'Annunzio left the hall, only to return almost immediately when an insult by one of the agents provoked the legionnaires to the point of attempting to kill the offender. The comandante

calmed everybody down: "What is going on? Be calm, don't get excited, the destiny of the *patria* is once again on the knees of its protecting God." The episode is symptomatic, both of the leniency of justice in D'Annunzian Fiume and of the personal nature of its application.

The direct impact of D'Annunzio's personality was extremely important to the morale of his troops, as well as to the willingness of the citizenry to accept the sacrifices, inconveniences, and occasional suffering they were required to undergo during the occupation of the city. It is significant that virtually every memoir of Fiume from the period tells at least one story of personal contact between the author and the comandante, indicating not only D'Annunzio's intense effort to personalize his rule but also the significance of his personality in shaping the loyalty of his followers. The charisma of the comandante was unmistakably stamped on the personalities of Fiume, for the participants in his political melodrama began to imitate him in all aspects of their lives. Perhaps the most striking example of this mimesis is the language of the city. From the most cultured intellectual to the poorest volunteer, all became masters of oratory, and even the simplest conversations often became elaborate discourses. Leon Kochnitzky recalled hearing himself say one day,[5] "one hundred twenty days and one hundred twenty nights," when he normally would have said "four months." While such excesses were, of course, most pronounced in the immediate surroundings of the Command, they spread throughout the city. "Officers wore white gloves, strong perfume, ate candies . . . and pursued the charms of women."[6]

It is probably impossible to attempt to reconstruct the level of sexual activity in any time or place, and in the case of D'Annunzian Fiume the problems are multiplied a hundredfold. Nevertheless, even making ample allowance for the inevitable exaggerations, it seems safe to say that Fiume must have been an amazing place. Paolo Santarcangeli, a very balanced observer, wrote that "it was a period of madness and baccanale, ringing with sounds of weapons and those, more subdued, of lovemaking."[7] To be sure, Fiume was already quite "liberal" in such matters long before the arrival of the legionnaires, but some words reportedly given by D'Annunzio to his officers in October or early November leave little doubt about the dimensions of the phenomenon:

> I have something to say to you young men, and it is strange that it is I who must say it, I, who have undergone the demands of youth so forcefully. But I can say it because from the moment I arrived in Fiume, I have maintained a Franciscan chastity, while you—you have exceeded all limits. We are surrounded, the conflict may be imminent, it is necessary to keep your muscles sound, and at the very least try not to go into the brothels when the soldiers are present. . . ."[8]

The notion of the comandante subjecting himself to a rigorous chastity hardly fits with his character and, in fact, bears little relationship to the truth. Comisso, for example,[9] refers to a certain Lily de Montressor, a singer in a port night club, who was frequently smuggled into the palace through a back door late at night and who left at dawn enriched by five hundred lire. Further, for most of the period, D'Annunzio was constantly in the company of the famous pianist Luisa Baccara, who remained his companion for the rest of his life.

Yet, the activity around him was so intense that the comandante was obliged to call for moderation from his men. We may well believe Comisso's impression that "the loving was without limit."[10] The young Giuseppe Maranini, in his first letter to his fiance from Fiume, wrote that "everyone enjoys himself here . . . and makes love with the Fiuman girls, who are famous for being beautiful and not difficult."[11]

This aspect of life in Fiume eventually became almost legendary and was perhaps the most common feature attributed by those outside to the City of the Holocaust. Turati, for example, wrote to Anna Kuliscioff in the spring of 1920 that "Fiume ha[d] become a bordello, a refuge for criminals and prostitutes of more or less 'high life,'"[12] and this observation was mild compared to that of other observers who often maintained that the majority of D'Annunzio's followers stayed in Fiume simply because of the licentiousness of the life there.[13]

Experimentation with drugs also existed in Fiume, although the extent of drug abuse is impossible to determine. It is certain that many used cocaine, a habit that stemmed from the Great War. Cocaine had been used by some pilots in order to stay alert during their flights, which frequently lasted several hours under extreme climatic conditions. In this manner, the drug came to be associated with valorous enterprises, and it was evidently introduced into Fiume by aviators. Comisso gives the impression that its use was fairly widespread among the younger officers,[14] a fact Giuriati confirms in his memoirs.[15] In addition, Giuriati recounts the successful suppression of a cocaine "ring" in the fall of 1919, when the *carabinieri* discovered a stash of the drug in a local pharmacy. The pharmacist was arrested and the cocaine supply sequestered; but this does not seem to have ended drug abuse in Fiume. In *Il Tappo*, the so-called organ of the officers' mess (and one of the finest examples of the wit that abounded in Fiume), a mock advertisement appeared early in December: "Futurist painter will perform any work. Fantastic impressions 'morphine style.' An absolute innovation."[16]

Clearly, then, Fiume was in the grip of a postwar frenzy, a general explosion of exuberance and licentiousness following the long years of trench warfare and enemy occupation. It must be said that this explosion was probably to be expected in a city that believed itself to be on the verge of fulfilling a cherished dream, and was not entirely due to the arrival of "D'Annunzian" forces. What was quite out of the ordinary was the durability of this frenzy, for by all accounts it lasted right up until the end of D'Annunzio's reign. As Santarcangeli writes, "it seemed that the celebration would never end,"[17] despite the increasingly difficult economic plight of the city and the numerous obstacles to annexation that emerged. There was a continuing feeling that those days would be remembered as an explosion of patriotic and romantic sentiment, and everyone wished to participate in the experience. The baccanale, then, was patriotic, and citizens and legionnaires alike participated willingly in the festivities. It is typical of the period that there were motion picture cameras at the gates of the city to film the "holy entrance," and on at least one occasion the comandante was offered a huge sum of money to participate in a documentary film (unfortunately, the first film cannot be found, and the second was never made). But one does not need to see such films to appreciate the theatricality of life in D'Annunzio's Fiume or to recognize the importance of this ongoing festival in mobilizing the legionnaires and citizens to support the command's projects. The effectiveness of the mobilization of the Fiuman masses can be better appreciated against the background of the severe economic and social difficulties through which Fiume passed in the autumn and winter of 1919.

THE ECONOMIC CRISIS

While the city had suffered considerably during the war, the financial condition of Fiume was far from desperate. On 6 September, less than a week before D'Annunzio's arrival, an editorial in *La Vedetta d'Italia* noted that despite the substantial civic debt, Fiume was in good condition to face her obligations, that the city did not lack resources: "The monetary wealth of her inhabitants is notable. . . ."[18] This was not to say that there were not serious problems, but most people hoped and believed that the most pressing of the city's economic concerns would be speedily resolved once annexation had been achieved.

Fiume's nationality raised some difficult problems, for example, the recovery of funds that had been deposited in foreign banks. One citizen discovered that his savings had been seized by the Austrian government, on the grounds that they were "Yugoslav funds." Fiume was not alone in exercising the option of assigning the city to its favorite nation, and as the unfortunate merchant in question observed in an angry letter to the *Vedetta*,[19] such problems could only be solved subsequent to the resolution of Fiume's sovereignty. Significantly, the newspaper observed that annexation constituted the key to the solution of the city's economic problems in general, for in addition to liberating some sequestered funds in foreign banks, it would enable Fiumans to get a favorable exchange rate with Italy.

The question of currency exchange was a constant affliction, for the day-to-day fluctuation in the rates (and that from one bank to the next) was remarkable. It was hoped to stabilize the rate at two and one-half Fiuman crowns per Italian lira, but Fiumans feared that if annexation did not take place, the crown might fall below fifteen hundredths of a lira (as eventually occurred). Speculation was naturally widespread, and by the end of September D'Annunzio had to negotiate the takeover of the local branch of the Austro-Hungarian Bank by the National Council, in an effort to guarantee a stable rate of exchange and help to protect the lira from speculators.

The attempt to give some stability to the currency was worked out by various men—Giuriati, Oscar Sinigaglia, several members of the National Council, and Ettore Rosboch, an official of the Fiuman branch of the Bank of Italy. In addition to creating a Credit Institute under the aegis of the National Council, they tried to negotiate with the Italian government for a conversion of the foreign currency in Fiume into lire. These negotiations were carried out in large part by Sinigaglia in Rome.[20] Obviously the government could not publicly undertake the conversion, but since the Banca Italiana di Sconto (a private institution) was willing to do it, all that would have been required was, in Giuriati's words, "that the government lend its consent and, although secretly, its guarantee."[21]

Nitti could not bring himself to approve the operation—it would have given his enemies a powerful weapon to use against him, strengthened the accusation that he was secretly in league with D'Annunzio, and seriously weakened his bargaining position with the Allies—and the currency chaos in Fiume became more serious as the autumn advanced.[22] At the same time that the Credit Institute was created, the Command decided to issue new Fiuman crowns, which were old Hungarian banknotes stamped with a new *Città di Fiume* seal. It was the Command's intention that these notes would become the official money of the city and would in time replace Hungarian and Yugoslav notes.

This strategy required a series of parallel measures: all banks were asked to keep separate records, one in Fiuman crowns, the other in Yugoslav crowns. The purpose of this measure was to ensure that Fiuman money could not be the object of speculation. Civic leaders reasoned that if they refused to change Yugoslav currency into Fiuman money, eventually the Yugoslav notes would stop circulating. However, as so often happens, the measures had the reverse effect; as soon as the new money was issued, merchants raised their prices in Fiuman currency (as much as thirty percent), speculators began hoarding the Fiuman bills (one could sell thirty-five Fiuman crowns for one hundred Yugoslav crowns), and a wave of counterfeit Fiuman money threatened to throw all economic transactions into near-total confusion.

Apart from the reactions of the citizenry to the new currency, the issue of Fiuman money caused a series of economic problems for unanticipated reasons. The price of wine is a typical example: the Command levied a twenty-five percent sales tax on liquor and required that the tax be paid in Fiuman currency. Thus, many dealers found themselves in the curious and unhappy situation of having to pay taxes (in Fiuman currency) on the basis of prices they had paid in another coin. A dealer who had purchased a bottle of wine for twenty Yugoslav crowns was required to pay five Fiuman crowns in taxes, but since one Fiuman crown was worth three Yugoslav crowns at the Credit Institute in late October, the effect of the sales tax was to nearly double the retail price of wine; the unhappy merchant paid the equivalent of fifteen Yugoslav crowns in taxes on a bottle he had purchased for twenty.

To make matters worse, the requirement that only Fiuman currency be recognized in transactions with the command had the effect of making it virtually impossible for many citizens to buy food (since food rations came from the Office of Supplies), and in late November the fiscal measures had to be modified. Merchants paid their taxes in the same currency as that in which they had made their purchases, and the Office of Supplies accepted Yugoslav crowns from the citizenry.

One could continue almost endlessly, describing the monetary chaos, but the matter was well summarized by *Il Tappo* at the beginning of December:

> The money that has free circulation in Fiume is that with the new seal, *Città di Fiume*, stamped on the notes which had the old stamp with the same words on it. However, these bills—for the greater convenience of the public—are rarely found in circulation. The purpose of this measure is to avoid problems for the people. Thus, the money that actually circulates is Yugoslav. Here a distinction must be made (but it is very simple): some of the notes are good, others are false. To tell the difference one need simply look at them. The bills with no seal stamped on them are not good, but they can nonetheless be used. Those of one thousand crowns are good, but nobody wants them. Those with a Hungarian seal are sometimes accepted, sometimes not. Some of those with a Croatian seal are good, some are false, others are somewhat false. Then there are the Czechoslovakian notes, then those of the new Yugoslavia—which are nearly official, and which circulate very well—then the Styrian-Corynthian ones, then those with the red Austro-German seal. These depend on the day of the week.
>
> To change Italian money into crowns, the matter is even simpler: it is sufficient to read the Exchange Bulletin, which says, for example, 7.50. The moneychanger will give 7.10, the café 6.50, the hat store 6, the stationery store 5, the pizzeria 4, and so on. This is all done with the noble intention of enabling the youth of Fiume to learn mathematics without going to school. . . .[23]

All prime materials, including food, were rationed, but inflation continued to be rampant; at the end of September, in the course of twenty-four hours the price of meat went from thirty-six to fifty-six crowns per kilo. *La Vedetta d'Italia* added that milk and eggs had virtually disappeared from the city. The Command resolved the problem of food shortages without inordinate difficulties, even though there were periods of severe shortages throughout the sixteen months of D'Annunzio's government. The availability of food and other prime materials varied according to the severity with which the blockade was enforced.

It has only recently become possible to discover the details of the blockade,[24] and it is interesting that while Nitti had no great desire to feed D'Annunzio's troops, he was equally opposed to permitting the population of Fiume to die of starvation. Nitti kept in close touch with Giovanni Ciraolo, the president of the Italian Red Cross, from the first day of D'Annunzio's seizure of the city, in order to arrange the shipment of foodstuffs and medicine to Fiume. The first written documentation of these contacts is a letter from Nitti to Ciraolo on 17 December, in which he asked the head of the Red Cross to take measures necessary to guarantee the shipment of foodstuffs. Further, since various financial and bureaucratic problems had developed, the president of the Council of Ministers actively facilitated the operation by putting 700,000 lire from the Bank of Italy at Ciraolo's disposition to pay for the food and shipping expenses. In essence, then, Nitti both sent supplies to Fiume and gave the city the credits to pay for them.

The first shipment by the Red Cross arrived in Fiume by rail on the afternoon of 25 October, composed of twenty-five cars containing more than 900 quintals of pasta, 850 quintals of rice, nearly 800 quintals of flour, more than 400 quintals of barley, 100 quintals of meat, 500 cases of milk, and 40,000 eggs. Further, Ciraolo shipped potatoes, gasoline, and medicines by sea from Venice and Ancona.

This substantial shipment at the end of October represented roughly half of what the National Council had requested of the Red Cross in order to meet its monthy needs. On 29 September Grossich advised Ciraolo that the city needed 4,000 quintals of white flour for bread, 1,200 quintals of rice, 600 quintals of white flour for pasta, and 600 quintals of barley each month, in addition to 1,000 cases of condensed milk, tapioca, coffee, and other foodstuffs. But Grossich's letter was based on a rather surprising figure—that of a population of 60,000 persons—and hence his request would have been sufficient for all citizens of Fiume, and for a double ration for the legionnaires. Ciraolo did not fall into this trap—Nitti would have punished him unhesitatingly if Fiume had been oversupplied, and indeed Nitti had already instructed Ciraolo to guarantee that foodstuffs would not be given to the legionnaires—and he therefore shipped far less than Grossich had requested.

During the period of D'Annunzio's occupation of Fiume, an enormous quantity of aid arrived in the city, thanks to the good offices of the Italian Red Cross: roughly 60,000 quintals of cereals, more than 400,000 eggs, 2,500 cases of condensed milk, and so on, for a total cost of 13 million lire. Despite this aid, many in Fiume continued to believe that Nitti wanted to "bring the city to its knees" through the application of the blockade. Ciraolo was furious at these suggestions and wrote an indignant letter to Riccardo Gigante, the Mayor of Fiume, on 18 December, stressing the role Nitti had played in the humanitarian efforts of the Red Cross. Ciraolo observed that the supplying of Fiume had been the greatest logistical enterprise ever carried out by the Italian Red Cross for an entire population, and continued by expressing his great esteem for Nitti: "I found in His Excellency a silent, compact but dedicated collaborator, who helped me day by day to resolve the many technical and financial problems. . . . The [Red Cross] by itself would not have been able to organize such a formidable effort without the support of the head of the government. He has always forbidden me . . . to reveal how much he has done. And you will have observed that in fact, not even in the most difficult days, during the most heated debates, has any mention been made. . . . My obligation to remain silent continues, but my conscience . . . obliges me to communicate to you what I have written."[25]

As we shall see, the moment in which this letter was written is extremely important, because it coincided with a particularly grave period in the negotiations between the Command, the National Council, and the Italian government. Nonetheless, it is clear that Ciraolo told the truth when he said that the aid received by the Fiumans would not have been possible without Nitti's initiative. The good will demonstrated by the president of the Council of Ministers in alleviating the difficulties of the city suggests that the president was prepared to tolerate D'Annunzio's presence in Fiume for a relatively long period. It is significant that Giovanni Giolitti, who succeeded Nitti the following summer, refused to send hospital beds, doctors, and gauze to Fiume when city officials requested them. Nitti had generally replied favorably to such pleas.

Despite the gravity of the economic crisis, all those who visited Fiume in these months spoke of the elegance of the shops, the abundance of pastries (which would continue to be produced until the middle of the following March) and of whipped cream in the coffee, from which we may conclude that food was not in critically short supply. As we shall see, D'Annunzio exploited the common belief that Fiume was on the verge of starvation by shipping hundreds of Fiuman children to Italy, but this was more a political maneuver than a measure to save children suffering from malnutrition.

There was one area in which the crisis was virtually total, and where the solution was not readily at hand: employment. The situation in the port—the nerve center of the city's economy—was catastrophic. The mineral oil refinery, which normally employed five hundred workers, was shut down because the unrefined oil that had been ordered from Rumania was not passing through the blockade. The torpedo works, once the largest in the Austro-Hungarian Empire, was at a standstill, and local businessmen were suggesting that its equipment be used to repair the railroad lines. But without steel imports, no work could be done in the torpedo factory. The shipbuilding factory Danubius had no contracts, and its working force was down to one-quarter of its prewar level. This was particularly damning to the city's economy, since numerous smaller enterprises depended on the functioning of Danubius for their own business. The rice mills were silent, pending the arrival of rice from India at the end of the winter, and the seed oil factory had closed down, because while seeds were plentiful at the home office in Genoa, the government would not permit them to be shipped through the blockade. In short, the observation of General Scipioni on 23 November, that the commercial life of Fiume was "virtually nil,"[26] seems entirely appropriate.

One must remember, however, that even if there had been no blockade, it would have been impossible to restore the city's economy to anything remotely resembling its prewar level. The torpedo works and the shipyards offer the most illuminating examples of the problems the Fiumans faced. The Whitehead Torpedo Works had been bombed by the Italian Air Force during the first days of Italy's entry into the war, and the Austrians had transported all the crucial equipment from Fiume to St. Pölen, near Vienna. Hence, when D'Annunzio arrived in Fiume he found that the only machinery left in the torpedo works was that required to test the torpedoes; nothing remained for their construction. Given the need of the Italian government for an efficient torpedo works, the minister of the Italian Merchant Marine negotiated the transfer of the necessary machinery from St. Pölen to Fiume in 1920, and in that year Whitehead produced ten steam compressors (for Italian companies). This was hardly sufficient work for a major factory, and until the issue between D'Annunzio and the Italian government was resolved, no further steps could be taken. This case is instructive, however, for it shows that collaboration between Italy and Fiume continued, even though a formal state of siege existed.

The case of Danubius is more complicated,[27] and perhaps more in keeping with the general "tone" of D'Annunzian Fiume. In December 1918, when the shipyards were overrun by Fiuman workers, the Hungar-

ian director was driven out and replaced with a local official. In the
spring of 1919, American and French groups were negotiating with
Hungary for the purchase of Danubius, when the revolutionary government of Béla Kun came to power, promptly suspended all negotiations,
and arrested the president of the Ganz Society (the corporation that
owned Danubius, at least nominally). Relations between Rome and
Budapest were quite good, so the Italian government, along with the
Banca Italiana di Sconto and the Terni Society, negotiated the purchase
of Danubius. The negotiations were far from easy, since any transfer had
to be ratified by the president of the Ganz Society. This obstacle was
overcome by obtaining his release and then smuggling him into Fiume
in disguise, where he duly signed the papers of sale. This transaction was
completed in early 1920, but the maneuvering had gone on throughout
the preceding fall and winter.

These two cases illustrate the extent to which the economic recovery of Fiume was outside the control of the Command. D'Annunzio
was totally dependent on the benevolence of Nitti for the functioning
of Fiume's major industries, and the acquisition of the torpedo works
and the shipyards guaranteed that Italy would exert enormous leverage
over the city's affairs.

THE REACTION TO THE CRISIS

In the face of the highly complex economic crisis, the citizens of
Fiume reacted with traditional simplicity; they blamed the whole situation on "foreigners" and other anti-D'Annunzian elements. By the
second half of September the city was in the grip of an intense wave of
xenophobia—a constant leitmotif of D'Annunzian Fiume, although generally in a less inflammatory form. As early as 17 September, the *Vedetta*
was calling for the expulsion of foreigners from the city: "We have tolerated them long enough. We have been too patient . . . we are at the
decisive moment, along with those of our brothers who have come to
defend us; but in order to be strong we want to be with them alone.
The others, the foreigners, the noncitizens, the immigrants from the ex-
monarchy, from Yugoslavia, from Hungary, have nothing to do here."

On the twenty-fourth, the paper carried a report that Croatian
butchers were refusing to sell meat to anyone who spoke Italian, and
two days later this had been inflated into a claim that Croatians (in Sussak) would only sell meat to people who swore they were citizens of
Yugoslavia. Such stories circulated quickly through the city, reinforcing
the notion that foreigners were attempting to sabotage the D'Annunzian
cause. In particular, the *Vedetta* seemed to believe that there was a
shadowy ringleader of the group that was monopolizing the meat supply:

"The little meat that arrives in the market is cornered every morning by an individual who, according to the statements of the butchers, sells it to French soldiers."[28]

The problem, of course, was not one of saboteurs or French agents but one of a lack of supplies, and the Command managed to find additional sources in relatively short order. By the end of the month there was meat on the butchers' counters, and there was even some milk available for babies and the ill. Hatred of foreigners, however, remained.

At the same time that the *Vedetta* had accused unnamed foreign elements of grabbing meat in the markets and shipping it off to the French Army or to Sussak butchers, it had made a more general accusation that the increase in the cost of living was due to "foreign speculators." In early October, these foreigners increasingly came to be labeled as Jews. On the seventeenth, Fiuman authorities arrested a certain Carlo Fishbein for currency speculation, and the description in the *Vedetta* was a classic of its sort: "He is what one would call a typical Jew, with a hooked nose and greedy claws, restless and active eyes behind the eyeglasses, all the cerebral activity concentrated in the spasmodic search for fruitful sources of income. . . ."

It was presumed that Fishbein had accomplices in his schemes to ruin the Fiuman economy, and he was accused by the *Vedetta* of participating in a Jewish cabal involved in speculative dealings in the city's money markets. Such activity, the newspaper maintained, was only the tip of the iceberg, and the next day, when another Hungarian was arrested for similar activity, the *Vedetta* remarked with grim satisfaction that he was, "naturally, an Hungarian Jew."

These remarks suggest that there was a certain anti-Semitic element within the Command (Baccich, the editor of the *Vedetta*, was a close friend of the comandante), and this impression is confirmed by other events during the same period. Perhaps the most dramatic of these was the launching of a handbill—in the style of the flight over Vienna—over Croatia in the middle of the month.[29] This handbill was extremely provocative, for while it called upon the Croatians to support D'Annunzian Fiume, it claimed that all the problems of the area stemmed from the machinations of the League of Nations, which in turn was "invented by international Jewish bankers as a mask for their speculations against all the peoples of the world." Suggesting that Croatians and Fiumans were both being exploited by the same evil forces, the handbill called upon the Croatians to unite with D'Annunzio in the defense of their freedoms and traditions.

At the same time, representatives of the Jewish Communities of Fiume and Trieste reported that various "high officials" of the command had given speeches in which they had suggested that the opposi-

tion to the annexation of Fiume came from "Jewish bankers."[30] The
matter was judged serious enough for the president of the Committee
of the Italian Jewish Communities to write a letter to D'Annunzio on
25 October,[31] in which he called upon the comandante to condemn
the anti-Semitic statements that had been emanating from Fiume and
to acknowledge the support the Italian Jews had given both to the Fiuman adventure and to the Great War. Moreover, he called D'Annunzio's
attention to numerous assertions that the comandante himself was a Jew:
"While the Command of Fiume dropped their battle cry against the
Jews on the Croatians, a Croatian clerical journal could find no better
way to arouse the populace against Italy and the command than to print
that you are the son of Palestinian Jews, repeating the tale that was so
dear to the reactionary and anti-Semitic sheets of old Austria and Imperial Germany. . . ."

The Roman Zionist newspaper, *Israel*, reported the episode,[32] along
with letters from Jews in Fiume, all of whom claimed that the comandante himself was not anti-Semitic and that the handbill had been written
without his knowledge. This last claim was certainly true, for the handbill was written by the noted Nationalist journalist Libero Tancredi; but
the matter of D'Annunzio's attitudes toward the Jews was a bit more
complex. Evidently the Jewish Community of Fiume had some doubts
about the situation, for they issued a public statement on 23 September
(transcribed on parchment and carried to D'Annunzio) that reasserted
their loyalty to "the cause": "The Hungarian, Austrian, and German
Jews of Fiume [the Croatian Jews did not sign the document] on the
anniversary of the plebiscite of October 30, 1918 . . . declare that they
are in favor of, and will support the annexation of, Fiume by Italy. In
the next elections, the 'National Union' list will be supported by all
those having the right to vote."[33]

When D'Annunzio received the document, he denied any anti-Semitism on his part, claiming never to have written an anti-Semitic line and
to have numerous Jews among his closest friends. Moreover, after a protest from Lieutenant Raffaele Cantoni, Baccich promised that the *Vedetta*
would desist from further attacks against the Jews. Insofar as can be
ascertained, the matter ended there, for the Fiuman Jews did not feel
it necessary to issue any further statements, and no trace of anti-Semitism reappeared in the pages of the *Vedetta*.

There seems to be no reason to doubt D'Annunzio's strong rejection
of Tancredi's handbill, even though certain anti-Semitic stereotypes appear here and there in the poet's writings.[34] It would seem, rather, that
the brief outburst of anti-Semitism was primarily rooted in local traditions. The bulk of the Jewish community was Ashkenazi, with its origins
in Eastern and Central Europe, and the Jews constituted nearly ten per-

cent of the population of Fiume. While a part of the community consisted of strictly Orthodox Jews, the remainder had not only abandoned
the rigors of Jewish law but had embarked on an assimilationist course
and were actively involved in the commercial and cultural life of the
city.[35] They were, therefore, typical of the Jews of the Hapsburg Empire, as were the attitudes of the Fiumans toward Jews. As anti-Semitism
was widespread throughout the old empire, it would be surprising to
find none of it in Fiume. This tradition played into the hands of those
who, like Tancredi, sought to exploit the fears of the "international
Jewish bankers' conspiracy." Given the xenophobia in Fiume in the
autumn of 1919 and the traditions of the empire, it is understandable
that the Jews should have been singled out. Indeed, it is remarkable that
the matter quieted down almost instantly. This failure of anti-Semitism
to take root in the superheated atmosphere of D'Annunzian Fiume sup-
ports the view of those who claimed that the city had been "Italianized,"
for while popular anti-Semitism was virtually unknown in Italy, it is unlikely that an anti-Semitic campaign could have been dissipated so
quickly in Austria or Hungary.

FIUME'S D'ANNUNZIO

Fiume and D'Annunzio were peculiarly well suited to one another.
Fiume's problems were serious, but not to the point of threatening the
city with starvation or epidemics, and the comandante portrayed Fiume's
travails as an act of redemption for all Italy. The image of a martyred
city suffering for its faith was grounded in the daily life of its citizens,
yet the suffering was not sufficiently grave to provoke mass anti-D'Annunzian sentiment.

The population of Fiume was uniquely suited to the poet-warrior's
campaign: a part was genuinely irredentist; another element enthusiastically embraced the idea of annexation for more selfish, opportunistic
motives, but with equal zeal; and youthful and idealistic groups were
attracted by the romanticism of D'Annunzio's adventure. Moreover,
Fiume actually represented a sort of avant-garde within Italian culture,
for in two major areas the city was well in advance of the "motherland":
Fiuman women had been granted the vote before the march of Ronchi,
thus institutionalizing the already important role they played in the political life of the town; and there had long been an interesting movement
among the Catholic clergy of the region demanding a drastic liberaliza-
tion of the priests' lives, entailing both the democratization of clerical
institutions and the possibility of a married clergy. Each of these tendencies grew stronger during D'Annunzio's government of Fiume and
each ultimately clothed itself in the mantle of "Fiumanism"; it is, how-

ever, highly significant that these proposed changes in the Church existed long before the arrival of the comandante, and it is unthinkable that he would have initiated them on his own. These aspects of Fiuman life were the result of the tensions and traditions of the city itself, and they simply became part of the world that D'Annunzio made his own.

In the following chapters, we shall be dealing with D'Annunzio's vision of a new world, the conception that fused a kind of political utopianism with the poet's unique ability to mobilize his followers into a coherent unit. The conventional wisdom about this period is that D'Annunzio imposed his vision of political and social reality on the population of Fiume, which was in turn dragged along in the wake of the comandante's activities. It should be clear from what has been said above, however, that a good deal of the enthusiasm and utopianism in Fiume did not come from its leader but was, rather, intrinsic to the city itself and would have existed without D'Annunzio. Undoubtedly the kind of chaos that reigned in Fiume lent itself to the comandante's initiatives, but one must be careful not to credit him for a greater impact than he actually had. D'Annunzio was not by nature a systematic man, and the radical transformation of the structure of Fiuman politics—along with the systematic attempt to change the relations between the city's classes—was the result of the reciprocal influence of D'Annunzio's charisma and the character of the city he governed.

The Definition of the Adventure

In early October Giuriati wrote to Sinigaglia that the question of Fiume had "stabilized" and that he and his allies in Fiume would do everything possible to "prevent the insinuation of centrifugal causes." But in the next paragraph, the head of D'Annunzio's cabinet confessed his conviction that it would be difficult to hold together the various elements in Fiume. As a result, Giuriati was forced to invent "diversions" for the populace, "such as that which I am preparing now: the election of Rizzo as deputy from Fiume for 16 November."[1]

As ever, the primary fear of the Giuriati-Sinigaglia axis was the expansion of the comandante's sphere of action, and Sinigaglia went to Fiume on 12 October to survey the scene. He spoke first with Giuriati, discussing both the failure to arrive at any definitive solution to the Fiume crisis and the possibility that D'Annunzio might take some unconsidered action. Giuriati reassured his collaborator that the situation seemed under control.

Sinigaglia spoke with D'Annunzio the same evening and attempted to spell out the political situation within Italy, "so that he would not have any illusions about the overly optimistic information given to him by Mussolini and Corradini."[2] While informing D'Annunzio that the elections in November were unlikely to represent a major triumph for the pro-Fiume forces, Sinigaglia was disturbed to learn that the comandante had in fact decided to "resolve the internal question before the elections," a phrase that could only imply some dramatic action. Sinigaglia strongly counseled against precipitancy, stating that any rash move was likely to harm the Fiuman cause. The issue of Fiume, he said, was more important than the results of the elections, and even if (as appeared likely) Nitti were to emerge greatly strengthened from the elections, he would eventually fall if he could not resolve the Fiume crisis. This was wishful thinking (and Sinigaglia probably knew it), but Sinigaglia was alarmed by the evidence that the more radical elements within the Command had apparently managed to convert D'Annunzio to their view of the situation. When D'Annunzio asked him what he thought of the plan to occupy Abbazia and Volosca, Sinigaglia told him that occupation would have serious internal repercussions and that it was crucial to convince the world that the Command, although deadly serious about the destiny of Fiume, had irrevocably decided not to move outside the city itself.

Despite these stern injunctions, Sinigaglia learned the following morning that D'Annunzio had decided to take action outside Fiume. Even more serious, neither Giuriati nor Rizzo, the two men most intent on dissuading the comandante from such adventures, had been consulted about the move. It was clear that D'Annunzio was relying on other opinions for his policies. Sinigaglia noted wryly in his diary that "it seems that this is the system, and that everyone gets the news before Giuriati and Rizzo."

THE *PERSIA* AFFAIR

For the first four weeks of D'Annunzio's occupation of Fiume, there were myriad rumors about his presumed intentions to carry his actions beyond the boundaries of the city, but there was little in the way of concrete action on the part of the command to confirm these stories. The *colpi di mano* were highly embarrassing to the government, to be sure, but they did not represent the kind of large-scale assault on the centers of power that was widely rumored. This situation changed on 10 October, when the Italian cargo ship *Persia* was commandeered and sailed to Fiume. The *Persia* was a unique prize, for it had been heavily laden with arms and munitions for the White Army in Russia and was to have sailed to Vladivostok for use in the war against the Bolsheviks. The maritime workers' union, the Federazione della gente del mare, after vainly attempting to convince the government not to supply the reactionary Russian forces with Italian arms, had its men take command of the ship in the straits of Messina and set a course for D'Annunzio's City of the Holocaust. No less than thirteen tons of military supplies thus found their way into the warehouses of the Command, and the city welcomed Captain Giuseppe Giulietti and the crew of the *Persia* with a celebration on the evening of the fourteenth.

Giulietti was the leader of the gente del mare, and he had given the orders for the hijacking of the ship to Fiume. For him, the maneuver served not only to demonstrate his organization's opposition to the supplying of the White Army but also to pressure the government into making various concessions to the maritime workers (concessions that had been guaranteed by Nitti but that were as yet undelivered). But the arrival of the *Persia* marked the beginning of a long alliance between Giulietti and the comandante (a collaboration which, as we shall see, would lead D'Annunzio to the verge of attempting a seizure of power in Italy the following year.[3] Further, the presence of the *Persia* in Fiume raised the possibility of a radical change in the actions of D'Annunzio's forces in Fiume: the federation was Socialist, and Giulietti was a close friend of the noted anarchist Enrico Malatesta. The forces of the war were beginning to form alliances with the genuinely revolutionary elements of Italian politics. Furthermore, D'Annunzio's response to Giulietti's gesture was extremely interesting and could only confirm fears that the comandante was planning actions of a new and more dramatic sort in the future. The evidence is in a fascinating letter from D'Annunzio to Giulietti on 15 October and in a speech to the people of Fiume later in the month. In his letter,[4] the comandante observed that the arrival of the *Persia* in Fiume "confirmed not only the sanctity but also the universality of our cause." The presence of the weapons of the *Persia* in Fiume gave the city "arms for justice," he said, and prevented those arms from being used against other peoples. "The cause of Fiume is not the cause of the soil, it is the cause of the spirit, the cause of immortality. . . . From the indomitable Sinn Fein of Ireland to the red flag which in Egypt unites the half moon and the cross, all the insurrections of the spirit against the devourers of raw flesh . . . are ready to become reignited from those sparks of ours which fly far away. . . ."

While many had feared an action by D'Annunzio within the boundaries of Italy or in Dalmatia, no one had contemplated the possibility that the comandante might seek to put himself at the head of an international movement. Yet in retrospect it seems almost inevitable that this should have occurred. The values D'Annunzio claimed to be defending in Fiume were indeed universal ones, and were directed against the victorious Allies. The outrage on behalf of Fiume against the course of the negotiations in Paris could easily have become a general cry of righteous indignation, on the grounds that those who were shaping the postwar world had failed to consider the legitimate demands of the oppressed.

The letter to Giulietti was the first statement in what became one of the most important themes of D'Annunzian Fiume, a theme that found its institutional incarnation in the project for a League of Fiume, an alliance of the oppressed peoples of the earth. This project did not take concrete form until the following year, when the outlines of D'Annunzio's ideology became clearer, but the comandante gave eloquent expression to the theme in one of his most celebrated speeches, on the occasion of the elections for a new Municipal Council.

As we have seen, the National Council had been created by its own membership late in October of the previous year. Many observers doubted the degree to which the council represented the true wishes of the Italian population of Fiume and wondered about the legitimacy of its power. In his memoirs, Giuriati refers to these suspicions in explaining the motivation for the municipal elections that D'Annunzio called for on 26 October: "In the first place, [there was] the need to expose the deepest thoughts of the Fiumans, holding a new plebiscite precisely at the moment when . . . the so-called Fiume compromise was being drafted in Paris. Further, [there was] the opportunity to offer the numerous journalists from all over the world who were gathered in Fiume (and particularly the American writers) proof . . . of the Italianness of Fiume."[5]

Giuriati's perception of D'Annunzio's motives was always limited (and, as we shall see, D'Annunzio frequently used Giuriati as a "screen" for his real intentions, particularly in foreign policy matters), and, as Sinigaglia's wry remark of the thirteenth demonstrates, many of the crucial decisions in Fiume were taken without consulting Giuriati. In reality, there were several motives for new municipal elections, and D'Annunzio undoubtedly hoped that the membership of the council would undergo a substantial change (it did not). First, as we have already seen, the National Council was not a particularly popular organization, especially with the lower classes of the city, and as D'Annunzio began to think about rallying the forces of the "have-nots" of the world around his banner, his sentiments inevitably clashed with those of Mayor Vio and other council leaders. Second, the continuing contacts between Vio and Badoglio revealed a fundamental clash of interests between the council and the Command,[6] especially after the mayor took the extraordinary step of establishing formal relations between the National Council and the Nitti regime, quite apart from any contacts between the government and the comandante. Hence, there had emerged a clean separation between D'Annunzio's policies and those of the National Council, and the comandante was intent on undermining the position of council members who were hostile to him. De Felice has analyzed this complicated situation with great insight, observing that the elections "demonstrate that . . . the comandante must have become convinced of the error he had committed a month earlier, in not assuming for himself all the powers of the city."[7]

In addition to the conflicts of interest between the Command and the National Council, D'Annunzio was beginning to recognize that the various maneuvers of the Nitti regime were designed to gain time for the government at his expense, and as the economic conditions in Fiume worsened it became increasingly clear that the comandante could not wait forever for action in Rome and Paris. D'Annunzio had to act to appease men like Keller and Cabruna, and the very nature of the political forms he had created for the city added their own internal logic to the situation. If Fiume were truly to become the source of a new fire to illuminate the West, it could not be permitted to smoulder indefinitely.

All these considerations found expression in a speech to the people of Fiume on the evening of 24 October, just before the election rallies. Entitled "Italy and Life,"[8] it is one of the most important and rhapsodic speeches given during the sixteen months of D'Annunzian Fiume, and it is necessary to look at it in considerable detail.

After briefly rehearsing the history of Fiume's attempts to achieve annexation on its own, D'Annunzio reminded the populace of the various expressions of sympathy the government had expressed for Fiume's destiny. On each of these occasions, he recalled, eloquent words had been spoken, but no action had resulted. The king himself had said that Fiume's 1918 appeal had created a "profound echo" in his heart; but, said the comandante, "the sailors did not disembark; the liberators did not appear. Where was victory halted? Who restrained her?" Now, he said, there was a new hoax in the air: the creation of a "free state" or a "free city" of Fiume, recently proposed at the Paris Conference. But this was not responsive to the desires of Fiumans; if Fiume became a free city, and "not a city of Free Italy," it would become subject to the intervention of the rest of the world.

D'Annunzio then enlarged the scope of his discourse, turning to the theme of the meaning of the Great War. To be sure, he said, the war had been fought for territorial acquisitions, but this was only one part of the significance of the struggle. The "great cause," he said, "is the cause of the spirit, the cause of immortality." These were the same words he had used in the letter to Giulietti, and from this moment on, D'Annunzio spoke of the need to reunite the Italian elements scattered through Fiume and Dalmatia with the mother country. He ran down the list: Idria, Postumia, Castelnuovo, the islands of the Adriatic. It was vital for the citizens of Fiume to continue to fight, for struggle held the meaning of this epoch of history: "We may all perish in the ruins of Fiume; but from those ruins the spirit will leap up, vigilant and strong."

The Fiuman struggle was, then, part of a global conflict between the major powers of the world and the exploited peoples who were forced to submit to their might. And just as the exploiting interests were united around the conference tables of Paris, the exploited peoples had to be fused into a solid body:

All the rebels of all the races will be gathered under our sign. And the feeble will be armed. And force will be used against force. And the new crusade of all poor and impoverished nations, the new crusade of all poor and free men against the usurping nations, the accumulators of all wealth, against the races of prey and against the caste of usurers who yesterday exploited war in order to exploit peace today, the new crusade will reestablish that true justice that has been crucified by an icy maniac with fourteen dull nails and with a hammer borrowed from the German Chancellor. . . .

Fiumans, Italians . . . when you proclaimed in the face of the Supreme Council that history written with the most generous Italian blood could not be stopped at Paris . . . you announced the fall of the old world.

Therefore, our cause is the greatest and the most beautiful which today has been directed against the evil of the world. It extends from Ireland to Egypt, from Russia to the United States, from Rumania to India. It gathers the white races and the colored peoples, reconciles the gospel with the Koran. . . .

Every insurrection is an effort of expression, an effort of creation. It does not matter if it is interrupted in the blood, provided that the survivors transmit the instinct . . . to the future.

. . . For all veterans, carriers of the cross who have climbed their Calvary for four years, it is time to rush toward the future.

The "rush toward the future" clearly indicated that something fundamental was changing within the Command. Previously, all statements from the comandante and those around him had limited the potential sphere of activity to Fiume, Dalmatia, and Italy. Yet the speech "Italy and Life" unequivocally called for international action based upon the revolt of the "have-not" countries against the major powers of the West. This appeal to what we now call the Third World was more in harmony with the ideas of Giulietti or Enrico Malatesta than with those of Sinigaglia, Giuriati, or Rizzo.

"Italy and Life" was a poetic extrapolation of ideas that had appeared in many of D'Annunzio's statements during the previous weeks, but it nonetheless marked a major turning point in the history of D'Annunzian Fiume. Even though the new policies would not emerge clearly for another two months, the outlines of the new direction could already be seen, and new actions would soon be under way. Fiume would serve as a model for the rest of the world and as a center to rally and finance movements of national liberation. The arrival of the *Persia* thus catalyzed numerous processes in Fiume: it enriched the stores of the city and made it possible for D'Annunzio to supply armies other than his own legions; it convinced him that radical socialists were capable of decisive, "D'Annunzian" action; and it demonstrated that the forces that were attempting to strangle Fiume were the selfsame elements that were dedicated to the suffocation of the Communist revolution in Russia.

It is no coincidence that October was the period in which Sinigaglia began to complain that the comandante was sending special agents all over Italy on mysterious missions and, more to the point, that these agents came with letters of authorization signed by figures in whom Sinigaglia had little confidence ("I do not understand a letter of presentation from Carli when you exist").[9] Taken in combination with Sinigaglia's discovery that Giuriati was often excluded from decision-making in the command, such laments constituted a cry of alarm. "I maintain that it is perilous to send all these people into action," he wrote to Giuriati, and the peril he sensed was implicitly directed against him and his allies.

It should not be assumed from this evidence that D'Annunzio had decided on a clean break with such figures as Sinigaglia or that there had been a coherent reevaluation of the comandante's policy in the early days of October. D'Annunzio's mind simply did not work along such lines, and it would be a serious mistake to overstate the ideological significance of his words at this time. Rather, the arrival of the *Persia* and the new contacts with the Left permitted the comandante to add another string to his bow, enabling him to appeal to men and organizations that had hitherto not been included in the Fiume adventure. To be sure, in short order these left-wing elements assumed pivotal importance in the enterprise and paramount significance in D'Annunzio's speeches and actions; but the comandante never cut his ties with the Nationalists, and he attempted to expand his activities rather than to shift his allegiance from one sector of the political world to another. Indeed, one of the original elements in D'Annunzio's "political theory" in Fiume was his ability to develop themes that transcended the traditional divisions in the political realm. The poetic themes of "Fiumanism" would prove attractive to both Left and Right and enable D'Annunzio to pose as a leader of *all* Italians (and of all citizens of the "new" postwar world). This problem shall be dealt with at length in the discussion of the new Fiuman Constitution of 1920, but it must be kept in mind that D'Annunzio was searching for a new political synthesis and not for the most profitable political alliance.

In addition to the doctrinal ambiguity of his political ideas, D'Annunzio's character made life extremely difficult for those who attempted to identify his future intentions. Among his other unpredictable qualities, D'Annunzio was almost totally incapable of saying no to his collaborators. Fiume attracted the most diverse types imaginable, in part because they all managed to find some sort of support for their projects there. D'Annunzio often guided these disparate forces, but he was also frequently carried along by them. Thus, Sinigaglia could write to Giuriati on 14 November that "in the public mind the idea is beginning to take root that while you and the comandante act with a sense of balance, there are too many crackpots there who compromise your situation and risk compromising the entire country."[10]

While Sinigaglia's point about the wilder elements in Fiume was belaboring the obvious, the complaint about "compromising" the country (the sort of phrase that runs all through Nitti's letters to Badoglio during the same period[11]) betrayed a fundamental lack of comprehension of what D'Annunzio's adventure in Fiume was all about. The comandante surely did not wish to "compromise" Italy, but the Italy he had in mind was quite different from Sinigaglia's. D'Annunzio believed that, given the proper leadership, the Italian people were capable of true greatness; Sinigaglia never once thought of taking his case to "the people." D'Annunzio's behavior was incomprehensible to the likes of Sinigaglia and Nitti, because the poet was experimenting with a new kind of political behavior. Traditional politicians were not interested in mass politics, whereas D'Annunzio actively sought to mold the masses to his will. While he was developing the techniques of the political festivals in Fiume, the comandante was taking the cause of "Fiumanism" to the peoples of the world; following the funerals for Bini and Zappegno, D'Annunzio had directed a passionate appeal to the "Italians of the United States,"[12] and following the election of a new National Council at the end of October, he sent a new appeal to the United States Congress. Similarly, he had entrusted to Achille Richard a mission to France,[13] hoping to convince the French government of the justice of his cause, and he later indulged in various campaigns of propaganda, both within and without Italy.

The frequently melodramatic themes D'Annunzio developed in Fiume were central to the new political era, and the failure of men like Sinigaglia and Nitti to understand the significance of the comandante's political "style" showed that they were blinded by outmoded ideas, which were losing their force in the piazzas of Italy and the streets of the Western world.

GOVERNMENTAL STRATAGEMS

Despite the radical themes in D'Annunzio's speeches and his new-found sympathy for such figures as Captain Giulietti, the government continued to try the route of negotiation to induce the comandante to leave Fiume. Badoglio was Nitti's negotiating agent, and his strategy was excellent: he realized that the comandante would only leave Fiume if he believed that his departure represented an act of supreme patriotism. To this end, the general attempted to convince D'Annunzio that his continued presence in Fiume constituted a menace to the stability of Italy and that if the Tittoni project (providing for Italian control of the city but leaving the port and the railroad lines under the control of the League of Nations)[14] was accepted by the Allies, D'Annunzio would either have to leave or take responsibility for the turmoil his refusal would inevitably produce within the country. Badoglio granted that

without D'Annunzio's seizure of Fiume, the Tittoni project would have
been unthinkable, but, he argued, to continue the occupation of Fiume
would risk plunging Italy into revolution: "The official Socialist Party
is delighted that all our attention and our energies are directed toward
the Fiuman cause. This [party] . . . is conducting a subversive action
with extreme violence, which the precarious conditions of the country
. . . permit us to fight very feebly and poorly. . . . It is thus necessary
to . . . reunite all to fight the internal enemy. . . ."[15]

While Badoglio used his persuasive powers on the comandante, concrete actions were being taken on the city's behalf: the Red Cross was
authorized to transport medical supplies to Fiume and a substantial
cash loan was sent to the city by the same route. On the twenty-eighth
Badoglio and D'Annunzio met, and the comandante gave his word that
if the Tittoni project proved acceptable to the Allies, Fiume would be
turned over to regular Italian troops.

Badoglio made much of this guarantee in his memoirs, but in practice it was only a.gambit by the comandante, who had no intention of
leaving Fiume. D'Annunzio already knew what Badoglio evidently did
not[16]—that the Americans had rejected the Tittoni proposal on the
twenty-fourth and that the government's proposal was merely a ruse to
induce D'Annunzio to leave Fiume, or at the least to remain inactive.
On the twenty-ninth D'Annunzio and Orazio Pedrazzi (the command's
informant in Paris) arrived together for the appointment with Badoglio
and told him of the American rejection of the Tittoni project and of a
new toughness in Tittoni's attitudes towards the Americans. The comandante argued that annexation was the only acceptable solution to the
crisis and followed his words with provocative actions: the colpi di mano,
which had been briefly suspended during the negotiations, were resumed. In early November one of the legionnaires was killed by the
regulars in a nocturnal conflict.

Despite these contretemps, negotiations served both sides: the comandante, because he desperately needed supplies; the government, because of the need to tranquillize D'Annunzio, pending some resolution
of the Fiume question in Paris. At the end of October Badoglio sent
badly needed coal to Fiume, relieving a potentially critical shortage, and
he permitted D'Annunzio to discharge some of the regular troops in the
city from active service. It was hoped that these favors would make
D'Annunzio more amenable to the requests of the government, and by
the end of the first week in November, Badoglio was quite optimistic
about the chances for a successful compromise. Colonel Domenico
Siciliani, the intermediary between Badoglio and the comandante during
the period of negotiations, had informed the general of the difficult
conditions within Fiume,[17] and Badoglio pressed the poet for an agree-

ment to an hypothetical situation on 10 November: would the comandante promise to turn the city over to Badoglio if the government guaranteed that it would accept nothing less than the Tittoni project? According to the general's account, D'Annunzio was amenable to this proposal,
and he asked for time to discuss the matter with his associates in Fiume.
In a mood of high optimism, Badoglio telegraphed Nitti that an agreement would be forthcoming if the government would commit itself to
the Tittoni proposal, come what may at the Peace Conference. Over the
course of the next two days, Nitti was persuaded to guarantee this position, provided the agreement remain secret. However, as dramatic events
shortly demonstrated, neither Nitti nor D'Annunzio would be called
upon to test the reliability of their respective guarantees.

THE ZARA EXPEDITION

While D'Annunzio had announced his intention to make Fiume a
center for the crusade of the Third World, his primary interest continued
to be Dalmatia. At the end of October he sent Giuriati on a mission to
Zara to speak with Admiral Enrico Millo, the military commander of
Italian-occupied Dalmatia, to find out the intentions of the Nitti government and the admiral's view of the situation. The irredentists were convinced that Nitti intended to abandon virtually all of Dalmatia to the
new Yugoslav state, in exchange for other territorial acquisitions from
the Allies. This conviction proved to be fully justified, as a telegram
from Nitti to Millo on 20 October demonstrates: "As soon as an accord
is reached with Allies and associates on the basis of our present negotiations, most of the occupied territory and the Dalmatian islands will have
to be abandoned."[18]

Millo was consequently asked to provide the government with a list
of Italian industries and leading citizens that might have to be transferred to the peninsula and suggestions for the aid of those Italian communities that would remain behind in Yugoslavia.

The admiral was not enthusiastic about Nitti's plans, and he responded with a warning about the likely consequences of the evacuation of
Dalmatia: "In the interior [the evacuation] would take place in an orderly manner, unless those who replace us demonstrate immediately that
they are inclined to vex and maltreat the population sympathetic to us.
. . . Nearer the coast, and more precisely at Sebenico, the probabilities
of a calm and orderly retreat diminish substantially . . . I do not speak
of Zara, because if, by terrible misfortune, the order to withdraw includes Zara as well, I foresee blood, acts of desperation, and destruction;
acts which I do not exclude at Sebenico as well. . . ."[19]

Millo also predicted that if the order to evacuate Dalmatia were given, D'Annunzio would not remain quietly in Fiume, and the admiral predicted a Fiuman expedition as soon as the decision to abandon the zone reached the comandante. If such an expedition were to take place, Millo said, he would not be able to control his own troops.

All of this was suspiciously familiar to the ears of the president of the Council of Ministers, and Nitti fired off an angry telegram to Millo, warning him not to get involved in schemes to prevent the evacuation. Nitti suspected that Millo, like so many of the military leaders, was on the verge of sedition, perhaps about to go over to D'Annunzio's cause. The specter of a dissident movement stretching from Fiume to Split and Zara was a real possibility for Nitti (although not so real as to provoke him to demand Millo's resignation, nor to accept it when offered shortly thereafter), and Millo himself had not decided what he would do if the order to evacuate Dalmatia arrived. As he said to Giuriati, "I confess that thus far I have been unable to make the decision to rebel—accustomed as I am, for fifty years, to obey orders. The Dalmatians hope in me; but I have not resolved the problem."[20]

Hence, while Millo claimed to have dissuaded Giuriati from recommending a Dalmatian expedition to D'Annunzio ("an action to be avoided . . . it seemed to me that I convinced him"),[21] he was in fact considering similar moves himself.

Giuriati's position in the talks with Millo was extremely interesting. Despite a history of opposition to Dalmatian adventures, Giuriati seems to have undergone a change of heart by the time of his arrival in Zara. Millo reported to Nitti that Giuriati had conveyed the clear impression that the command (and himself included) was committed to adventures outside Italy, whenever they thought it necessary, "with the goal of redeeming the oppressed."[22] In short, it appears that the evolution of the comandante's thinking about Fiume's role in the world at large was paralleled by a similar change on Giuriati's part. We shall see this "new" Giuriati again, when he conveyed these views to the Italian government during formal negotiations in November. For the moment, it is important to understand the extent to which the ideas of "Italy and Life" had penetrated even those who had been opposed to such principles from the beginning of the Fiume adventure.

D'Annunzio and the activists around him who were increasingly crucial in shaping the policies of the command were not content to leave the new conception of "Fiumanism" abstractly suspended in the air. Reinforced by the arrival of Leon Kochnitzky in late October, they undertook to demonstrate their resolve at a particularly dramatic moment in the relations with the Nitti regime. With elections scheduled for 16 November, the radical Fiumans hoped that a dramatic act would catalyze those forces within Italy that were potentially favorable to them. To this end, early on the morning of the fourteenth, D'Annunzio and the cream of his general staff (and, of course, Guido Keller) sailed to Zara, arriving later that morning.

Few events in the first few months of D'Annunzian Fiume made such an international impression as the trip to Zara, and it had vast importance for both D'Annunzio and Nitti. The comandante received a hero's welcome,[23] and after having met with Millo he spoke to the people of Zara in one of the memorable moments of his oratorical career. The weather was foul, and the piazza where he spoke was filled with mud and slush. Yet when, after asserting the legitimacy of Italy's claim to Zara, he unfolded the flag of Giovanni Randaccio before the crowd, they all knelt in the rain before it. The transformation of the banner from a piece of cloth into a religious symbol was now complete.

The most important aspect of the Zara expedition was the telegram Millo sent to Nitti that day. After informing the head of the government of D'Annunzio's arrival, Millo continued: "I have pledged my word that we will not evacuate the Dalmatia of the Treaty of London (stop) the troops and the volunteers [that had come with D'Annunzio] remain under my control (stop) with this action I believe that I have behaved as a soldier and an Italian."[24]

D'Annunzio left three military companies in Zara, and Giuriati remained in the city along with Millo to command the troops, as a symbol of the commitment of the Fiumans to Dalmatia. With Millo's promise to defend the territory promised in the Treaty of London, Nitti reached another critical moment in his dealings with the armed forces of the country. His angry telegram to Millo on the morning of the fifteenth speaks volumes:

> I have learned with sadness but without surprise what you communicated . . . you have no right to make statements on such matters. Military power is always subordinate to civil power. Further, as a matter of fact in the proposals presented to the Washington government . . . it is provided that Dalmatia, except for Zara and a few islands, be assigned to Yugoslavia. . . . Hence you, undertaking not to evacuate the Dalmatia of the Treaty of London, have made a promise which no Italian government will be able to maintain without putting itself in open conflict with the Allies.[25]

There are two points of great interest in this telegram. First, there is the rage at having been betrayed once again by one of his military leaders, repeating the pattern of the march of Ronchi. But while Nitti took great pains to remind Millo of the chain of command, he did not remove the admiral from his post (nor did he order him to expel the D'Annunzian forces that remained in Zara), perhaps because he feared that firing Millo might trigger a chain of seditious actions throughout the military forces. Moreover, Nitti's words to Millo demonstrated the accuracy of D'Annunzio's information about governmental intentions regarding Dalmatia. Nitti was indeed determined to abandon the region, and thus, from the comandante's point of view, the expedition was fully justified.

Curiously, the expedition to Zara has invariably been dealt with as if it were a stroke of poetic madness on the part of the Command, and many observers, both at the time and long after, have insisted that D'Annunzio permitted himself to be talked into the adventure by some of the wilder elements in Fiume. This, for example, seems to have been the "official" view of Nitti himself, as reported by Senator Albertini: "Instead of speaking with the few reasonable elements [in Fiume], D'Annunzio held a meeting with some forty-odd persons: the wilder elements gained the upper hand, and so the expedition to Zara was decided upon (it appears that it had been prearranged by the 'radicals' along with elements of the Dalmatian occupation forces) . . . D'Annunzio no longer controls the situation, he has no one in his hand, he has been overcome by madmen. . . ."[26]

This interpretation of the Zara expedition has little to recommend it, but it serves to illustrate how successful Nitti had been in convincing Italians that D'Annunzio's policies rested upon an irrational base. Badoglio shared this view, suggesting that the more radical elements in Fiume felt that if Italy was going to challenge the United States on the Fiume issue (by adopting the Tittoni plan unilaterally and then sending regular troops to the city), they themselves might just as well demand the entire package of annexation.[27]

While D'Annunzio was subject to strong emotional impulses, he was not nearly so foolish as Albertini implied. The expedition was based on a careful analysis of Nitti's maneuvers. The comandante realized that Nitti was stalling for time, hoping to keep the lid on Fiume until the November elections were held. If the election results strongly supported him, he could then use the Fiume "card" in the poker game in Paris. Strengthened by a landslide in November, Nitti might well go to the Allies with the claim that his country would not permit him to abandon any of the territories it had been promised in the Treaty of London, and at the same time he might continue to use D'Annunzio's presence in Fiume as a goad to force the Allies' hand. The one thing the Italian leader did not want was to be forced into action before the elections, and this explains his reluctance to take any decisive steps in Paris, Fiume, or Zara. He wanted the biggest "pot" possible in Paris (and he wished to remain in power in Rome), and it did not matter to him which chips he raked in: Fiume was desirable, but so was Albania, and he was willing to wait for the strongest possible hand to be dealt to him before he placed his final bet. Hence, he gave orders to Badoglio to negotiate with D'Annunzio but dragged his feet whenever any concessions were demanded from him. He attempted to dupe the comandante by offering him the lure of the Tittoni proposal, even when he knew there was no hope for its approval in Paris. He believed that time was on his side (particularly as the physical condition of the American President worsened through the autumn).

Similarly, he would not be rushed into action by the Zara expedition, which he recognized as an attempt by D'Annunzio to force him to define his position. Indeed, he quickly ordered the censors to suppress all news about the expedition until the elections were over. At the same time, he refused to precipitate a crisis by removing Millo or by challenging the presence of D'Annunzian troops in Zara, explaining his failure to act in terms of the delicate political position of the moment and promising his allies that he would take stern measures after the elections. As Jay telegraphed to Polk on the seventeenth, "if Nitti wins out the punishment to be inflicted on authorities found responsible . . . would show what government thinks of matter. [Sforza] also confidentially tells me that Milo [*sic*] was trusted as being famous disciplinarian."[28]

Nitti spared no effort in attempting to impose order on the chaotic Fiuman situation, even lending his support to a mission by the Grand Master of Italian Masonry, Domizio Torrigiani, to urge the numerous Masons among the leaders of D'Annunzian Fiume (including Ceccherini) to remain calm.[29] Finally, while all channels were exploited to tranquillize the comandante,[30] a series of discussions with representatives of the Command began in Rome in the middle of November, regarding the financial crisis in the city. In the course of the talks, Nitti's spokesmen repeatedly assured the Fiumans that the government actually approved of the occupation of the city and would soon take substantial measures to relieve Fiume's fiscal plight by guaranteeing a massive loan from private banks and eventually stabilizing the currency.[31]

Before turning to D'Annunzio's state of mind following the Zara adventure, one further element in Nitti's view of the complex Fiuman crisis must be mentioned: the question of Yugoslavia. Virtually to a man, the Italian leaders believed that the Yugoslav state was destined to collapse, probably in relatively short order. Furthermore, they were not content to stand by and let the new nation fall of its own weight but were secretly aiding rebel anti-Serbian forces within the country, as several letters from Sinigaglia to Giuriati demonstrate.[32] Obviously, the collapse of Yugoslavia would help to resolve the Fiume question, for Allied opposition to Italian control of Fiume was largely based on the contention that the city and its port were essential to the new nation's economic stability. On this point, D'Annunzio and Nitti were for once

in total agreement, and the comandante had already established contact
with Montenegrans and Croatians who were opposed to the creation of
Yugoslavia.[33] If Sinigaglia's information was correct, Nitti was only too
happy to see these contacts proceed and to have D'Annunzio serve as
an *agent provocateur* on behalf of Italian wishes in the Balkans.

FROM ZARA TO THE MODUS VIVENDI

D'Annunzio's expectations following his triumphal voyage to Zara
were similar to those following the seizure of Fiume; he was exhilarated
by his reception, and like any politician following a successful rally, he
assumed that the world would react the same way his audience had. The
comandante returned to Fiume convinced that the Italian people would
embrace his dramatic gesture and give him a tangible sign of their support.
The elections quashed these happy dreams with unequivocal firmness,
for not only was Nitti confirmed in office but the Socialists were greatly
strengthened in the Chamber of Deputies. Moreover, with the government's remarkably effective control of the press, the Zara expedition
was presented to the public as an act of rash irresponsibility (if not of
downright madness). Instead of hailing his exploit, Italian public opinion disapproved, and there were other small straws in the wind indicating a changing climate of opinion in the country. When, for example,
Colonel Mario Sani of the Fortieth Infantry attempted to convince his
regiment to defect to D'Annunzio in November, only two officers joined
him. In the country at large, furthermore, national glory was becoming
secondary to matters of food and income, as the menace of general
strikes and food shortages loomed over the major cities.

In this atmosphere, D'Annunzio's mood swung back and forth between two opposite poles. On the one hand, he considered the possibility of negotiating a compromise with Nitti along the general lines the
president of the Council of Ministers had proposed prior to the Zara expedition. If a satisfactory settlement for the city could be arranged,
along with some formal statement by the government to the effect that
D'Annunzio and his legionnaires had rendered a great service to the nation, the comandante for his part was prepared to give up the occupation
of Fiume. This position undoubtedly had a large sector of the Fiuman
public behind it, including important elements within the Command:
Rizzo, Reina, Giuriati, and Ceccherini, to name the most illustrious
figures. Furthermore, such a decision by the comandante reflected his
disappointment with the Italian public. He had, after all, taken a series
of dramatic and dangerous moves in the expectation that they would
shock the public out of its postwar lethargy and inspire the Italians as
the Fiumans had been inspired. Having twice failed to obtain a con-

sensus from his countrymen, D'Annunzio might have been expected to take a stand adopted by many leaders when they are rejected—deciding that the people were unworthy of great leadership and retiring from a position of command. This sentiment undoubtedly played a part in his behavior following the Zara expedition and was reflected in the secret mission Giuriati carried out late in November when he went from Zara to Rome to meet with Nitti's representatives.

There was, however, another side to D'Annunzio's post-Zara mood, namely, the emotion that characterized his policies in the months to come. Having failed to achieve his goals by force of example, D'Annunzio contemplated an act of violence, some spectacular enterprise that would turn the present unfavorable situation topsy-turvy. It is symptomatic of the ideological tenor of late 1919 that both D'Annunzio's supporters and his opponents regarded a possible expedition by the comandante outside Fiume in terms of bolshevism. Badoglio advised Nitti that the "bolshevist" element in Fiume was gaining the upper hand,[34] while Leon Kochnitzky wrote to the Belgian foreign minister on 22 November, predicting a dramatic action by the comandante to save Italy from the communist menace. Kochnitzky's letter gives an excellent insight into the mood of the palace in late November:

> All [in Fiume] view the menace to their country with anguish; they will perish, or they will save it.
>
> Mister Minister, as I write to you the comandante is in his room, two steps from here; he is preparing a message to the Italian nation. Great moments are soon to be upon Fiume.
>
> *Either the government will rally to D'Annunzio's thesis, annex Fiume and the territory of the Treaty of London and, aided by the poet and the army, vigorously exercise power, not hesitating to adopt repression to assure respect for law and the liberty of the citizens;*
>
> *Or else Nitti will be incapable of taking the necessary decisions, and in that case he will be overthrown and will drag down the crown in his wake.*
>
> I have every reason to believe that the army will follow D'Annunzio and . . . will march on Rome. . . .[35]

Any such plans for a march on Rome in November remained sealed in D'Annunzio's room, for no evidence exists that such an undertaking was being planned. Nonetheless, Kochnitzky's letter provides a view of one important element within the command: those who were convinced that sooner or later D'Annunzio would have to resort to arms in order to save Italy from its leaders and its internal enemies. By the beginning of December, such ideas would have gained the upper hand within the politics of the comandante's palace. In the interim, D'Annunzio was sufficiently in agreement with the "radicals" to authorize various provocative acts and *colpi di mano*: a group of *Alpini* passing through the Fiuman zone were persuaded to join the Legions; the supplies the French troops had left behind were sequestered in late November; and in early December the ship *Bertani* was hijacked from the harbor of Trieste by a group of *Uscocchi*.

Provocative actions were not limited to the Fiumans, however, and if the government was genuinely interested in negotiating in good faith with D'Annunzio, the second half of November was a particularly propitious time for such dealings. However, for a variety of reasons this was not possible for the Nitti regime, and the air of mutual suspicion that had characterized the first round of discussions was worsened by the events of late November. Giuriati went to Rome to test the possibility of reaching a compromise and immediately found that it was extremely difficult to ascertain the government's position: Sforza assured him of the government's desire to reach an agreement with D'Annunzio, while Salata claimed that such an accord could only be reached after the comandante had left Fiume. The discussions with Sforza clearly indicated the difference in perspective between the command and Rome, as this exchange between the two men demonstrates:

> *Giuriati*: My confidence in the people is based on the result of the war and on what I saw in the trenches. Our soldier exceeded the most optimistic prediction. He saved [us] despite the commanders and despite the government . . . today it is once again the people who save, the people of whom my comandante is the happiest and most glorious expression. . . .
> *Sforza*: . . . While you see the Italy of the future swathed in laurels and flowers, Nitti sees it swathed in millions [of lire].[36]

For Nitti, then, the paramount consideration was one of economics: Italy could live without glory, but she could not survive long without money. The key to the financial security of the country was America, and consequently, whatever he might think of the glory of D'Annunzio's enterprise, Nitti was determined to settle the Fiume crisis in a way that did not produce total rupture with the United States. Consequently, although Giuriati was permitted to believe that the government was more than willing to negotiate with the comandante about various matters, at the same time the head of the D'Annunzian cabinet was talking to Sforza and Salata, Badoglio was submitting a modus vivendi directly to the comandante in Fiume. The modus vivendi was little more than a restatement of the Tittoni plan of the beginning of the month, and it is indicative of D'Annunzio's frame of mind that he agreed to study the proposal at great length. On the twenty-sixth, following his conversations with Sforza and Salata, Giuriati returned to Fiume by way of Trieste, where he spoke with Badoglio and learned for the first time of the proposal the general had made to D'Annunzio (Sforza later

Francesco Saverio Nitti

claimed that he, too, had been ignorant of the modus vivendi).[37]

Arriving in Fiume, Giuriati and D'Annunzio exchanged views and considered what counterproposals ought to be made to the government, while Badoglio and Nitti threatened a complete blockade of the city if the government's terms were not accepted. On the twenty-ninth, the command's proposals were ready, and they were submitted to Badoglio. They included: (1) a statement of gratitude from the government for the actions of D'Annunzio and his men on behalf of the right of self-determination for Fiume; (2) a promise by the government to occupy the city and the territory of Fiume (substantially more than had been called for in the Tittoni proposal, which had, in any case, limited the area of Fiume to the city itself, excluding the port and the railroad lines), pending the moment in which Italy could accept the wishes of the people of Fiume; (3) a promise by the government to sustain and actualize the principle of the annexation of Fiume; (4) a formal announcement by the government to the Allies that the Tittoni proposal was defunct as a basis for resolving the Adriatic situation; (5) a promise to keep Millo in command of Dalmatia and to supply him with sufficient troops to defend the region against possible attacks from the Yugoslavs; (6) various economic actions on behalf of the city; (7) recognition of the valor of the legionnaires and permission for them to wear the ribbons and medals they had acquired in Fiume.

These proposals were accompanied by a letter from the National Council, authorizing D'Annunzio to act as the sole representative of the municipal government in the negotiations with Rome.

In rapid sequence, the government broke off negotiations with the comandante, and even before formal rejection of the Command's proposals arrived in Fiume, the citizens of the town discovered that a copy of the modus vivendi, accompanied by an inflammatory letter from Riccardo Zanella, had been distributed throughout Fiume and attached to the walls of the city. Zanella's letter warned the Fiumans of the dire consequences that might follow a rejection of the government's proposals, accused D'Annunzio and the National Council of keeping the proposals secret because they feared a popular consensus in favor of the modus vivendi, and urged the people to make their wishes known.

D'Annunzio concluded (probably correctly) that Zanella had acted in concert with Badoglio (and with the prior knowledge of Nitti),[38] and this highly provocative act, combined with the summary conclusion of talks on the part of Badoglio and the imposition of a harsh blockade on the city, suggested to the comandante that the government's sole interest was in forcing him out of Fiume, in order to leave Rome with a completely free hand to negotiate the destiny of the entire Adriatic region with the Allies.[39]

Despite D'Annunzio's analysis of the situation, the pressures on him to yield to the government's proposals were enormous. As Nitti and Badoglio had recognized, the population of the city (like the population of Italy in general) was tired of constant crisis and desperately wished for a state of normalcy. On 17 November, a commission under Rizzo's leadership, formed to study the economic conditions of the city, concluded that the currency had to be stabilized and that nine thousand tons of coal would be needed each month to keep services functioning at a bare minimum.[40] In an attempt to maintain some sort of normal rhythm in Fiume, the schools were opened on the nineteenth, and public officials continued to act as if stability were just around the corner. On the twenty-fifth, Riccardo Gigante was sworn in as the new mayor, having promised a broad program of public spending, including new housing for the poor; a lifting of the blockade; severe action against currency speculators; the construction of a new hospital; the opening of the public baths (not a single public bath was currently in operation); a new hydroelectric plant; a new aqueduct; and new public libraries, theaters, and evening schools.[41] But such programs would only be possible if Fiume received massive transfusions of money and if the industries of the city, now long stagnant, could regain their former levels of activity. As long as Italy remained an enemy, Fiume would be unable to prosper. This was the harsh reality against which D'Annunzio had to judge his response to the government's invitation to leave Fiume.

On the other hand, there were some signs that D'Annunzio might be able to ride out the crisis and eventually see his ideas prevail. The foremost indicators of this chance were the worsening of Wilson's health and the rumors of America's imminent abandonment of the peace talks. The United States Senate's opposition to the Versailles treaties was well known, and it was generally believed that Italy could obtain many more concessions from the British and the French than from the Americans. Consequently, D'Annunzio agreed to a new round of negotiations in early December, hoping that while negotiations were in progress, some event would clarify the situation.

On 8 December the government submitted a new version of the modus vivendi for the consideration of Rizzo and Giuriati in Rome (assisted by Sinigaglia and Giovanni Preziosi), whose content was quite different from that of the earlier text. Italy undertook to guarantee Fiume's right to decide its own destiny, taking formal recognition of the repeated expressions of the city's desire to be annexed to Italy, and would "only consider acceptable a solution consonant with that which Fiume declared to desire."[42] While the government absolutely refused to issue a statement of gratitude to D'Annunzio and the legionnaires and would make no promises to the comandante about the disposition of Admiral Millo, it seemed to Rizzo and Giuriati that the new modus vivendi might prove acceptable to their leader, and so they left immediately for Fiume.

The city was in a state of extreme agitation, the conflict between the moderates and the radicals having finally burst into the open in the form of a move to eliminate Major Carlo Reina from his post at the head of the general staff of Fiume. Reina had long been a supporter of the "minimalist" thesis: that D'Annunzio and the legionnaires should be concerned only with the resolution of the Fiume crisis; seek to solve it in the best way possible, and then leave the city. Issues concerning Dalmatia, a march on the interior, alliances with foreign revolutionary movements or domestic radicals were all foreign to Reina's view of the meaning of the march of Ronchi. Understandably, this attitude put him in direct conflict with those, like Keller, who saw in the comandante's actions the basis for a new world. Further, Reina made no secret of his opposition to such men and openly collaborated with such figures as Castelli, Nitti's official informer, and contact with the more conservative forces of the National Council.[43]

While Giuriati and Rizzo were in Rome, the radicals brought a series of charges against Reina, who in turn charged a group of officers of the Battalion of the Grenadiers with plotting to form a "soviet," which would select their own commander. Two investigations were held, with the result that Reina was removed from his command, sentenced to two months in prison, and ordered to be transferred to Zara. The charges against the grenadiers were found to be without foundation (but they indicate, once again, the widespread fear of anything smacking of bolshevism), but the radicals were convinced that there were plots under way to undermine the integrity of the Fiuman enterprise. "These turbid elements that surrounded D'Annunzio, which were already ubiquitous and which made him do whatever they wished well before the arrival of Rizzo and Giuriati . . . after their arrival formed a Committee of Public Safety, occupying the headquarters of the armored cars, which they keep ready to go day and night, and formed a group of centurions called 'of death' as a bodyguard for themselves and for D'Annunzio."[44]

This was the information relayed to Badoglio and Nitti, slightly distorted, but quite close to the reality of those turbulent days. The group of "centurions" (actually called "*La disperata*"), created by Keller, was composed of those men who had arrived in Fiume without documents and who consequently had not been given official recognition by the Command. These lost souls had been living in the shipyards when Keller organized them into a highly irregular military group—what the comandante's "action secretary" called a new military order. Their behavior far exceeded the bounds of eccentricity; every evening they retired to an abandoned store, where they held military exercises with live ammunition![45]

In addition to Keller, the Committee of Public Safety included Alberto Cais di Pierlas (an officer of D'Annunzio's Quartermaster Office) and Beltrami. Their influence on the comandante was substantial, because they reflected one of D'Annunzio's two conflicting emotions during the period of negotiations with the government. They represented the desire to make of Fiume something more than a gambit in the maneuvers for control of the territory of the former Austro-Hungarian Empire, and they strongly endorsed the sentiments the comandante had expressed in late October.

On 11 and 12 December, D'Annunzio met with General Badoglio and his representative, Colonel Siciliani, in an attempt to gain further concessions. Significantly, the last request he made of Badoglio was that he be permitted to remain in Fiume after the occupation of the city by regular troops, at the head of a group of volunteers. Badoglio would have none of this, and the comandante finally told the general that the terms seemed acceptable to him but that he would have to obtain the consent of the National Council before signing the document.

THE DEFINITION OF THE ENTERPRISE

It is probably impossible to reconstruct the events of the middle of December with complete confidence, but most of the crucial elements are fairly clear. When D'Annunzio told Badoglio of his decision to sub-

mit the modus vivendi to the National Council, he did so in a mood of
mixed resignation and anger. He did not want to leave Fiume, but the
internal situation had become virtually insupportable: the blockade
threatened the city with starvation, the divisions within the ranks of
the legionnaires had become gaping rifts, and Zanella's propaganda had
convinced a substantial part of the population that the command was
acting against the best interests of the town. Hence, D'Annunzio turned
to the National Council, hoping against hope that they would reject
the government's plan. As he telegraphed to Millo on the fourteenth:
"I have called the council to collaborate with me, so as not to take
responsibility for a decision that does not come from my heart."[46] At
the same time, he was under no illusion about the likely outcome of the
council's deliberations, and he advised Millo that it was necessary to
plan for the return of the Fiuman forces from Zara, so that they could
be dissolved. Badoglio, in the meantime, was frenetically planning the
occupation of Fiume, and he and Nitti exchanged telegrams regarding
which troops would be used and how the legionnaires would be transported to Italy.

D'Annunzio's telegram to Millo ended on a prophetic note: "A
beautiful thing is about to end. A light is going out. . . . There is much
impure substance around me, but today I am only spirit. . . ." In the
end, the "spirit" would gain the upper hand.

The National Council met on the afternoon of the fifteenth, while
rumors spread through the town.[47] Many citizens were convinced that
a fundamental conflict was going on between D'Annunzio and the
Council, for it was not generally known that the comandante had agreed
to submit to the council's decision. As a result, many viewed the meeting of the National Council as an attempt to subvert D'Annunzio's
authority. That afternoon, Madame Thérèse Ruelle, a Belgian supporter
of D'Annunzio, spoke in the Fenice Theater, and in the middle of her
address the poet suddenly walked onto the stage. In highly emotional
terms, he described the situation to the audience; the Fiume question
was about to be resolved, and the legionnaires would soon leave the city.
It was five o'clock, and D'Annunzio's radical supporters began to spread
the news that, because of the decision of the National Council, the comandante and his followers were being forced to leave Fiume.

This was all in keeping with D'Annunzio's desire that "the people"
should force him to reject the modus vivendi, and when, at eight o'clock,
the council made its decision (by an overwhelming vote of forty-eight
to six) to accept the government's proposal, an angry mob had gathered
beneath the balcony of the palace. Some five thousand people, consisting largely of legionnaires and the women of the city, demanded the
appearance of the comandante, and when he finally emerged with the

text of the modus vivendi in hand, he was welcomed with wild applause. Paragraph by paragraph, he read the government's proposal to the crowd, and he asked them, "do you want this or not?" Mixed cries reached his ears, and at the end of the recitation, the crowd demanded the rejection of the proposal and renewed resistance by their leaders. "But resistance means suffering. Is that what you desire?"[48] His own wishes became evident when, a moment later, he unfolded the banner of Randaccio over the balcony and invited the Arditi to sing their war songs. With this new act of defiance, D'Annunzio promised the crowd that he would submit the question of the modus vivendi to a plebiscite, and the populace burst into a new celebration that lasted late into the night.

On the following morning, D'Annunzio advised the National Council of his decision to hold a referendum on the modus vivendi, and the vote was scheduled for the eighteenth. In fact, the result of the referendum was a forgone conclusion, as the comandante knew only too well. Despite numerous irregularities and scenes of violence at the voting booths, an enormous majority voted to accept the modus vivendi. But, given the excuse of violence at the polls, D'Annunzio suspended the referendum on the afternoon of the eighteenth, at the same time he was making new demands of Badoglio (including the obviously unacceptable request that the government promise that all of D'Annunzio's statements in Fiume be guaranteed passage through the censor). The following day, he announced that the results of the plebiscite were nullified and that he would make the final decision himself—a decision that was by then clear to everyone.

There were two fundamental motives for D'Annunzio's rejection of the modus vivendi: one emotional, the other "political." The emotional basis has been discussed at some length, and in the last analysis it must be clear that D'Annunzio could not bear to tear himself away from an enterprise he called "the loveliest of the lovelies." However, his final rejection of the government's compromise was not entirely irrational. He did not trust Nitti, and he had good reason to suspect the honesty of the proposal. Furthermore, probably unbeknownst to the comandante, the practical impossibility of actualizing the modus vivendi had been demonstrated at Paris on 9 December, with the submission of an Allied memorandum to the Italian foreign minister. This memorandum, which became public on the twenty-first, called for the creation of a bastard "Free State of Fiume," to be composed of forty thousand Italians and two hundred thousand Slavs and Slovenes. Given Nitti's unswerving conviction that Italy could not risk open conflict with the Allies, this memorandum rendered impossible the government's ability to guarantee the provisions of the modus vivendi. To be sure, at the time of the plebiscite, no one in Fiume knew about the memorandum, but its existence demonstrates that D'Annunzio's instincts were sound and that he had correctly analyzed the situation when he told Millo on the fourteenth: "For my part, I do not see any guarantee apart from my presence and that of the legionnaires."

The negotiations were quickly concluded. On the twentieth, Badoglio gave the poet twenty-four hours to sign the agreement, and when D'Annunzio responded with a reiteration of his previously unacceptable demands, the general declared the negotiations terminated, turned over his command to General Caviglia, and left for Rome to assume his new position as chief of the general staff and head of the Royal Army.

With this seemingly final rupture, the moderate forces within the command had received a fatal blow, and Giuriati resigned as *Capo del gabinetto* on the twenty-third. D'Annunzio had anticipated this development, and two days earlier he had wired an invitation to Alceste De Ambris, one of the leading anarchosyndicalists in Italy, to come to Fiume. De Ambris would replace Giuriati, giving further evidence of the triumph of the radicals and the impending transformation of the Fiuman enterprise into an attempt to create a new model for the Western world. The search for that "something more," which characterized the attitude of Keller and Cais and those who had formed the Committee of Public Safety, soon became the dominant theme of D'Annunzio's words and actions in the new year.

On 31 December 1919, D'Annunzio explained the meaning of his decision to remain in Fiume and outlined the direction he had plotted for the future:

> Today a miraculous year ends: not the year of peace, but the year of passion . . . not the year of Versailles, but the year of Ronchi.
>
> Versailles means decrepitude, infirmity, obtuseness, pain, cheating . . . Ronchi means youth, beauty . . . profound newness.
>
> Against a Europe that suffers, stammers, and stumbles; against an America that has yet to rid herself of the goal of a sick mind that still yet survives an avenging disease . . . against all, against everything we have, the glory of giving the name to this year of torment and ferment. . . .
>
> There is no spot on this earth where the human spirit is freer and newer than on these shores . . . let us celebrate this creation and preserve this privilege. . . .[49]

D'Annunzio had decided to give a new meaning to his Adriatic adventure, a meaning above and beyond the goals of "completing" a victorious Italy and defending the right of self-determination of the Fiuman people. As Renzo De Felice has observed, the invitation to Alceste De Ambris (for the explicit purpose of drafting a new constitution for Fiume) was issued at least partly in order to lay a new basis for this enterprise, "which otherwise would have quickly exhausted itself . . . and—however things developed—give a historic justification to his rejection of the modus vivendi."[50]

8
The D'Annunzian World

Until very recently, the period from late December 1919 until the signing of the Treaty of Rapallo in November 1920 was considered a time of relative inaction on the part of D'Annunzio and his supporters. The ten or eleven months that make up this period witnessed the gradual erosion of the comandante's position in Fiume, and there were relatively few of the highly dramatic events that had characterized the first four months of the enterprise. As supplies slowly dwindled and the struggle for existence became ever more difficult, D'Annunzio's support from the populace (and from many of the officers and soldiers as well) became progressively weaker. While the first period was characterized by an almost constant influx of new volunteers, 1920 saw a significant emigration of forces from Fiume. The first four months had been notable for the high level of enthusiasm displayed by the Fiumans themselves, but in the new year D'Annunzio had to deal with demonstrations against his rule, a formal rupture with the National Council, an active campaign by Zanella and the Autonomists to drive him out of the city, and protests from workers' groups. Against this background, most scholars have considered D'Annunzio's apparent inaction as indicative of a turning inward on his part and also of his lack of political ability to structure the chaos that was Fiume in 1920.

Thanks to the researches of Renzo De Felice,[1] this view of D'Annunzian Fiume in the first ten months of 1920 has been sharply revised, to the extent that we must now say that the period in question provides the key to the meaning of the Fiuman enterprise. Far from being a period of quiescence for D'Annunzio, 1920 was full of activity; but it did not produce the effects that the comandante hoped for. Further, Fiume in these months provides a microcosm of the passions, fears, and dreams that characterize our own world. Consequently, this period is crucial not only for understanding D'Annunzio's importance, but also because it offers an opportunity to untangle many of the strands that make up the fabric of politics in our own time. Unfortunately, this is also the most difficult period to reconstruct, mainly because the documentation we possess is in large part fragmentary and incomplete. Because of the nature of the evidence, the reconstruction of this "moment"–in both this chapter and the one following—will be attempted by looking at various aspects of the period, without undertaking a sequential narration.

THE "FIFTH SEASON": THE WORLD OF GUIDO KELLER

When the rupture with Rome over the modus vivendi became clear, D'Annunzio, as we have seen, called Alceste De Ambris to Fiume. This was a decision of no small importance, demonstrating the extent to which the comandante had moved to the Left during the four months he had ruled Fiume. De Ambris's politics were well known; one of the leaders of Italian revolutionary syndicalism, committed early on to intervention in the Great War, he had won his socialist spurs in the syndicalist struggles of two continents (having spent two years in Brazil), he had been one of the major spokesmen for the trade-union movement (traveling to the United States at the war's end to deliver a series of speeches and press conferences), and he was the secretary of the Unione Italiana del Lavoro. De Ambris was a friend of Mussolini and had served as an intermediary between the Fascist leader and the comandante in late November, when he had carried a letter from Mussolini to Fiume (containing the usual suggestion that the poet not indulge in any actions within Italy).[2]

De Ambris arrived in Fiume at one of the moments of greatest tension for D'Annunzio. As we have seen, the duplicity of the government, the internal conflicts within the city, and the possibility that he might have to abandon Fiume combined to produce a mood of mixed anger and frustration in D'Annunzio, and his encounter with the robust and energetic De Ambris convinced him of the desirability of a future collaboration. When negotiations with the government collapsed, the comandante immediately wrote De Ambris: "I believe that your presence and your help are necessary. You will be able to render the highest service to our cause."[3] When Giuriati resigned a couple of days later, it became possible for D'Annunzio to make the revolutionary socialist the head of his cabinet.

The invitation to De Ambris must be viewed in the light of the multiple forces acting upon D'Annunzio. Above all, it reflected the profound disillusionment the comandante felt for the nationalist forces that had theretofore played such a major role in the Fiuman enterprise. For four months he had played the Sinigaglia-Giuriati game (with some notable exceptions), hoping that Nitti would fall and that a new government in Rome would annex Fiume. With the definitive failure of this strategy in late December, the comandante was compelled by circumstances to find a new orientation for his enterprise. This is not to say, however, that he had to *improvise* a new strategy, for he had already begun to shift the direction of the Fiuman adventure toward the ideas of men like Captain Giulietti. While the basis for this decision was in large part emotional, the comandante had good reasons for it in the experience he had had with the two groups. While the men of the Right had urged caution and patience, those of the Left (in the form of the leader of the Gente del mare) had provided guns and a ship for Fiume, had undertaken a program of propaganda on Fiume's behalf within Italy, and were urging the comandante to ally with the revolutionary forces of the country. In early January D'Annunzio decided to execute an abrupt about-face and throw in his lot with the forces of revolution.

On 5 January, in response to an appeal from D'Annunzio, Giulietti sent his brother to Fiume with a five-point proposal.[4] The plan called for a march on Rome by an army consisting of the comandante's forces, the Gente del mare, and the Socialists (along with such figures as Errico Malatesta). The goal of the action was revolutionary in two senses, for Giulietti wished to install a new social order ("guaranteeing everyone the fruits of his own labor") and resolve the Adriatic crisis, including the annexation of Fiume. In order to achieve this, Giulietti required a formal statement of support from D'Annunzio, in order that he might approach the leaders of the revolutionary forces. D'Annunzio's reply the following day was indicative of his state of mind and also revealed a level of activity outside Fiume that had not been evident to those outside the most private counsels of the command:

> The meaning of my enterprise and of my most obstinate resistance is becoming clearer every day. . . . All the desires . . . of revolt—the world over—turn toward the fires of Fiume, which send their sparks far away. . . .
> Since last October I have intervened directly in the Egyptian movement against the "devourers of raw flesh" . . . the Croatians turn toward me, as well, wishing to divest themselves of the Serbian yoke. . . . The revolution of the "separatists" is ready. It should explode . . . before the fifteenth of March. . . .
> I have the arms, as well; I have the shells of the *Persia*, millions of them. I lack what Machiavelli called "the spine of War". . .[5]

D'Annunzio was ready for the enterprise (a few lines later, he assured Giulietti that nobody was more prepared than he for "the grand action"), but he wanted to be certain that funds (Machiavelli's "spine") would be available, both for the march on Rome and for the broader actions he was planning throughout the world. We shall return to this "grand design" at length in a subsequent chapter, but it must be stressed that D'Annunzio's adherence to the proposal for an alliance with the revolutionary forces of Italy was viewed by the comandante as part of a greater plan of action. Furthermore, he was determined to make Fiume the center of the revolution:

> Today, any effort at liberation must start at Fiume. For a vaster social enterprise I must begin here. My spirit is based on these shores for all forward jumps, particularly for a leap to the other shore. . . . Here the new forms of life are not only conceived, but are fulfilled. . . .
> I have gone back to the people who generated me. I am mixed with their substance. . . .
> I must be able to resist and rule here *until the day you announce.* . . .

D'Annunzio's emphasis was significant: revolution, yes, but only if the Fiuman enterprise was absolutely guaranteed. Further, the stress on his close ties with "the people" and his passionate devotion to "this shore," where the "new forms of life" were to be fulfilled, point toward an enterprise that the comandante considered of paramount importance for his future plans: the creation of a new institutional system for Fiume, which would in turn provide a model for the new world of "free spirits."

The plan for a march on Rome with the Socialists failed, although many of those whom Giulietti approached were willing to attempt it. He held a series of meetings and obtained the support of Errico Malatesta and Nicola Bombacci. However, the maximalist Giacinto Menotti Serrati refused to join the plot for a coup d'etat. The director of *Avanti !* could not bring himself to join with D'Annunzio, and as time passed, the impossibility of an alliance between the Fiumans and the Socialists became ever clearer, despite numerous declarations of a desire for such an alliance on the part of D'Annunzio and his supporters. If it had been difficult for the Socialists to consider joint action in the first days of January, it became even more so once De Ambris had become the head of D'Annunzio's cabinet. An alliance between leading interventionists (with heretical Socialist views) and the party that had opposed the war was too much to ask for in 1920.[6]

Despite the failure of Giulietti's attempt to arrange an armed coup, a revolutionary direction was surely more congenial to D'Annunzio's personality than a long program of negotiation and parliamentary maneuvering. In the end, D'Annunzio's policies were based upon his viscera, and he found himself thrilled by his role in Fiume and excited at the possibility—indeed, the necessity—of transforming the enterprise into something with a more "profound" significance. In late 1919 the themes of "Italy and Life" found their way back into the poet's speeches, and his address on the last day of the year struck the note that would become dominant in 1920. "We have laid the foundations for a city of life, an entirely new city," he told his listeners, and he used a metaphor that was new to his rhetoric: "It lives, and radiates splendor. It has the vigor and the splendor of a fifth season upon the world. It is a spontaneous Latin season, an unheard Latin harmony."[7]

Previously, the comandante had spoken of Fiume as a martyr, or as a virile source of resistance, or as a fire that would consume the evils of a corrupt world. With the end of the old year, however, he began to speak of Fiume as a special source of creativity, as a unique realm where life took on a new meaning and where the future lay close at hand. In a sense, the failure to reach a compromise with Nitti left the poet with a tabula rasa on which he could design his own system for the postwar world. D'Annunzio's enthusiasm at this prospect has not been generally understood (as it was invariably misunderstood at the time), and De Ambris was one of the few to recognize it: "The most intimate and real sense of this enterprise evaded almost everyone. . . . Only a few young, naive persons really understood D'Annunzio and his work, those whom the war had opened up to that heroism which labors for the pure Idea, for the sacrifice that seeks no gain. . . ."[8]

Of all the people in Fiume, this description most closely describes Guido Keller, and much of the enthusiasm for the new world that the comandante (and De Ambris) attempted to create in 1920 was due to the ongoing contact between the Command and men like Keller. As we have seen, such men played a significant role in convincing D'Annunzio to reject the modus vivendi in December, and they continued to exercise great influence over the comandante. D'Annunzio was in constant contact with the legionnaires (in contrast to his virtual isolation from the citizenry), taking hikes in the countryside every day with a different company, eating with his officers, and generally sharing in the pervasive atmosphere of exhilaration. Further, as time passed, the composition of the legionnaires underwent a significant change; with the elimination of such moderating forces as Giuriati and Reina at the beginning of the year and with the gradual emigration of the more traditionalist elements from the ranks (the most important being the departure of Captain Rocco Vadalà of the *carabinieri* in May), the more adventurous elements became dominant in the city.[9] They had chafed at the unwelcome discipline of the first four months, and in 1920 they exploded in a variety of ways. Keller captured their sentiments with characteristic accuracy in his journal, *Yoga*, in late 1920: "When the redemptive mission of the holocaust succeeded, something was expected of them. Under the ash of their involuntary physical inactivity, generous sparks kindled their hearts, and . . . they gradually understood . . . that life is born from struggle, as harmony is generated from discordant sounds."[10]

Keller attempted to organize these "proud and fiery spirits" in his *Yoga* group, which he termed "a union of free spirits tending toward perfection,"[11] but it was not a very large or impressive body. Nonetheless, Keller's desire to establish something new at Fiume, especially after the period of "ashes," which had lasted until the failure of the modus vivendi, found full expression in the plans of the comandante in the new year, and in those of a large number of the legionnaires. In particular, the Arditi shared both Keller's insistence upon establishing something original and durable in Fiume and his conviction that the long period of physical quiet had generated a creative urge among the legionnaires. As late as May, articles in *La Testa di Ferro* were defending the apparent stasis in Fiume by pointing to a presumed internal dynamism. Mario Carli, for example, pointed out to his readers that "one does not move only with one's feet" and that humanity moves forward with methods other than the locomotion of men's legs: "The apparently static condition of the legionary enterprise conceals a dynamism that is not evident to all eyes. . . . But what a movement of passion, of constructive energies, of brains bursting into flames. . . !"[12]

It was in the very nature of their world for the legionnaires to avoid traditional institutions, and Keller and his friends usually slept outside the city in order to symbolize their detachment from their physical confines. Yet Keller's remarkable ability to galvanize the men around him into action enabled him to experiment with new forms of organization that, in their turn, inspired D'Annunzio and found a kindred spirit in De Ambris's radical syndicalism. Carli was right when he claimed that a teeming world of creativity lay beneath the apparently dormant surface of D'Annunzian Fiume, and the quality of the creations that emerged from that world was extremely high. There is much of Keller's brand of creativity in the Carta del Carnaro, the brilliant constitution for Fiume that was composed by De Ambris in the first two and one-half months of the year and then rendered in D'Annunzian language (with some important additions) during the summer. Moreover, it is quite impossible to read the project for a new democratic organization of the armed forces (written by Captain Giuseppe Piffer, D'Annunzio's personal secretary, and the comandante in October[13]) without seeing the influence of Guido Keller and the wild men of *La Disperata*. Keller was a true contemporary of the Dadaists whom, it is necessary to remember, Swiss authorities considered more threatening to their traditions than Vladimir Ilyich Lenin.[14]

Keller's greatest influence on life in Fiume came from his readiness to improvise drastic measures to protect the city from what he considered to be "unhealthy" influences. Just as the Committee of Public Safety had been created on the spur of the moment, Keller and his band

of *enragés* (given their habit of going through Fiume stripped to the
waist, we might call them the *sans-chemises* of the Fiuman revolution)
served as a vigilante group, ready to take action against all and sundry,
even against D'Annunzio himself. The most entertaining example of
such actions was the projected escapade of the Castle of Love.

Keller and Giovanni Comisso, his comrade in arms, had become
alarmed at the influence of D'Annunzio's lover, the pianist Luisa Baccara.
While the comandante was inclined to undertake all manner of adventures, Baccara, fearing that he might be killed at sea, continually implored him not to risk his life in such expeditions. Keller could not tolerate this influence on the Command, and he plotted with his kindred
spirits to get the woman out of Fiume. Desiring to accomplish this in
"a fantastic manner," Keller and Comisso produced a plan to remove
Baccara from the scene that was one of the most imaginative schemes
of the year. They learned of a medieval festival called the Castle of
Love, which had been celebrated in Treviso. The ceremony was simple:
the prettiest girls in town were placed in a wooden castle, which was
then "besieged" by men from the surrounding area, who launched food,
money, flowers, and other gifts at the women. Comisso and Keller proposed to reenact the festival, with the bath house on the beach serving
as the castle, and Baccara as the *Madonna Castellana*. At the height of
the assault, the Arditi of *La Disperata* would kidnap her and spirit her
out of town, in order to "put her in a cage like a hen and carry her to
a desert island." Nor was Baccara the only target of the band; as Keller
recalled several months later, during the festivities they hoped to eliminate *all* their enemies: "At the end of the celebration, amidst the frenzy
of the dance, the men of the past . . . and those threatening to the celer-
ity of the . . . enterprise would have been seized, tied, and put on a
boat and carried away."[15]

This scheme failed when D'Annunzio surprisingly refused to permit
the festival to be held, saying that the world would see in it the hand of
that decadent figure they believed the comandante to be. "It is too
D'Annunzian,"[16] he said, and Luisa Baccara remained in the city (and
would remain the poet's constant companion for years to come).

Keller and his immediate circle of friends were simply extreme cases
in the world of the legionnaires, a world that is extremely difficult to
capture in the language of historical analysis or political science. The
English writer Osbert Sitwell did well in the fall of 1920:

> The general animation and noisy vitality seemed to herald a new land, a new
> system. We gazed and listened in amazement. Every man here seemed to wear a
> uniform designed by himself: some had beards, and had shaved their heads com-
> pletely so as to resemble the Commander himself . . . others had cultivated huge
> tufts of hair, half a foot long, waving out from their foreheads, and wore, bal-

anced on the very back of the skull, a black fez. Cloaks, feathers and flowing
black ties were universal, and every man—and few women were to be seen—
carried the "Roman dagger."[17]

Despite this atmosphere of rampant individualism, with everyone
believing he had a major role to play in the creation of a new world,
there was a remarkably low level of violence and disorder. Apart from
the duels and fist fights that characterized the ambience of the soldiers
themselves, life in Fiume went on apace (albeit under severe economic
strains). The occasional acts directed against the Italian citizens of Fiume
by the legionnaires frequently had a bizarre tinge to them, as when, in
May, the command had to issue a warning to the populace not to turn
over property to men claiming to be members of a secret police force.
In a document signed by Sani and Coselschi, the citizenry was advised
that some miscreants, dressed in army or legionary uniforms, and showing false identification, had been searching and seizing Fiumans and
their homes.[18] But, surprisingly, such incidents were quite rare.

This was not the case, however, with regard to the Slavic population
of Fiume, and despite the numerous proclamations of sympathy toward
the Croatians that emanated from the palace, there were several violent
encounters between them and the legionnaires. At the moments of the
most intense economic suffering in the city, the troops would vent their
spleen on Croatian merchants and on anything that smacked of a "foreign" presence. The most ferocious anti-Croatian riot took place on 14-
15 July, when legionnaires and citizens sacked Croatian establishments
for nearly forty-eight hours (destroying several Fiuman stores as well).[19]

Of all the moments of violence in 1920, none was so potentially explosive as that directed against a group of departing soldiers in the first
week of May. Given the atmosphere in Fiume in 1920, representatives
of the traditional order found themselves extremely uncomfortable, and
the exodus of these men became substantial in the late spring and early
summer. The most famous of these episodes was the departure of Captain Vadalà of the *carabinieri*, who, with the consent of D'Annunzio,
led several hundred troops out of the city on the evening of 6 May.
Vadalà was alarmed, it seems, both by the dramatic changes in the
politics of the Command (the new constitution had been widely rumored
since its completion in the middle of March) and by the undisciplined
behavior that had come to characterize the legionnaires. As the captain
marched out of Fiume, legionnaires, particularly the Arditi, decided to
take matters into their own hands, and they attacked Vadalà and his
followers at Cantrida, along the armistice line. The result was three
deaths (one *carabiniere*, one vice brigadier, and one civilian) and scores
of wounded. Thanks to the intervention of General Ceccherini and other

officials, a full-scale massacre was avoided,[20] but the incident serves to illustrate the intensity of the passion with which the legionnaires were prepared to defend their "cause." Their most violent acts were reserved for those of their own ranks who abandoned the city, just as in any group of "true believers" the heretic is treated with greater severity than the infidel. The Arditi newspaper, *La Testa di Ferro*, devoted its entire front page to the encounter on the ninth, listing the "traitors" and hailing those Arditi who had been wounded in the assault, "spilling a robust blood for the city of holocaust, which could not have been spent more gloriously." Nonetheless, the attrition was substantial. In the week of Vadalà's departure, a total of 705 soldiers left the city,[21] and the Command was forced to step up its campaign of recruiting new volunteers in Italy in order to replenish its manpower supply.

With exceptions such as these, it must be said that the legionnaires were remarkably well behaved and astonishingly well disciplined (in their own manner, to be sure). Numerous sources support this view, but perhaps the most remarkable evidence for the good behavior of the legionnaires comes from the report of a female journalist from the *Times* who visited Fiume in early September (one of the most agitated periods of the year). While stressing that the legionnaires weren't organized in either the English or the German manner, she nonetheless reported that "the discipline among the troops (for the most part Arditi, dressed in every kind of uniform) seems excellent . . . these Fiuman legionnaires are not a wild group of adventurers; like their leader, they are idealists, enthusiasts. . . ."[22]

The discipline of the legionnaires was quite good, but it was not achieved by the traditional means of giving orders from on high. Men like General Ceccherini, accustomed to normal military discipline, labored against severe obstacles to maintain control over their men. As the general himself observed three years later, "it was not possible to install a regime of iron discipline and military authority there, where the somewhat blind generosity of D'Annunzio permitted all manner of infraction."[23] The general remained in the city primarily because he could not bring himself to leave his son behind, and this tiny generational conflict reflects much of Keller's world in Fiume. The youthful energies of those who chose to remain there were directed in large part against the symbols and methods of the world of their parents and other disciplinarians. As their adoption of bizarre modes of dress and their experimentation with drugs indicate, these men were interested in new models for their behavior, and new techniques were consequently necessary to structure their actions. Along with these techniques, new ideas—indeed, an entirely new worldview—were evolved to maintain the devotion of the legionnaires to Fiume and its comandante.

We have already suggested that D'Annunzio was involved in the creation of a new form of liturgy in Fiume, a liturgy that would play a very important role in the evolution of civic festivals and the development of mass politics in the modern world. But the mere forms (the daily marches in the countryside, the speeches from the balcony, the dialogues with the crowd, the elaboration of new "civic" holidays) were not in themselves sufficient to keep the legionnaires in that state of constant enthusiasm that characterized what we have termed Keller's world. During the course of 1920, D'Annunzio created a new quasi-religious world view, which came to be the "official" language of Fiume and which was adopted not only by the political leaders of the Command but also by many of the religious figures in the city. The most eloquent testimony to this fact is found in the words of Don Celso Constantini who became the apostolic administrator of Fiume in May. Referring to the evolution of the Carta del Carnaro, he wrote: "The life of Fiume, agitated, tumultuous, torn by diverse political currents that were a mixture of idealism and materialism, was already sufficiently pagan without it having been necessary to publicly proclaim a humanistic cult."[24]

In a subsequent letter to the comandante, Don Celso complained that D'Annunzio had contributed to the rebirth of a pagan cult, in which hedonism and esthetics took precedence over ethics, "and Orpheus over Christ."[25] One might wish to challenge Costantini's choice of words, but in effect his protest was well founded, as the behavior of some Fiuman priests had amply demonstrated. Toward the end of March, a group of Capuchin priests came to the attention of Fiuman authorities as a result of their attempt to radicalize the church from within. For some time, a number of Capuchins had been promoting a movement to permit priests to marry, and they were promptly accused of being Bolsheviks. Stung by this accusation, they issued a "Public Confession" in March,[26] explaining their position and calling upon Fiumans to support them. Briefly, they demanded three basic changes in the policies and the structures of their order. They wanted the right to marry, they wanted local control over the funds of the order, and they wanted a democratization of the hierarchy. In particular, the "modernists" wanted their provincial superior elected from below, rather than appointed from above. On the marriage issue, which was understandably the most highly publicized of the three, they claimed divine support: "For us, the man who marries is more honest than he who lives, not with one, but with several women, and notwithstanding that, is scandalized by the others. We will not prevent anyone from getting married . . . since this is the law of God, confirmed and consecrated by Christ."[27]

By the middle of April, the "modernists" had encountered so much opposition from within their order that they were prepared to join

D'Annunzio and leave the fold. Their superior went to the Fiume *Questura* (police headquarters) and accused them of "rebellion," asking the authorities to expel the renegade priests. Under the threat of imminent expulsion, the "modernists" went to the comandante, requesting his support in their efforts to reform their order. D'Annunzio saw no great threat to public order in this movement (and hardly wished to establish a precedent by expelling people from Fiume for rebellious acts), and he ordered the *Questura* to keep its hands off the entire question, leaving the church to deal with the revolt.

The church dispatched Father Paterniano from Rome to Fiume to handle the minicrisis. He took a hard line with the rebels, demanding that they publicly recant or face expulsion from Fiume. The plan was to break up the group and send its members singly to various distant dioceses. True to their convictions, however, the "modernists" refused to retract their "Public Confession" and they undertook to model their resistance to their superiors on that of the Fiumans to Nitti. By the second week in April they had hung a large banner from the monastery window, reading: *Hic manebimus optime*, "We will remain here splendidly." This was the slogan D'Annunzio had hurled at Nitti the previous fall, the same slogan that appeared on the postage stamps of Fiume when its independence was proclaimed the following autumn. The Capuchins, like the legionnaires, had become part of Keller's world.

In the end, seven of the "modernists" left the order, inspired by that mixture of materialism and idealism that had so dismayed Don Celso. The seven demanded civilian clothes and "severance pay" from the order or, barring that, free food and lodging in the monastery.[28]

While the penetration of D'Annunzian ideals into the realm of religion was of considerable significance, the transformation of religious symbols into the rhetoric of the Fiuman revolution was of far greater importance, and the comandante achieved a potent fusion of sacred and profane elements in his orchestration of civic festivals in the new year. One spectacular example of the powerful effect he achieved was the celebration of San Sebastian's Day, the twentieth of January. San Sebastian was D'Annunzio's favorite saint (D'Annunzio had written a cantata with Claude Debussy celebrating the death of the martyr), and the celebration was staged with great care. Late in the morning, in the church of St. Vito, the women of the city presented the comandante with a bayonet made of gold and silver, and the gift was passed to Padre Reginaldo Giuliani, the priest of the Arditi. Giuliani blessed the bayonet, which was then given to D'Annunzio by a group of women: "To you . . . chosen by God to radiate the light of a renewed liberty through the world, the women of Fiume and of Italy . . . religiously offer this holy weapon, this blessed bayonet, in which our spirit and our hearts are fused with our meager gold and silver, so that with it you may carve the word *victory* in the living flesh of our enemies."[29]

D'Annunzio responded by recalling the martyrdom of San Sebastian. He reminded his listeners that after the saint had been killed by the arrows of his enemies, a woman had come and tended to his corpse, removing the fatal lances one by one. "I want to believe that the blade of this proffered bayonet, my sisters, was made with the steel of the first and last [arrows]."

D'Annunzio used this image to merge the ceremony in Fiume with the myth of the martyred saint:

> The archer of life cried out in his death agony: "I die in order not to die."
> He cried, bleeding: "Not enough! Not enough! Again!"
> He cried, "I will live again. But to live again it is necessary for me to die."
> Immortality of love! Eternity of sacrifice!
> The paths of immolation are the surest; and the blood of the hero and the heroine is inexhaustible.
> You know this, sisters in Christ, brothers in the living God. This is the sense of this mystery. This is the meaning of this gift.[30]

After the church ceremony, D'Annunzio walked into the piazza, where the legionnaires passed in review before him. Antonio Grossich, the mayor of the city, was so moved by the spectacle that he exclaimed, "he's a saint!"[31]

We have already observed that in D'Annunzio's view of the world, religious experiences were not restricted to church functions, and that the comandante had attempted to fuse the symbols of the church with the civic functions of the Command for several months. In this manner he was able to achieve a civic enthusiasm based not only upon his own charisma and the loyalty and devotion of his followers but also upon the symbols and personalities of the Catholic faith. This religious quality of D'Annunzio's "political thought" is crucial to an understanding of the efficacy of his leadership in 1920. The basis of his appeal to the Fiumans in 1919 had been the cry to hold steadfastly to their desire to be reunited with the mother country, hoping that the heroic gesture of the march of Ronchi and the various efforts to bring pressure upon Nitti would eventually bear fruit. Yet despite D'Annunzio's great charisma, and the unquestioned dedication of the vast majority of the populace to the goal of annexation, such a program was essentially passive; it depended upon the action of others (in this case, none other than the hated *Cagoia*) for its eventual success. As we have suggested, the very nature of D'Annunzio's regime demanded that the citizens be drawn together into an emotional unit that was, in turn, given a symbolic importance. As Leon Kochnitzky put it, "Fiume is the mournful symbol of all the injustices of an execrable period" and as such demanded action to redeem its suffering. Those who were brought into the emotional "community" that D'Annunzio created with his political drama inevitably became frustrated by their dependence on others for the redemption of their cause. One can view the conflict of December 1919 as a conflict between those who participated in the D'Annunzian community and those who remained outside it, who were simply attempting to bring Fiume into the world of normal Italian "business as usual."

The passivity of the first four months of the enterprise was shattered in the December convulsions, and the new year was to be a year of action. To return once again to the metaphor of San Sebastian, Fiume may have suffered for four months, but it would be reborn in the new year. Fiume may have been martyred, but martyrdom purified the city in a later triumph. Furthermore, the city's leader was armed with sacred weapons in order to carve victory into the bodies of her opponents. This transformation of the mood of Fiume from one of anticipation to one of determined initiative had a significant impact on the spirit of Fiumans in 1920. The D'Annunzian festivals in the new year, as we have seen, were festivals of creative exuberance, and they truly made Fiume a "city of life." In no other document is this spirit so vibrant as in Kochnitzky's description of the festival of San Vito, the patron saint of Fiume, in the summer of 1920, and it deserves to be cited at length:

> The illuminated piazza, the banners, the great written proclamations, the boats with their beflowered lanterns (even the sea had its role in the festival) and the dances. . . . They danced everywhere: in the piazza, in the streets, on the dock; by day, by night, they danced and sang, not with the voluptuous softness of the Venetian barcaroles, but rather it was an unrestrained bacchanale. To the rhythm of martial fanfares one saw soldiers, sailors, women, citizens in bohemian embraces, recapturing the triple diversity of the primitive couples hailed by Aristophanes. One's gaze, wherever it fixed, saw a dance: of lanterns, of sparks, of stars; starving, in ruin, in anguish, perhaps on the verge of death in the flames or under a hail of grenades, Fiume, brandishing a torch, danced before the sea.
>
> In the impoverished homes of the old city, the women had removed the sacred images. The tiny lights glowed in front of the figure of Gabriele D'Annunzio.
> Others may call this hysteria. It is the *Bal des Ardents*.
> Under the gaze of the hostile and cowardly world. . . . Fiume dances before death.[32]

Notwithstanding such boisterous exhibitions (to which the tradition of the *colpi di mano* must be added as a typically Fiuman manifestation), the action in Fiume in 1920 consisted, for the most part, in that frenzy of intellectual activity that Mario Carli quite rightly termed the real dynamism of D'Annunzian politics. Throughout the first part of the year, the comandante and his followers produced a series of projects

which, if actually put into effect, would have had unfathomable consequences both in Italy and throughout Europe. As we shall see in the following chapter, the Command drew the blueprints for a new order on a
vast scale—a new constitution, an international revolutionary organization
to combat colonialism and imperialism, a series of initiatives designed to
destroy the unity of the new Yugoslav nation, a radical reorganization
of the army, and several attempts to produce a revolutionary seizure of
power in Italy. The failure to transform the world was due to various
factors, the most important of which was the failure of D'Annunzio himself to elaborate a clear "political" vision of the necessity for concrete
action at the proper moment. Yet no man can overcome an endless series
of obstacles, and the practical barriers to the creation of the "new world"
envisioned in the Fiuman workshop were virtually without end.

THE OBSTACLES TO REALIZATION

The economic drama of Fiume was continuous in 1920 and merits
a book of its own; only an outline of the crisis can be given here. Due
to the lack of any solid "balance sheet" for the city, one is forced to
guess about the actual state of affairs, but it is unquestionable that the
city frequently arrived at the brink of a real disaster.[33] The chaos within
Fiume was considerable, owing to the failure of the Command to achieve
a resolution of the currency problem. In the middle of January, *La
Vedetta d'Italia* reported that many merchants had stopped taking small
notes (of one or two crowns) issued by the Command because of the
rampant counterfeiting of such bills, and consequently many citizens
found themselves unable to spend their "money."[34] In subsequent weeks
the Command (and the National Council) attempted to convince the
citizenry that the small notes were genuine, but their efforts met with
little success. By early February, the National Council had passed a law
requiring merchants to accept the small bills, but the council still had
to establish an arbitrary maximum amount that merchants had to accept.
This monetary confusion continued, unabated, throughout the year.

The economy of the town had virtually ground to a halt, as we have
already seen, even after the shipyards had been purchased by a group of
Italian industrialists in February.[35] While the *Vedetta* triumphantly announced that "this means that Fiume is Italian, and that Italy is defini-
tively in Fiume," unemployment in the city remained between eight
and ten thousand, and there was virtually no activity along the water-
front. No real commerce existed until November, and the shipyards and
torpedo works limped along at about one-quarter capacity. Although
almost all basic commodities were rationed, the city never seems to have
been threatened with starvation.[36] Indeed, at one point D'Annunzio

complained that the palace was spending too much money on food, to which Sani replied in a fascinating document: "As far as prices are concerned, I can guarantee that everything is going up, and that nothing can be done. I wanted to call your attention . . . to the fact that *all* the members of your household staff order food in profusion, for a consumption that evidently you can not sustain. It would be a good idea for the kitchen to receive orders from only one person, *who has your trust*."[37]

Thus, food was clearly available in Fiume, and the copious quantities that were ordered for the comandante's table evidently spilled over into the laps of his servants. The problem of excessive spending by the Command was another leitmotif of Fiuman life, one that consumed a great amount of poor Sani's time. On 16 October 1920, in a document that provides us with a synopsis of the fiscal situation of the Command, Sani presented the comandante with a long list of abusive practices. In it, he illustrated the profligacy that characterized the spending practices of the troops under D'Annunzio's command. For example, (1) while the budget called for salaries totaling ten thousand lire per day, the actual cost was three times that figure; (2) several expenses were impossible, such as bills for dental work (there were two dentists in Fiume who performed their labors free of charge); (3) numerous officials, finding themselves with nothing to do, and "infamous for the immoral and incomprehensibly costly tenor of life" they led, had created special "missions" for themselves and their friends. On these "missions" (within Italy), they invariably traveled first class, stayed in the finest hotels, and dined in the most costly restaurants; (4) the sailors received the same pay they would have received had they been at sea; (5) two captains had moved into the finest hotel in Fiume and were charging their bills to the Command; (6) although Fiume's official representatives in Rome received free lodging from friends of the Command, they nonetheless charged the Command for rent.[38]

To be sure, the legionnaires were not always in a position to distribute money with such careless abandon, and one frequently finds D'Annunzio forced to take extreme measures to raise funds for his needs. Since the administration of the city was divided between the Command and the National Council (the Command paying for the legionnaires and the council for municipal expenses), there was often considerable debate about who should pay for what. On 18 May, for example, D'Annunzio wrote an angry letter to Grossich, accusing the council of dragging its feet about a loan that had been promised him, and he heatedly observed that he had been unable to pay his troops because of the council's procrastination.[39]

Conditions in the city were subject to sudden fluctuations (depending on the generosity of the Italian government, the availability of credits from sympathetic industrialists, the success of the *colpi di mano*, and the strictness with which the blockade was enforced), and the rapidity of these changes can be seen in two speeches given by De Ambris, the first at the end of February, the second late the following month. In February, he told the Fiumans that food had been guaranteed and that while the economic situation was difficult, it was not desperate. He hoped to resolve the currency problem and suggested that if "non-Fiumans" were eliminated from the factories of the city, there would be a significant increase in the work force.[40] Almost exactly one month later, the situation seemed to have changed drastically: "The economic reserves are exhausted, or nearly so. It must not be forgotten that Fiume has existed thus far on credit for its food and its heating supplies. At the moment our creditors are not inclined to give us further help and are, on the contrary, demanding to be paid. . . . At the same time the public and private warehouses . . . are today virtually empty, and there is no possibility of resupply. . . ."[41]

There were some political explanations for the drastically different tone of De Ambris's messages. In February he was seeking to bolster the morale of the population, whereas at the end of March he wished to convince the people that they would eventually have to declare the city's independence (as provided in the new constitution) and seek to reactivate its economy on their own. Yet the short supply of heating fuel was a serious problem in the harsh Adriatic winter, as was the high level of unemployment. In addition, the efforts of the Command to come to grips with the economic problems of Fiume accentuated the already existing tensions between it and two groups: the National Council and the non-Italian population.

The issue of non-Italians, to which De Ambris referred in his speech in late February, had come momentarily to a head in that period, as it did once again in April, when a strike by the largest workers' organization, the Sedi Riunite, forced the Command to intervene in the city's economic affairs. On 26 February some thirty-six workers were expelled from Fiume for their political activities, which included attempts to disrupt the few factories that were functioning.[42] The workers were all Slavs, and the Sedi Riunite protested this action against its members. De Ambris replied with a stern message, maintaining that Fiume had to defend itself against "foreign elements who condemned Fiuman workers to unemployment." He continued with a statistical analysis of the working force of the Danubius shipyards. Of 877 workers, he said, there were only 200 Fiumans. The remainder consisted of roughly 200 Italians from the newly acquired territories, nearly 300 Slavs from the same areas, some 100 Slavs from officially Yugoslav territory (Sussak), 51

Hungarians, 15 Austrians, 4 Dalmatians, and 1 Pole. The proportions were more or less the same in the category of white-collar employees, demonstrating that Italians and Fiumans actually made up less than half the working force. Thus, De Ambris observed, while Fiume teemed with unemployed citizens, foreigners continued to hold their positions in the businesses and factories of the city. While De Ambris did not say it, he knew the explanation for this situation; it was cheaper for Fiuman factory owners to hire Slavs, and the Slavic workers were easier to fire than were Fiumans, who carried far more political weight. De Ambris stressed that his position was not based upon any hostility to the working class as such, and indeed the Command had permitted workers' organizations to distribute their literature and hold public meetings in which the policies of the Command had been roundly denounced.

In like manner, De Ambris insisted that the Command was not about to undertake a purge of foreign elements, which had been treated with what he called "friendly equity." (As a matter of fact, unbeknownst to the citizenry, the new constitution had provided for the creation of public schools for the non-Italian population, a proviso that eventually generated a heated protest from the Italians when it became known.[43]) Nonetheless, a "purge" did take place. On the twenty-eighth, the Command announced that all noncitizens of Fiume who had arrived after 30 October 1918 would have to leave the city within ten days.[44] This seems to have been largely a political maneuver, for there were so many exceptions to the expulsion decree (those whose work was considered indispensable, those over sixty, those who were sick, those who enrolled in the legions) that very few persons actually had to leave Fiume. The effect of the measure was probably more psychological than economic in nature.

The conflict with the National Council was more profound and created more problems for the Command than the tensions between Italians and Slavs.[45] The majority of the National Council had voted for the modus vivendi, had little or no interest in the grandiose schemes that emerged from the palace in 1920 (and were frightened by the prospect of a Republican government), were deeply concerned about the possibility of a complete economic collapse of the city, and resented the usurpation of traditional powers by the Command. They were dismayed by the continuing *colpi di mano*, believing (with some reason) that a continuation of this practice would inevitably produce a direct conflict with regular troops, and above all, they were alarmed by the presence of Alceste De Ambris at the right hand of D'Annunzio. Early in March, the Executive Committee of the Council had already forced Grossich (whose loyalty and dedication to D'Annunzio were beyond question) to urge the comandante to alter his foreign policy "or suffer the consequences."[46] In particular, they wished the *colpi di mano* terminated and demanded a clear definition of the powers that were to remain in the council's hands. On 15 March, the situation was considered so serious that the executive committee summoned De Ambris to a meeting the following day, in order to explain his behavior to them.[47]

De Ambris's response to this cursory summons is highly illuminating.[48] He refused to appear before them and offered D'Annunzio the opportunity to remove him from his position. After this gesture, De Ambris made a scathing attack on the council, in which he suggested that profiteering and economic irresponsibility were not the sole province of the legionnaires. The gist of De Ambris's assault was that the National Council feared him because its members were guilty of failing to meet their responsibilities to the populace. Many Fiumans suspected that some of the wealthier citizens of the town—some of whom served on the council—were hoarding goods, hoping to make larger profits once the situation was stabilized. Goods were indeed being hoarded, for De Ambris was able to report that nearly one hundred sacks of rice had been uncovered in the back of a store, and a supply of furs had been found in another warehouse. As a result, he had ordered that a complete inventory be undertaken; but the National Council rebelled against this measure, maintaining that only they could initiate such action. De Ambris's response was highly critical: "Can one stand passively by while goods that are indispensable to the life of the city are withheld in this manner from the market . . . ?"

De Ambris pointed out that the Command had been forced to take action because the council had failed to do so, and he claimed that if the city had waited for the council to undertake the badly needed measures, "we would have spent weeks and months idly waiting." He concluded with an ultimatum: "I, too, agree that the limits of the powers of the National Council must be defined; but I declare at once, that for my part, if this means putting the Command in a position in which it must consider itself only a spectator to the inactivity and insufficiency of the National Council, I would find it utterly superfluous to remain at the post that your generosity has given to me."

The antagonism between De Ambris and the leaders of the National Council is well illustrated by this exchange. This ongoing conflict will occupy us at some length when we turn to a discussion of the reaction to the Carta del Carnaro, but it is essential to stress that this tension increased throughout the year. If there was any hope of patching over the rift that had been opened by the crisis of December 1919, it vanished with the appointment of De Ambris to replace Giuriati and with the drafting of the constitution in March; from that moment on, it was simply a question of the intensity of the struggle and the identity of the winner.

THE *COLPI DE MANO* AND THE BABIES' CRUSADE

The tradition of the *colpi de mano* continued to be lively in 1920, both as a means of providing supplies for the blockaded city and also—more rarely—obtaining funding for some of the comandante's foreign adventures. This latter undertaking was most clearly exemplified in the case of the *Cogne* in the fall, which will be discussed in the context of the Lega di Fiume. More common was the first type of coup, and the *Uscocchi* who were responsible for the maritime activities became almost legendary figures in Fiume during the year. In the middle of May, there were five ships in the harbor as a result of their activities, which had provided the legionnaires with a wide variety of supplies, ranging from arms to foodstuffs. The range of the Fiuman pirates was surprisingly large, and Italian ships from Trieste to the straits of Messina were subject to the sudden attacks of these imaginative enterpreneurs.

The most important *colpi de mano*, however, took place on land; for they were directed against Italian military personnel and their property, and produced the most intense reactions on the part of the government. The two incidents that best illustrate this sort of action both took place relatively early in 1920: the capture of General Nigra in late January, and the so-called adventure of the Horse of the Apocalypse in April.

General Arturo Nigra had been one of the Italian officers most vociferous in his opposition to the D'Annunzian enterprise, and he had incurred the wrath of the legionnaires for his unrelentingly hostile attitude. In order to teach him "a lesson," the legionnaires, having learned (as a result of tapping the telephone lines) that the general was due to travel from Sussak to Trieste on the night of 26 January, ambushed his car on the road to Trieste and brought him to Fiume. Nigra's attitude under the circumstances was hardly surprising; he maintained that he had always been a warm supporter of D'Annunzian Fiume and protested that he had been the victim of a serious misunderstanding. The Command treated Nigra as a guest of honor at the palace, according him full military salutes on public occasions and, after a series of threats from Nitti and Caviglia, released him on 9 February. The *Bollettino Ufficiale* explained the *colpo* with an uncharacteristic touch of wry humor on 10 February. The general, it said, "manifesting his faith in the sanctity of the cause of Fiume and his high esteem for the defenders of the threatened city, did nothing but recall to us that he had been a good Italian, a good soldier, and a loyal man. Since the circumstances that had made the severe measure [of his capture] necessary had been eliminated in this manner, yesterday General Nigra was liberated. . . ."[49]

Needless to say, the detention of an Italian general in Fiume for more than a month not only strained the patience of the government but produced genuine alarm among the members of the National Council. However, this was a mere ripple compared with the tidal wave of protest created by the affair of the "Horse of the Apocalypse" in the spring. Late in the afternoon of 18 April, a group of *Uscocchi* made off with forty-six horses from a military stable near Abbazia and transported them by sea to Fiume. The enterprise was undertaken as a protest against the mistreatment of several ex-legionnaires, who had been arrested in Trieste as soon as they attempted to return to Italy, and it produced an immediate reaction from Caviglia. On the nineteenth, the National Gouncil received an ultimatum from the head of the Forty-fifth division of the Italian Army, General Ferrario: if the horses were not returned within three days, Fiume would receive no more grain. The following day, the terms became more severe: if the horses were not returned, all railroad traffic in and around Fiume would be terminated. The city was threatened with a total blockade.

D'Annunzio responded with an angry message, refusing to yield to the blackmail of the Italian authorities and accusing them of starving women and children under the pretext of defending Italy. Within a few days, however, the matter was settled, and the Command arranged to transport the horses to the regular troops across the lines. But the last laugh was on Caviglia; instead of returning the well-fed horses that had been captured by the *Uscocchi*, the legionnaires led forty-six emaciated beasts from the city to the Italian boundary. The entire episode permitted the comandante to issue one of his most memorable statements, full of humor and glee:

> How could [Caviglia], excellent Italian, be offended by our need to substitute his potent beasts for our starving skeletons, and offer them our gentle cure instead of the . . . tedium of the stables?
> Yesterday we ate fourteen of them, skinnier than the cows of Egypt. . . . We shall send him the seven and seven skulls as a trophy, to assuage his wrath. . . .
> We have committed armed aggression against loyal troops.
> We have stolen forty-six quadrupeds.
> We have offended Italy.
> We do not know how to think "Italianly."
> We are not Italians.
> We deserve only to be starved, manacled, and executed.
> We shall resign ourselves.
> But I must further confess that last night, I stole the Horse of the Apocalypse, to add it to the forty-six quadrupeds on the criminal barge.
> He has his marvellous general's harness, and a divine thunderbolt in each holster.
> *Cum timore*.[50]

The *colpi de mano* served an important function in the civic festivals of Fiume. During the long period that began with the failure of the modus vivendi, they counteracted the sense of inaction that hung over the heads of the legionnaires, and helped give a feeling of power to the citizens of the city. Along with the ideological innovations of the year, the *colpi de mano* illustrated the courage and the creativity of D'Annunzian Fiume. The comandante also hoped that these actions would produce a sympathetic response in Italy, but for the most part this hope was not fulfilled, and the command was forced to take other actions to generate a public response to its plight. The most famous of these was the project of sending hundreds of Fiuman children across the blockade into Italian homes, ostensibly to save them from starvation in Fiume, but actually in order to publicize "the cause" throughout the country.

This "babies' crusade" was organized in conjunction with various groups within Italy,[51] foremost among which were the Fasci di Combattimento and patriotic womens' groups. The first group of children, some two hundred fifty in all, left Fiume in late February. D'Annunzio took the opportunity to compare the moral condition of Italy to the physical state of the ancient world under the scourge of leprosy. Just as the ancients believed that only the blood of babies could cure a leper, so he hoped that the transfusion given by the babies of Fiume would cure Italy of the "leprosy of faithlessness and the moral misery into which she has fallen."

Somewhat surprisingly, Nitti, falling into the propaganda trap the comandante had laid for him, gave orders that no further groups of children would be permitted to enter the country. D'Annunzio was consequently able to denounce the government with righteous indignation: "If the veto is not removed, I shall load my innocents onto one of my ships and send them ashore at one Adriatic port after another. And I will open fire, without hesitation and without scruple, on whosoever dares to interfere with their course or seeks to impede their landing."[52]

The result of the episode was easily predictable; for a brief period, Italian public opinion rallied to the Fiuman cause, and demonstrations on behalf of the Fiuman babies were held throughout the country. The veto against further expeditions was quietly removed, and by the late summer there were nearly four thousand Fiuman infants living in Italy. But such measures could not possibly resolve the Fiuman crisis and only served to heighten the antagonism between the Command, on the one hand, and the National Council and Italian government, on the other. Eventually D'Annunzio had to face the fundamental issues his rule in Fiume had raised: would he become the center of an international movement or would he concentrate his energies on annexation? Further, if he undertook to lead a new crusade on behalf of the oppressed peoples of the earth, was it not necessary to give Fiume a coherence and an integrity it had not yet acquired? The comandante sought to resolve these two problems in the most imaginative undertakings during the sixteen months of D'Annunzian Fiume: the Carta del Carnaro and the Lega di Fiume.

The March toward the Future

On 13 April 1920, the *Bollettino Ufficiale* of the Command published an interview with D'Annunzio conducted by Doctor Brajer of the *Neue Freie Presse* and "various Hungarian journals."[1] The comandante told his interlocutor that the Fiume adventure had to be viewed in the context of an unjust peace, which had forced other countries and peoples to bow their heads after "a more or less verbal and platonic" protest. This was not the case in Fiume, he said, where an act of rebellion had been launched "against every kind of persecution and threat, against the misgovernment of Italy, against the richest and strongest nations of the world."

He spoke at some length of his project for a League of Fiume, to be opposed to the League of Nations ("that conspiracy of privileged thieves and robbers"). The Lega di Fiume would gather together the oppressed peoples and nations of the world, from the Irish and the Egyptians to the Indians, the Austrians, and the Hungarians, all suffering at the hands of the nations that had designed the Versailles Treaty. By then this theme had become familiar in Fiume, and Brajer pressed the comandante for information on a new topic, which had been the subject of recent rumors in the city: the possibility of a new form of government for the "city of life." D'Annunzio began with a cautious and somewhat evasive response:

> I know that much has been said in recent days about the creation of an independent state, but this has often been spoken of with little knowledge. . . . The Command has indeed considered giving a new form of political organization to Fiume, but independent of any partisan goal and with the sole aim of guaranteeing . . . the principle that has guided us from the enterprise of Ronchi. . . .

The guiding principle of annexation was, then, to be guaranteed, and D'Annunzio continued by observing that the economic situation of the city was extremely difficult and that the reserves were about to run out. Consequently, the Command was forced to find some way to reactivate the economy of the city, give some stability to the currency, and stabilize the existing situation so as to enable Fiume to resist until the moment of annexation.

This general reply did not satisfy Brajer, who asked the comandante if he had some more concrete notion of the form that a new organization of Fiume would take. D'Annunzio's answer suggested that the plans for the new state were very far advanced indeed: "If we have to draft a new constitution, we will create a constitution of liberty infinitely different from the old statutes. . . . Even if, after a very short time (as we devoutly wish), the annexation should prevent us from applying the constitution in all its forms, it could still remain as an example to all the world of the aspiration of a people and of a group of spirits. With such a constitution we will be able to reunite the communal liberties . . . with the most recent institutions which move the world of today."

Both the timing and the language of the comandante's reply were significant. As we shall see, the Command was engaged in a bitter struggle with the National Council in late March and early April, and the notion of a new, libertarian constitution was anathema to the council's leaders. Moreover, in his description of the possible form of the new constitution, D'Annunzio evoked the images of "Keller's world," particularly in his reference to a "group of spirits" and in his reiteration of the hope that Fiume would serve as a model for the entire world.

The most significant element in D'Annunzio's reply to Brajer, however, was the grammatical shift in the last sentence—from the conditional to the future—when he spoke of the libertarian achievement he hoped for from the new charter. This was perhaps a slip of the tongue on the part of the comandante, for the content of the new constitution was already well known to him. The document, the Carta del Carnaro, had been drafted by De Ambris, and its provisions undoubtedly exceeded the most pessimistic anticipations of the leadership of the National Council. The head of the comandante's cabinet had been working on the subject since his arrival in Fiume in January, and D'Annunzio received the final draft on 18 March.[2] Its content was revolutionary, as the second paragraph indicated: "The Republic of the Carnaro is a direct democracy that has productive labor as its base and the largest possible functional and local autonomy as its governing principle. It confirms, therefore, the collective sovereignty of all citizens, without regard to sex, race, language, class, or religion; but it recognizes major rights to the producers and decentralizes the power of the state as much as possible, in order to assure the harmonious blending of the elements that form it."[3]

The republican nature of the proposed state suggested that the comandante was prepared to undertake a radical break with the past (even if he did change the name of the new state from *republic* to *regency* in the final text).[4] Fiume had remained in a state of suspended animation for eight months, hoping that it would be possible to bring about the annexation with Italy; but this long wait had produced serious crises within the city. As we have seen, the economy was at a standstill, and the ability of the Italian government to turn the food spigot on and off at will had made it necessary for the Command (and the National Council) to keep a weather eye turned toward Rome. It was desirable to reestablish the economy of the city on an independent basis, while still attempting to achieve annexation.

In addition to the strategic reasons for the proclamation of a new state in Fiume, there were ideological reasons, and these were paramount in the plans of both D'Annunzio and De Ambris. Both men were convinced that Fiume could become something far more important than an appendage to a victorious Italy, and both were determined to create a new institutional structure in Fiume that would serve as a model for the new world emerging from the rubble of the Great War. As we have suggested more than once the very nature of the community D'Annunzio had created in Fiume demanded actions of an increasingly dramatic nature and imposed the need for a new opening toward the future on the leaders of the enterprise. Both D'Annunzio and De Ambris were well suited for such a role, and their collaboration on the new constitution was particularly felicitous. While the two men did not always agree on strategy and tactics, they were remarkably in tune on matters concerning the new state, and even though D'Annunzio rewrote the entire document in August, he did not make a single fundamental change in the structure that De Ambris had laid out in the first three months of the year. There were additions—important ones—but the basic edifice remained as it had been designed by the radical syndicalist and submitted to the comandante in March. In its final form, the Carta del Carnaro combined De Ambris's revolutionary vision with D'Annunzio's poetic insights into the nature of mass politics. While the Carta often verges on the utopian, the thoroughness with which D'Annunzio demonstrated his knowledge of the workings of crowds, of public festivals, and of politicoreligious symbols in the civic life of the people makes it a remarkably modern document. Indeed, one is tempted to say that the Carta del Carnaro, despite the typically archaic language that the poet often used, is a document that was conceived years before its time, for it not only contained an original syndicalist structure but also anticipated the demands of mass politics. It offers the contemporary student of political thought a challenging originality, the likes of which one is hard pressed to find in other statutes of the modern period.

THE CARTA DEL CARNARO

Although in the final text the comandante called the new state a regency (for various tactical reasons), it was a decentralized parliamentary republic. In normal circumstances, there was to be no strong chief executive, and the execution of the laws was entrusted to seven rectors (for foreign affairs, finance and the treasury, public instruction, interior and justice, national defense, public economy, and labor). Each rector was elected by one of the three legislative institutions and served a one-year term. He could be reelected once but then had to wait a year before he could serve again. The rector of foreign affairs also served as president—a position that seems to have been almost entirely honorific.

There were two elective parliamentary bodies, which came together once a year to form a third institution, the so-called Arengo del Carnaro. D'Annunzio named the two houses the Consiglio dei Provvisori and the Consiglio degli Ottimi (De Ambris had termed them the Economic Council and the House of Representatives). The first was to consist of sixty members, elected by universal suffrage (all citizens who had passed their twentieth birthday were entitled to vote), according to the following proportional scheme:

1. Ten members from the industrial and agricultural workers
2. Ten from the *gente del mare*
3. Ten from the employers
4. Five from the agricultural and industrial technicians
5. Five from the employees and the administrators of private agencies
6. Five from teachers, students in schools of higher education, and the other members of the Sixth Corporation*
7. Five from the "free professions" (medicine, law, etc.)
8. Five from the civil servants
9. Five from the cooperatives

These nine groups corresponded to the nine "Corporations" of the Syndicalist state designed by De Ambris.

The Consiglio degli Ottimi was composed of one representative for every thousand citizens, who was elected directly by universal suffrage. The term of office was three years for the Ottimi and two years for the Provvisori.

The division of powers between the two houses was implicit in the composition of the relative bodies. The Ottimi were responsible for the

---

*The "Sixth Corporation," described below, comprised all those involved in education and artistic creativity.

civil and penal codes, the police, defense, the secondary schools, the
fine arts, and the relations between the central government and the
communes. The Provvisori, on the other hand, dealt with business matters: commercial and maritime law, all questions dealing with labor,
transportation, public works, tariffs, customs duties and trade, technical and professional instruction, industry and banking, and the exercise
of the free professions.

The Arengo, which gathered all the Ottimi and Provvisori into a
single body, was entrusted with the legislation of foreign policy, finance,
higher education, and any eventual reforms of the constitution.

The Carta del Carnaro was an extraordinarily optimistic constitution, providing for only one annual meeting of the Ottimi ("in the month
of October, with a sharply concise brevity") and two of the Provvisori
("in May and November, using a laconic style in its deliberations").
There was an enormous range of matters purposely left undefined, for
the framers of the constitution desired to leave the maximum possible
initiative to the local governing bodies, the communes. Given "full
autonomy," these were modeled on the medieval and Renaissance bodies
of the same name: "They exercise in themselves and for themselves all
the powers that the constitution does not attribute to the legislative,
executive, and judicial officers of the regency."

The democratic form of the regency was to be extended to the
communes, whose laws had to be approved by their members (and by
the central government) and could be reformed by a vote of a simple
majority of the population.

The communes were similar to the states in America during the
period of the Articles of Confederation; they were expected to negotiate
treaties among themselves and make mutual arrangements for reciprocal
legislation and administration. However, the central government had the
power to intervene in the communes' affairs; it could challenge communal laws it felt were unconstitutional (bringing them to the Supreme
Court, the so-called Corte della Ragione), and it could intervene to reestablish order when asked to do so by either the communal authorities
or by one-third of the voters in the commune. In this manner, not only
would the internal order of the communes be guaranteed but the regency could safeguard the communes from one another. This last option
was of the utmost importance, for it is clear from other sections of the
Carta del Carnaro (in particular, those sections dealing with public education) that D'Annunzio and De Ambris expected there to be Croatian
communes within the regency, and they were careful to ensure that the
central government could guarantee peaceful relations between the Italian and the Slavic elements.

At the apex of the structure was the office of the comandante, an office that was to be filled only at times of extreme peril to the regency. The language of the text speaks for itself: when the regency sought a single man to "gather, excite, and conduct all the forces of the people to battle and to victory," a comandante could be nominated in the Arengo, for a term to be determined by that body. The Carta recalled that in the days of the Roman Empire, the Republic would occasionally select a dictator for a period of six months, and this period (which De Ambris proposed in his original draft as the maximum term of office for the comandante) was to serve as a guideline for the Arengo.

The judiciary contained some innovations, prompted in part by De Ambris's commitment to the cause of the working class. There were five separate judicial institutions: the communal judiciary (Buoni Uomini), the Labor Court (Giudici del Lavoro), the normal civil courts (Giudici togati), a court for major crimes (Giudici del Maleficio) and the Corte della Ragione. The Buoni Uomini were selected by the communes in a manner left up to them, while the Giudici del Lavoro were elected by the Corporations, in a manner similar to the selection of the Provvisori: two judges were elected by the industrial and agricultural workers; two by the *gente del mare*; one from the agrarian and industrial technicians; and so forth, through the remaining Corporations.

The fundamental judicial organization, the Giudici togati, was to be composed of lawyers selected by the members of the Corte della Ragione. Interestingly enough, this was the only body of the five for which a degree in law was required (although three of the five members of the Corte della Ragione had to have legal degrees), and the Giudici togati heard all cases involving civil, commercial, and penal law that did not fall within the competence of the Buoni Uomini or the Giudici del Maleficio. This latter body, which tried all cases that comported a penalty of three or more years in prison, was to be composed of "seven sworn citizens" and directed by one of the Giudici togati.

Finally, atop the judicial structure, came the Corte della Ragione, which regulated all conflicts between the legislative and executive bodies. In addition, the Corte dealt with all constitutional issues, with acts of high treason, abuses of power, and acts against the "rights of citizens." Finally, the Corte served as the supreme court of appeal, selected the Giudici togati, and settled issues of jurisdiction among the other courts.

This brings us to one of the major innovations of the Carta del Carnaro, and perhaps the most controversial element: the "Corporations." The statute dealing with the Corporations begins with a polemical note: "Only the assiduous producers of the common wealth and the assiduous producers of the common strength are complete citizens of the Regency, and with it constitute a single working substance, a single ascendant fullness."

To encourage this assiduous activity, every citizen was required to be a member of one of the nine Corporations (the tenth, as we shall see, was part of a higher realm). The membership of the Corporations was defined as follows:

1. All salaried workers, artisans and small landowners
2. Technical personnel in private firms (but no partowners)
3. Blue-collar employees of private firms, neither "workers" nor owners
4. Employers, owners, and "management"
5. Civil servants
6. "The intellectual flower of the people," more specifically, teachers, students in higher education, all those who practiced the fine arts, along with decorators, etc.
7. Practitioners of the "free professions"
8. The administrators of the cooperatives
9. The *gente del mare*

Each Corporation was given the juridical standing of a private citizen; it could tax its members in order to provide for its financial needs, could organize its members (according to their desires) and could take appropriate action on their behalf. As in the case of the communes, the framers of the constitution were not anxious to spell out the activities of the Corporations in great detail, for they hoped that the new organizations would flourish spontaneously. In a long comment on the Carta, De Ambris illustrated the functioning of the Corporations in quite simple terms. The executive, he said, would compile a census of all citizens, and each citizen would receive a card enrolling him in a Corporation. Once this process was complete, the members of each Corporation would elect their Provvisori, who would then in turn constitute the provisional leaders of the Corporation itself. From this moment on, the Corporation would develop as its members saw fit and as its talents rendered it possible:

> If the members are ignorant and lazy, . . . the Corporation will necessarily live an embryonic and primitive life, limiting itself to the election of its representatives . . . and little else. But if, instead, the members have an ardent, vigilant, and vigorous class consciousness, . . . the Corporation will be able to create in itself the organs for a fuller and more complex life, organizing cooperatives, social security, schools, banks. . . .
> . . . There is virtually no limit to the development of the Corporation. . . .[5]

It is interesting that while the Corporations are described in a single, terse paragraph in De Ambris's draft of the constitution, in the final version written by D'Annunzio they receive a lengthy and eloquent treatment. After describing the "functional" aspects of the new institutions, he turned to aspects of civic life that had received no mention whatsoever by De Ambris: every Corporation "invents its insignias, its emblems, its music, its chants, its prayers; institutes its ceremonies and its rites; participates, as magnificently as it can, in the common joys, the anniversary festivals, and the maritime and earthly games; venerates its dead, honors its leaders, celebrates its heroes."

These themes of the festivals of D'Annunzian Fiume have almost always been cited as evidence of D'Annunzio's tendency to transform political matters into theatrical gestures and as demonstrations of his lack of political realism. As we have attempted to show however, it seems more appropriate to suggest that D'Annunzio inserted such elements into the constitution because of his comprehension of the nature of modern political processes, and that the Carta del Carnaro is one of those rare documents that truly express not only the institutional necessities of the modern world but its emotional needs as well. This will become clearer if we look more carefully at some of the additions D'Annunzio made to De Ambris's original draft.

The libertarian quality of the Carta has already been stressed, and it was thoroughgoing. In addition to complete parity of the sexes, the constitution guaranteed freedom of the press, of speech, and of religion. Interestingly enough, the Carta dealt with possible abuses of these freedoms:

> Every religious cult is admitted, is respected, and may erect its temple;
> But no citizen may invoke his faith and its rites to evade fulfilling his obligations as prescribed by law.
> The abuse of statutory liberties, when this tends to an illicit end or disturbs the equilibrium of civil society, may be punished by appropriate laws;
> But these may in no case damage the perfect principle of these liberties.

Religion was very important to D'Annunzio, and he elaborated the three religious beliefs which, in his opinion, lay at the heart of the new state:

> Life is beautiful, and deserves to be severely and magnificently lived by man made whole again by liberty;
> The whole man is he who knows how to invent his own *virtu* every day so that he may every day offer a new gift to his brothers;
> Labor, even the most humble, even the most obscure, if it is well done, tends toward beauty and ornaments the world.

It is ironic that these words were written into the Constitution of the Free State of Fiume by D'Annunzio rather than by De Ambris, for in them (to the surprise of those who have viewed the comandante as the "John the Baptist" of fascism) is the essence of European radical socialism. Indeed, these three sentences conjure up the Karl Marx of the *Economic and Philosophical Manuscripts* of 1844. The young Marx, like many other heirs of Hegelianism, had been engaged in the search for a way to end human "alienation," and D'Annunzio saw the structure created by the Carta as a means of organizing a society in which human creativity would blossom in a way rarely seen in the history of mankind. It is by no means accidental that he employed the language of the Comunes in his new constitution, for he wished to recreate in the regency of Fiume the ferment of activity that had produced the Renaissance. He hoped that this constitution would produce a new, unalienated man.

While some of the language D'Annunzio used to describe the transformation he hoped to achieve in Fiume is mystical, the idea itself belongs to a tradition of rationalism. The fact that he chose to create a new state rather than a new religion suggests that D'Annunzio saw his role in the framework of the perfectibility of man, rather than himself as the leader of a new spirituality. At the same time, the presence of "religious" themes in the Carta del Carnaro indicates the extent to which the new state (like others in the modern period) had assimilated religious motifs into its own, secular catechism. We have already seen how Don Celso Costantini was alert to the encroachment of the new constitution on religious terrain, and the accuracy of his appraisal is confirmed by the reaction of Guido Keller to the Carta. In a lengthy comment[6] (never published during his lifetime), one finds a Keller quite different from the "free spirit" of *Yoga* or the irrepressible adventurer of the *colpi di mano*. "Humanity is in continuous progress," he wrote, and "the marvelous mystery of life is only the total of the greatest problems the human mind sets itself, the solution of which only religion or philosophy can make clearer." Keller proceeded to analyze the progress of the human spirit, concluding that the goal of the modern state was to make labor meaningful, to remove it from the oppressive atmosphere of the industrial age, and to enable men to fulfill themselves in their labor. "Labor will be a pleasure, one of the necessary human needs. And . . . *as work tends to enlarge life and to a greater consciousness, it is itself a sort of prayer, because, as it widens the sphere of the known and the knowable, it opens new paths to human activity and spiritually elevates the idea of the unknowable, of divinity.*"

Keller's words help to explain one of the more perplexing sections of the new constitution, the famous Tenth Corporation:

> The Tenth . . . is reserved for the mysterious forces of the people in the throes of labor and elevation. It is almost a figure of offering to the unknown genius, to the appearance of the new man, to the ideal transfiguration of the works and of the days, to the fulfilled liberation of the spirit. . . .
> It is represented in the civic sanctuary by a glowing lamp, which carries inscribed

upon it an ancient Tuscan word from the epoch of the *Comunes*, a stupendous
allusion to a spiritualized form of human labor:
Fatica senza fatica.

"Fatica senza fatica"—labor without exhaustion, labor as the fulfillment of man's creative energies, was the goal of the regency. The corporate
structure that De Ambris drafted for the new state was designed to provide
each man with the maximum possible participation in the world of his
own labor, and the decentralization of the government was intended to eliminate the sense of "distance," characteristic of so many modern nations,
between the state and the citizenry. Moreover, the Carta guaranteed a wide
range of services and rights in order to make life dignified: primary education, physical education, "remunerative labor with a minimum wage
sufficient to live well"; social security for illness, injury, involuntary unemployment, and old age; the right to personal property when "legitimately
acquired," the inviolability of the domicile, habeas corpus, and
compensation "in the event of judicial error or an abuse of power."

The framers had, then, advanced a modern conception of the rights of
citizens and the necessity of providing them with opportunities to participate
in, and control, the institutions that shaped their lives. Moreover, the
regency was designed to encourage the development of the qualities of its
citizens, for the appearance of the "new man" was very much at the center of D'Annunzio's concerns. The sections on public instruction provide a
clear insight into the process the comandante believed would produce the
new citizen. In referring to public schooling, he wrote: "Here the free
man is formed. And here the reign of the spirit is prepared . . . the *Reggenza* . . . places the culture of the people at the summit of its laws. . . ."

Education has been a central interest of all men who believed it
their destiny to usher in a new era of human history, and particularly
of those who wished to reshape human nature. While D'Annunzio certainly believed that both of these events could be achieved in the context of his new state, he took great care to ensure the free development
of the citizenry. Not only did he not prescribe any specific content for
the educational system; he stipulated that the schools would be "value-
free" and that no indoctrination in religious or political matters would
be tolerated. There was to be a sort of civic indoctrination, but of a
peculiarly "D'Annunzian" sort: an indoctrination in beauty and music.
Here again, D'Annunzio's understanding of the workings of mass politics
enabled him to spell out the details of techniques that were necessary
to sustain the enthusiastic participation of the multitudes. He called for
the creation of a College of Ediles, charged with maintaining the decorum
of civic life. The Ediles were required to keep the city beautiful, to
organize the civic festivals, and to instill a sense of beauty and elegance
in the citizenry. The Ediles were called upon to impart an almost

religious faith in the elegance of the creations of the people. It would be the duty of the college to "persuade the workers that the ornamentation of the most humble abode with a sign of popular art is a pious act, and that there is a religious sentiment of the human mystery and profound nature in the most simple sign which is transmitted from generation to generation. . . ."

This was not simply a device to manipulate the body politic, for it constituted one of D'Annunzio's own personal beliefs. In 1935, he reflected that "the popular song is almost a musical revelation of the world. In every popular song (true, earthly, born of the people) there is a dream image that interprets Appearance. The primordial melody, which manifests itself in popular songs . . . seems to me the most profound word about the essence of the world."[7]

For this reason, D'Annunzio proclaimed in the Carta that "music is a religious and social institution," adding that "a great people is not only that which creates its God in its own image but that which also creates its hymn to its God." In order to institutionalize music in the regency, the last paragraphs of the constitution called for the creation of choral and instrumental groups (funded by the state) in every Commune. Further, an enormous theater, capable of seating some ten thousand spectators, was to be built, where the people could attend concerts "entirely *gratis*, as the Church fathers termed the grace of God."

Typically, one of the last great celebrations in Fiume in the final days of the enterprise was a concert by Arturo Toscanini and his orchestra, invited by the comandante to breath "the most resonant air in the world."[8] The play on words eloquently summarized D'Annunzio's passionate devotion to Fiume and to the new world he hoped to create there.

THE POLITICAL CRISIS

The new constitution was drafted by De Ambris in the middle of March, made public at the end of August, and finally promulgated hastily in early September. The long delay between its preparation and its public appearance was due to the political situation in Fiume and in Italy. De Ambris urged the comandante to make the design for the new state public in late March, and D'Annunzio replied on the twenty-ninth, stating his conviction that a public meeting on the question would be "useful." However, the meeting was not held, nor was the constitution released. The most obvious reason for keeping the Carta inside the comandante's palace was that it had generated an intense and widespread opposition even before the specific details of its text became known. According to General Caviglia,[9] it was clear as early as 21 March that there was a substantial monarchist sentiment in Fiume opposed to the idea of a Republican constitution and also that "the finest officers, preoccupied and disgusted with the revolutionary attitudes of the Command . . . openly showed their intention to remove themselves from this perilous tendency." Caviglia believed that these officers were prepared to lead their troops out of the city if a Republic was proclaimed.

Caviglia's informants in Fiume were not always reliable (one gets the impression that he expected the collapse of the enterprise from one day to the next for over seven months), but in this case they accurately reported the state of alarm in the city. Nowhere is this better illustrated than in De Ambris's speech (already referred to in another connection) on 30 March. He began with a reference to the agitation of the previous two weeks and claimed that the concern of the citizenry and the legionnaires stemmed from a fundamental misunderstanding of the purposes of the Command: "It was thought: a Republic, and thus an explicit renunciation of the idea of annexation . . . Republic, thus positive action, an open struggle against the political form which sustains Italy. . . ."[10]

De Ambris responded to each point, promising the populace that in no case would the Command take any fundamental decisions about the future of Fiume without the full support of the people and, further, stipulating that there was absolutely no chance that the goal of annexation would be abandoned by the comandante. He pointed out, however, that there *were* pressing reasons which might force the Command to propose an autonomous state to the citizenry; that there was no immediate prospect for annexation ("there is not a single politician in Italy, not even among the most sincere friends of Fiume, who dares speak out on behalf of annexation. . . ."); that the economic situation was becoming increasingly difficult, and placing the city on an independent basis might help to reactivate the economy; and finally, that there were signs that the major powers ("that international capitalist 'trust' which goes under the name of the League of Nations") were planning to create either a "free state" of Fiume or a "cushion state" between Italy and Yugoslavia, in which Fiume would lose her identity. Under such circumstances, De Ambris suggested, it might be better to anticipate the actions of the major powers and confront them with Fiuman independence as a fait accompli, rather than await their decisions passively.

He then turned to the question of the form a new Fiuman state might take. After declaring that it was premature to address the question, he discussed the hostility that many had expressed against the idea of a republic: "It is strange that in Fiume, where there is fear of nothing, there is fear of a word . . . what is a state without a prince? Call it a free state, like the Congo, or a free city. . . . A state that does not have a king at its head is a Republic; and since I do not believe that there is a

pretender to the throne of Fiume, you will permit me to remain im-
mune to the phobia of those who hesitate before the latin word which
means simply a public thing."

This attempt to beg the fundamental question indicates the intensity of anti-Republican sentiment in Fiume and the rather narrow para-
meters that defined the scope of the Command's possible actions. The
opposition to a new Republic in Fiume was not limited to the conservative members of the National Council but extended to the ranks of the
legionnaires, and D'Annunzio could not risk alienating the most powerful segment of his political base.

At the same time that anti-Republican sentiment in Fiume was
forcing the Command to backtrack in its march toward the future,
similar setbacks were being registered in the parallel attempt to enlist
the support of the Italian and European Left on behalf of the Fiuman
enterprise. D'Annunzio's quest for an alliance with the forces of radical
socialism outside Fiume did not end with the rebuff of January, and in
early March, the comandante arranged an encounter between Leon
Kochnitzky and Giovanni Bonmartini, of the Ufficio Relazioni Esteriori
of the Command, with a certain Engineer Vodovosoff, an "official messenger" of the new Union of Soviet Socialist Republics."[11] D'Annunzio
hoped it would be possible to establish formal relations between Fiume
and the new Russia, an achievement that would have greatly facilitated
subsequent advances in the direction of organized European socialism.
However, Vodovosoff torpedoed the plan, stating that not only did the
Russians have no confidence in D'Annunzio, but he himself was unwilling to risk alienating the Italian government by meeting with the comandante. The Fiuman representatives protested, observing that Fiume
was about to proclaim a new institutional structure, which, although
dissimilar to that of Moscow, was nonetheless destined to create "new
social forms." This seemed to interest the Soviet courier, who told Kochnitzky and Bonmartini that the Russians were prepared to abandon their
preconceptions about D'Annunzio if the actions of the Command demonstrated their falsity.

The Russian response to D'Annunzio's trial balloon was much more
open-ended than that of the Socialists, who were unmoved even when
the Command demonstrated genuine sympathy for the working class
and took concrete steps to aid the Fiuman proletariat. The unrelenting
hostility of the Socialists to any sort of alliance with a movement led by
De Ambris and D'Annunzio was demonstrated once and for all by a
series of episodes in early April, following the first major episode of
class conflict in D'Annunzian Fiume.

The steady inflation of the postwar period had taken its toll on the
working class, and the difficult economic situation was aggravated by a

series of provisions that made the tenor of life in the "City of the Holocaust" dreary and oppressive. With the short supply of heating oil and electricity, the city was cold and dark, and a law of 31 March terminated the production and sale of those fabulous sweets and pastries that had been a tradition of Fiuman life since the days of the Austro-Hungarian Empire.[12] No cakes, pies, biscuits, chocolates, or caramels were permitted in the city, and while this in itself did not constitute a major economic sacrifice for Fiumans, it illustrates the depressing atmosphere that permeated the town. Food was rationed, but even so, many workers were unable to purchase their supplies as a result of the monetary crisis, and the National Council had been unresponsive to suggestions that action was necessary. On 6 April the two largest workers' organizations, the Sedi Riunite and the Camera del Lavoro, directed a specific request to the council, demanding an increase in the daily ration for workers (at a lower price) and the establishment of a minimum wage of fifteen lire a day (to be paid in Italian currency).[13] The National Council responded to these demands with a vague and evasive document, granting some price reductions and some increases in the rations, agreeing to pay salaries in lire, or their equivalent (to be computed each week), and promising in principle to raise salaries.

The workers did not want agreements "in principle," and on the evening of the sixth they announced a forty-eight-hour general strike (excepting public services), stressing that this was a purely economic measure, with no political motives. They further announced (in an attempt to demonstrate their good faith to the council) that they would break sharply with anyone who attempted to give the strike political overtones. With this caveat, the strike began at nine o'clock on the evening of Tuesday, April sixth, and the following day the workers supervised the distribution of food supplies and other rationed goods to the populace and awaited the reaction of the National Council and the Employers' League. It soon became clear that the employers were in no hurry to negotiate; their group had not even felt it necessary to hold a meeting. Consequently, D'Annunzio summoned the leaders of the conflicting groups (along with representatives of the National Council) to the palace the following morning to begin negotiations. The comandante was in full accord with the workers and impatient with the delays the employers' group was imposing upon the city. The head of the Employers' League offered a long series of objections to the workers' demands, but he was interrupted by D'Annunzio, who advised him that in his view the workers were entirely justified in their desires. When the employers' representatives replied that they were not in any event empowered to negotiate a minimum wage, the comandante angrily closed the meeting, ordering the two groups (and the council representatives) to return that afternoon with authority to fix the wage scale.

At five o'clock on the afternoon of the eighth the employers returned with a counterproposal: they would pay 100 crowns a day as a minimum wage. The workers predictably rejected this out of hand, and the meeting was deadlocked. Both sides agreed to submit the matter to arbitration, and D'Annunzio served as arbitrator. When the comandante proposed a minimum wage of 13 lire a day, both sides accepted the figure.[14]

D'Annunzio's active intervention on behalf of the workers of Fiume (and his famous speech "Questo basta e non basta,"[15] which followed the episode) was motivated not only by the just demands of the workers' representatives but also by his anger at the relentless persecution of the proletarian organizations that had been undertaken by the leaders of the business community in this period. The essence of these actions can be gathered from an angry letter he wrote to Grossich in the first hours of the strike: "The council acted in favor of the shopkeepers by fixing prices in lire, but did not take similar action on behalf of the workers. The threat to the Sedi Riunite was made at a particularly inopportune moment. . . . The command was not even advised of the expulsions *of a political nature* which were carried out, while the Command must bear the burden of the responsibility for them. . . ."[16]

The National Council had initiated a campaign against the workers' organizations at the very moment when De Ambris and D'Annunzio were attempting to create the new syndicalist state in Fiume. The acts against the radicals in Fiume (whether by threats or expulsions) must be viewed in the context of the internal conflict that had been generated by the arrival of De Ambris and that had been heightened by the drafting of the Carta del Carnaro. Despite D'Annunzio's unqualified support of the workers in the general strike, the council continued to move with great vigor against the strike leaders. When the workers protested the delay in the activation of the agreement more than a week later, the council took the opportunity to arrest some five hundred persons and, with the aid of Vadalà and the *carabinieri*, have the offices of the Sedi Riunite sacked and the organization removed from the premises. Moreover, numerous "undesirables" were expelled from the city, and all attempts to reverse this steady stream of repression proved unsuccessful.[17]

It is most unlikely that D'Annunzio actively participated in the repression of a group he had taken such great pains to support just a week earlier, and it is possible that many of these actions took place without his knowledge. It is more likely, however, that the comandante, having despaired of an effective alliance with the Socialists, had simply resigned himself to an uneasy coexistence with the National Council. This can be gathered from a report for the journal *Umanità Nova* written by the anarchist Randolfo Vella in the summer,[18] following a trip to Fiume.

From this report it emerges that a few days prior to the general strike
the Sedi Riunite had asked the comandante to dissolve the hated National Council and thus demonstrate his dedication to the workers. D'Annunzio had expressed his support (undoubtedly enthusiastically seconded
by De Ambris) but had required formal commitments from the Socialists' organizations. The Fiuman Socialists replied that they would need
the approval of the national party for such a policy decision, and to this
end contacts were established in Trieste in the days immediately following the strike. The goal was to obtain the support of the Italian Socialist Party for a sharp "opening to the Left" in the internal policy of
Fiume, and the Command sent Leon Kochnitzky, accompanied by the
Fiuman Socialist Samuel Maylander, to carry on the negotiations.[19]
Kochnitzky was dismayed by the overwhelmingly negative reaction of
Giuseppe Passigli, the editor of *Il Lavoratore*. It may be assumed that
Passigli's response reflected the sentiments of the national party, and
the caustic article that *Il Lavoratore* published on 13 April ("D'Annunzio
vuol proclamare la repubblica . . . sociale")[20] left little doubt about the
decision of the Socialists: "The workers of Fiume must not trust anyone
aside from the Socialist Party . . . they must be on guard. . . , The workers must have faith only in their strength and their solidarity . . . with
the Socialists. With no one else."

When Kochnitzky wrote his memoirs of his days in Fiume, he noted
that "the Socialist Party must bear a tremendous responsibility" for the
failure of D'Annunzio's projects.[21] In the case of the programs of the
Carta del Carnaro, he was undoubtedly correct. At the moment when
the Socialists rejected the comandante's invitation to support him, D'Annunzio had no realistic possibility of basing his actions on the political
programs of the Left. If he continued to support the workers, he would
do so against the desires of those who had constituted the base of his
regime in Fiume (as the departure of Vadalà and other like-minded
troops demonstrated the following month). Without the support of
the workers' organizations in Fiume (and, by extension, of the Italian
Left), no such action could be undertaken. Consequently, it seems
reasonable to conclude that the comandante was compelled by circumstances to leave the National Council with an open field, and the full
wrath of the conservatives fell on the Sedi Riunite and the Camera del
Lavoro. Even D'Annunzio's attempts to meliorate the situation (by granting dozens of pardons for those arrested) served little (the police, under
the control of the council, simply ignored the pardons),[22] and the balance
of power in Fiume swung back toward the council leadership.

This is the background against which the failure of the Command
to promulgate the new constitution must be viewed. Far from represent-
ing a lack of decisiveness,[23] the long delay in issuing the Carta del Carnaro

seems rather to suggest a certain political realism on D'Annunzio's part. He could have chosen to proclaim the Fiuman Republic and let the chips fall where they might, but it had become clear that he could not win this game, and he preferred to wait for a more opportune moment. In the meantime, he dispatched De Ambris to Italy in a frenetic attempt to find a solid base of support outside Fiume,[24] hoping to accumulate enough powerful allies (and enough money) to be able to launch his programs on his own strength. This meant not only shelving the project for the Carta but also temporarily restricting the plans for the Lega di Fiume.

THE LEAGUE OF FIUME

The project for the creation of a League of Oppressed Peoples had deep roots in D'Annunzio's thought, for he had conceived of his Fiuman enterprise in "universal" terms almost from the beginning. The comandante was not content to see the scope of his action limited to the city of Fiume, and he had established contacts with other foreign movements very early on. The full story of the Lega di Fiume remains to be told, and we shall not attempt a thorough analysis here. However, it is now possible to give at least the basic outlines of the project, which logically divides itself into two broad areas: the creation of the Lega itself, and the so-called Balkan intrigues, which eventually became the basic program of the "external relations" of the Command.

The guiding spirit of the Lega di Fiume was Leon Kochnitzky, the Belgian poet who had come to Fiume late in the fall of 1919, left the city during the crisis of December, and then returned in January to become the head of the Ufficio Relazioni Esteriori.[25] This Fiuman "foreign office," acting with very little money and only a handful of men, attempted to enlist the support of foreign movements—and foreign powers—in behalf of the Fiuman "cause." At first Kochnitzky (with the assistance of Eugenio Coselschi, Ludovico Toeplitz, Giovanni Bonmartini, Henry Furst, and others) was content to gather statements of support from the representatives of movements sympathetic to D'Annunzio. By early spring there was abundant evidence that an "anti-League of Nations" would be able to count upon a wide range of support, and Kochnitzky decided to request the creation of a formal organization.

There was good reason to be optimistic about the league, as one learns from a long series of memoranda that Kochnitzky prepared for D'Annunzio during the last week of March and the first half of April,[26] listing the nations and movements that were either already committed to the project or that were expected to join the cause in short order. On 27 March, for example, the head of the Ufficio Relazioni Esteriori informed D'Annunzio of a veritable torrent of support for the enterprise:

> The preparatory work for the convocation of the "League of Fiume" is by now well advanced: Mohammed Salem [Bey] has promised to bring Indian and Irish delegates to Fiume within a few days, who, along with our Egyptian friends and Fiuman and Dalmatian representatives will be able to reunite in Fiume before Easter. . . .
>
> The preparatory meeting would be organized as follows:
>
> Certain support: Fiumans, Dalmatians, representatives from the islands, Egyptians, Indians, Irish.
>
> Probable support: Croatians, Montenegrans, Albanians, Hungarians.
>
> Possible support: Flemings, Turks.

There was a remarkably high level of traffic of representatives of various groups throughout Italy during the spring of 1920, as the plans for the Lega went forward. While many of the meetings took place in Fiume, others were held throughout the country and were frequently observed by informers of the Ministry of the Interior. The files of this ministry reveal that the famous aviator Tommaso Cartosio served as a "contact man" between the Command and Arab representatives in Italy.[27] It was evidently difficult for the agents to sort out exactly what was going on, and the confusion that characterizes many of their reports is not without its humorous side. Being unfamiliar with Arab titles, and taking almost all written documents as gospel, it became possible for a single man (for example, Abdul Said) to appear several times in the agents' reports and thus multiply into a small Arab army (thus one finds Abdul Said, Dott. Said bey, Abdul Hamed Fuad Elui di Said, Abdul Sais [sic], Dott. Sais, and so forth). Further, there was a report in March that a certain lawyer named Costa was the secretary of the "League of Oppressed Peoples," of which Said Bey was the president. In fact, it seems that Said was one of the Egyptians who was in contact with Kochnitzky, and while the league never materialized in the form Kochnitzky worked for, Said at least had the pleasure of spending three months in a series of luxury hotels in Rome and then leaving the country (and a debt of some ten thousand lire).

While the agents of the Ministry of the Interior were trying to decipher the network of foreign representatives that crisscrossed Italy and Fiume, they discovered that at least some of the plans emanating from the Command were quite serious. By 3 June, for example, they learned from the Maritime Ministry that the Egyptians had received 250,000 rifles (shipped from Spain by way of Libya) as a result of their dealings with D'Annunzio. These arms had been purchased from the Command (perhaps they were the arms from the *Persia*), and the transaction had been arranged by Kochnitzky in late March.[28]

Kochnitzky saw the league as the vehicle for shattering the old order and establishing a world governed by the principles expounded in "Italy and Life." It was, then, part of the sharp turn to the Left that characterized the policies of the Command during this period, and Kochnitzky significantly maintained that it was essential to acquire the support of the Soviet Union for the Lega. He considered this inevitable, claiming that Communist Russia, "like all spiritually alive elements of our time," could not fail to recognize the value of the new "International." Further, Kochnitzky urged D'Annunzio to support the Hungarian Communists and to issue an attack against Horthy's regime.[29] Such a stance would demonstrate the principles of "Fiumanism" upon which the new league would rest. Similarly indicative of Kochnitzky's conception of the Lega is a statement in a note to the comandante on 29 March; "While the presence of representatives of the Montenegran Court seems scarcely desirable in Fiume for various reasons, it would instead be useful if one or more leaders of the Montenegran insurrection against Serbia attended." We shall shortly see the nature of the monarchical representatives in Fiume and the extent to which Kochnitzky failed to grasp their importance to the policies of the Command. It is crucial, however, to stress that Kochnitzky's conception of the Lega di Fiume was of a piece with the design for the Republic of the Carnaro. Both committed the Command to an alliance with radical socialist forces, and both demonstrated D'Annunzio's willingness to embrace the fundamental tenets of the European Left. Consequently, the plans for the league were subject to the same pressures as the plans for the Carta del Carnaro; as the internal position of the Command was weakened by the attacks of the National Council, and when attempts to ally with the Socialists failed (whether within Italy or on a Europe-wide scale, as in the case of the talks with Vodovosoff), the project was threatened. Kochnitzky was aware of these problems, and explicitly linked the destiny of the league to the political situation in Fiume: "I know very well," he told the comandante on 29 March, "that we can run into grave difficulties, given the internal situation in Fiume, and the numerous expulsions of the working-class element. . . ."

The league was placed in serious jeopardy by the events of early April, and by Easter, Kochnitzky's messages to D'Annunzio were tinged with apprehension. On Easter Day he wrote: "I hope the League of Fiume will not give the world the grotesque spectacle of the 'League of Nations': impotence-indecision." But the grandiose plans of the Belgian poet could not survive the shock of the first half of April, and the League of Fiume slowly disappeared, at least in the form Kochnitzky had conceived for it. To be sure, there were other factors in D'Annunzio's decision to abandon the project for the League; above all, the necessary

funds were lacking for an undertaking on such a vast scale, and there
was no indication that money was forthcoming. Moreover, one of the
cornerstones of Fiuman policy—opposition to the expansion of American
influence—was by no means universally shared, even by the most ardent
supporters of the plans for the Lega. Giuriati discovered that the Egyptians[30] were unwilling to join in an anti-American campaign, and he was
forced to report to the comandante that Egyptian nationalists felt they
needed America. Finally, there was considerable opposition within the
Command itself to the creation of a multinational organization, especially one that included Arabs. Kochnitzky advised D'Annunzio that
Colonel Sani "has declared himself openly hostile to any statutory freedom for the Arabs, and he does not consider any Moslem to be trust-
worthy."

By the end of the third week in April, it was clear that the league's
days were numbered. On the eighteenth, Kochnitzky wrote that the
Command had failed to keep its promises to the Arabs ("the scrupulous
orientals"), and he foresaw a "backlash" from the Arab world if action
was not taken in short order. The loss of the Moslems, he felt, would
shipwreck the enterprise, and he wrote D'Annunzio that "the League
of Fiume is becoming transformed into a tool for Balkan use that will
certainly be able to render signal services to the Consulta and to the
city of Fiume. It will no longer be the shimmering globe that is worthy
of the hands of Gabriele D'Annunzio alone."

Ironically, the formal announcement of the Lega to the people of
Fiume took place ten days after this letter was written. On 28 April the
Bollettino Ufficiale announced that the league had "already obtained
the explicit adhesion of Ireland, Egypt, all of Islam, and all the peoples
engaged in the just struggle against the barbarous domination of the
Serbs: Croats, Montenegrans, Albanians, Bulgaro-Macedonians."

On the same page that carried this announcement, there was a message from D'Annunzio to the Conference of San Remo suggesting that
the moment for action was near. "It is necessary to fight to the finish
and run the risk of provoking an unlimited conflagration." The comandante stressed that this was not an empty threat: "I have not only
mined the port. My mine-setters work everywhere." D'Annunzio was
telling the truth. The port of Fiume was literally mined, and he had
promised to blow it up if any military action was taken against him.
Moreover, he was confident that in very short order an explosion would
take place in the Balkans.

As De Felice has recently observed,[31] there was nothing new in the
idea of provoking disorders with Yugoslavia. It had long been a possibility among Nationalist and military circles in Italy, and there is evidence that elements within the Italian government were favorably dis-

posed toward such action (Badoglio, in particular, seems to have been a supporter of the plan).[32] The idea had also attracted D'Annunzio for some time. Giuriati claimed in his memoirs that D'Annunzio had "cultivated the hope of organizing a concentration of malcontents" from the first weeks of the Fiuman enterprise,[33] and no one knew this better than the chief of the cabinet. In late November, Giuriati had established contact with Colonel Pettorelli Lalatta (who went under the *nom de guerre* of Colonel Finzi), a man who had been establishing contacts with Croats, Slovenes, and Montenegrans in order to promote insurrections against the Serbs. Giuriati believed that the situation in Fiume could facilitate Pettorelli Lalatta's efforts, and on 27 November he put one of his own men, Captain Trombetti, in contact with "Finzi": "I believe it is necessary to coordinate your efforts with Dalmatia. We will take care of Zara; we will also take care of Millo. Trombetti can be helpful to us for Split."[34]

Nothing further is known about Giuriati's activities during the winter of 1919-20—indeed, Giuriati does not even refer to them in his memoirs —but he must have made considerable progress, for in his famous letter to Giulietti of 6 January, D'Annunzio was able to guarantee a series of Balkan uprisings within three months: "I have worked profoundly to give a new face to the Adriatic question. Even the Croats, wishing to unshackle the Serbian yoke, turn to me. . . . The revolution of the 'separatists' is ready. It must explode before the spring recalls the farmhands to work the soil, that is to say, before 15 March. . . . I can lead the movement. I can enter Zagreb as a liberator. All is ready for this."[35]

As this letter suggested, D'Annunzio had coordinated his efforts with Admiral Millo, the other Italian actively working for an uprising in the Adriatic. Giuriati had gone to Zara on 21 February with two Croatian separatists (followers of Stefan Radich) and had arranged for a pro-separatist journal to be published in Zara (in the Croatian language).[36] Throughout the winter and early spring D'Annunzio and Millo worked together on the "Balkan intrigues," and the comandante was frequently able to obtain money and supplies (in particular, gasoline for his ships and airplanes) from the admiral.[37]

Despite this activity by Giuriati (an activity in which Sinigaglia was also involved),[38] the uprisings in the spring did not take place. The prime reason for the failure of any sort of movement seems to have been a lack of funds, for there was no lack of activity on the part of the Command. The early spring of 1920 was filled with meetings, secret missions, and attempts to acquire money and arms. Here, as in the case of the Lega di Fiume, the situation was not without humor. One of the key figures in the contacts between the Command and the Croatian separatists was Doctor Ivo Frank, who, along with Doctor Vladimir Petrovich-

Saxe, seems to have made the voyage from Fiume to Zara in February. Frank presented himself as a representative of the separatist movement, and indeed, Sforza believed that Frank was a figure of great importance, as he wired Nitti on 2 March: "Doctor Framk [*sic*] has been in Fiume for some time. . . . It seems to me that there are various lines running from Fiume . . . Framk has everything in readiness . . . he does not need arms, but twelve million lire at once. . . . On this condition Framk believes success guaranteed. . . . For my part, I must add that . . . recently in Croatia certain events have taken place which indicate that Framk's Party is growing stronger. . . ."[39]

However, Nitti's information was altogether different, as his telegram to Caviglia from San Remo on 16 April reveals: "We are dealing with an adventurer, who, I believe, is playing a double game, and is working for the restoration of the Hapsburgs. I have given orders for him to be captured, arrested, and expelled."[40]

It is impossible to ascertain the truth about the mysterious Doctor Frank (who, like the Arab delegates to the League of Fiume, is to be found with numerous versions of both his first and last names in the documents), but the fact remains that he, along with Saxe, was at the center of the machinations of the Command. This sort of maneuver provides us with a model for the "Balkan intrigues," which in turn came to define the "foreign policy" of the Command almost entirely in the last six months of the year.

Whatever Frank's real function, he played a major role in what Giuriati believed to have been the most substantial accomplishment of the Command's "ambassadors":[41] the series of treaties between the Command and the representatives of various Balkan nations and nationalities in the summer of 1920. Giuriati published two of the five documents in question in his memoirs (albeit without the names of the Balkan signatories), and the others have come to light in the past few years as a result of the research of Federico Gerra.[42]

The two treaties Giuriati reproduced in his memoirs were both signed in Venice on 5 July 1920. Giuriati and Host-Venturi represented the Command, while Frank and Saxe (or Sachs, as he signed the treaties) represented Croatia. In addition, one treaty bore the signatures of two Albanians and of His Excellency Jovan Plamenatz, the President of the Council of Ministers and Foreign Minister for the King of Montenegro. The treaties represented a guarantee on the part of Fiume to arm and supply a rebel army within Yugoslavia and provide it with millions of lire in order to wage a civil war. The numbers of guns and the quantities of money and ammunition were impressive: 9,000 guns, 7 million bullets, and 1 million lire to Albania; 9,000 guns, 6 million bullets, and 7 million lire to the Croats; 9,000 guns and 7 million bullets, plus 3 million lire to Montenegro (although, as we shall see, the comandante had already made his own, secret arrangements with Plamenatz). The bulk of these supplies were to be delivered in a matter of weeks, for the treaty stipulated that the insurrections would begin on the first of August in Montenegro, on the ninth in Albania, and in Croatia on the twenty-fourth.

In return for these supplies and funds, the Balkan parties undertook to do all they could to destroy Yugoslavia. Moreover, the treaty that promised guns and money for the Albanians, Montenegrans, and Croatians established D'Annunzio as a legitimate representative of Italy! "[The Balkan parties] declare that they recognize in the comandante of the city of Fiume the loyal and legitimate representative of victorious Italy, so that all aid received from the above-mentioned comandante must be considered as received from Italy, and all obligations contracted toward the above-mentioned comandante must be considered as contracted toward Italy. . . ."

Surely, the Balkan representatives had little to complain about in this treaty, and the language that might appear to bind them in a contractual relationship with Italy was in fact merely a rhetorical flourish; the only obligation the Balkan parties assumed was that of waging war against Yugoslavia. One might well ask, however, precisely what advantages Fiume expected to derive from the arrangement. The answer becomes evident when one looks at the other treaty of 5 July, between Fiume, Croatia, and Slovenia. This pact stipulated the boundaries that would exist between those countries and Italy after the "liberation" of the Croatians and Slovenes. Moreover, it called for the creation of a Dalmatian Republic, which would eventually hold a plebiscite to decide whether it would be independent or part of the Republic of Croatia. The cities of Zara, Sebenico, Split, Trau, and Ragusa were to remain "perpetually independent" and were to be constituted into a loose federation or maritime league.

There were elements in this treaty that resembled certain provisions of the Carta del Carnaro, particularly in the delicate area of public education. Article 17, for example, provided that each of the signatories should create primary schools wherever 100 students of a nationality different from the majority lived, so that the minority students could have their own lessons. Similarly, signatories were required to create secondary schools wherever there was a group of five hundred minority-group students. Furthermore, wherever one-third of the population was of a nationality different from that of the dominant group, that minority would be permitted to use its own language in legal and political acts.

This treaty also had its peculiar side; although the text outlined the future boundaries of Slovenia, there was no Slovenian signatory. Giuriati "explained" this omission by observing that while there were several

Slovenes available to sign, none of them was a true representative of all the people. In the text, this matter was dealt with by a declaration of the Croats to the effect that once the liberation of Slovenia had been achieved, the Slovenes would undoubtedly see fit to ratify the treaty!

Despite the often preposterous nature of the texts of the treaties that Giuriati and Host-Venturi signed on behalf of the Command in Venice (only a single copy of this document was drafted, and it remained in the comandante's possession), there was little doubt that D'Annunzio was extremely popular among the leaders of the "oppressed nationalities" within the boundaries of Yugoslavia. Had the comandante been able to produce the millions he had promised the Balkan revolutionaries, he might well have been able to organize a series of insurrections of the sort the treaties called for. In any event, the commitment on both sides was a durable one, for on 19 October the agreement was renewed, with a new set of dates for the Balkan uprisings and a new quantity of arms and money to be provided by the Command (now the Regency of the Carnaro), and Macedonia and Voivodinia had been added to the list of Balkan allies. The total guaranteed by D'Annunzio was impressive: 130,000 rifles and 20 million lire.

The new treaties in the fall reflected a suddenly changed financial situation in the regency. Throughout the summer, representatives had raced about Italy in a desperate attempt to find the money D'Annunzio needed to finance the Balkan uprisings. Indeed, so intense was this activity that De Felice has written that the last six months of the Fiuman enterprise "were lived by D'Annunzio essentially in the hope of the anti-Serbian revolt in Yugoslavia and in the nightmare of the vain quest for economic means. . . ."[43] Finally, in September, the *Uscocchi* captured the large steamer, the *Cogne*, in Catania, and sailed it to Fiume.[44] D'Annunzio immediately offered the ship for sale to the Italian government, asking 20 million lire as ransom. This figure, precisely what the comandante needed for his Balkan allies, was immediately rejected by the Italian government, and in late October, having failed to extort a single lira from Italy, D'Annunzio began selling the cargo of the *Cogne* (silk, cotton soft goods, automobiles, airplanes, Swiss watches, and miscellaneous other goods) in small lots. That this sale was directly connected to the necessity of underwriting the Balkan uprising is beyond doubt, for on 27 October the Albanian, Croatian, Voivodinian, and Montenegran signatories of the treaty of the previous week wrote a letter to D'Annunzio, in which the following paragraph appeared: "Taking notice of your generous offer concerning the sale of the *Cogne* to underwrite our common enterprise, we beg you to consider. . . ."[45]

The Balkan representatives considered themselves relieved of all responsibilities, and while they promised to fulfill their previous obligations in the event that D'Annunzio produced the money in a very short period, it was clear from the tone of the document that the game was at an end, at least for the time being. As we shall see in the final chapter, the comandante continued to believe that a revolution would occur in Yugoslavia, right up to the last days of his Fiuman adventure. But, as he had written to Giulietti at the beginning of the year, he could not become the liberator of the Balkan peoples without the "spine of war." Even the intervention of Senator Borletti in the *Cogne* affair (obtaining 12 million lire in ransom from a group of industrialists[46]) was not sufficient to meet the desperate needs of the Command.

There is one more treaty in the series of pacts with the Balkan nationalists, and in many ways it is the most interesting one of all, because it suggests a range of activities on the part of the comandante that have not been credited to him. On 12 May, D'Annunzio signed a secret treaty with Jovan Plamenatz, on behalf of the king of Montenegro.[47] This treaty is by far the most "serious" in terms of its language; there is no request that Montenegro recognize D'Annunzio as a legal representative of Italy, no stipulation of boundaries that could not possibly be enforced, and no grandiose promises of aid. The treaty with Montenegro was quite simple; it stated the mutual desire of the two parties to achieve the restoration of the Montenegran monarchy and to see an anti-Serbian movement spread throughout Yugoslavia. Consequently, D'Annunzio undertook to provide arms and other supplies to the new Montenegran army, "according to his means and up to the extreme limit of his possibilities." This was the only treaty with the Balkan representatives that involved a military quid pro quo. The Montenegran representative promised that his country would form an alliance with Italy, granting her the right to establish a naval base in the mouth of the Cattaro in the event of war "or risk of war."

This document suggests two important aspects of the Command's activities in the fall of 1920. In the first place, while Host-Venturi, Giuriati, and others (such as Zoli, after the summer was over) were signing agreements with various groups in order to stimulate uprisings wherever possible in Yugoslavia, D'Annunzio himself was also engaged in serious diplomatic contacts. Although his representatives signed treaties full of all manner of promises and guarantees, the comandante himself— insofar as is known—signed only the one, relatively modest treaty with Plamenatz. This suggests that D'Annunzio used his "representatives" to stimulate the Balkan uprisings but was prepared to lend his own name only to pacts with the likes of Plamenatz. Moreover, neither Giuriati nor Host-Venturi knew about the secret treaty with Montenegro,[48] a fact that indicates that the comandante wished to keep many of the threads of his foreign policy in his own hands, and it may well be that many of the details of the "Balkan intrigues" have remained unknown.

Finally, the treaties of the summer and fall of 1920 help us to understand the mood of desperation that had increasingly characterized the Command since the April crisis. D'Annunzio (along with De Ambris) was convinced that the world was about to enter a new epoch of history and that he was destined to play a major role in the transformation. Only money was lacking, and for more than seven months D'Annunzio sought desperately for it, making promises left and right and guaranteeing that he would participate in the impending uprisings of the Balkan peoples in the autumn, once the money had arrived. There was a growing element of panic in the situation, after the summer months had failed to produce a single dramatic event in favor of "the cause."

Along with the deteriorating psychological mood of the Command, the quality of D'Annunzio's staff began to diminish. Typical of the turnover in personnel in the summer and fall is the change that took place in the "Foreign Office"; Leon Kochnitzky, depressed and somewhat angered at the failure of the Lega di Fiume, resigned his position on 2 July and left Fiume at the end of the month. His place was taken by Eugenio Coselschi, previously the private secretary of D'Annunzio, a man constantly accused of stealing money from the Command's treasury, a supreme opportunist, and a sometime poet. In August, he drafted a document purporting to summarize the doctrine of "Fiumanism."[49] In this document the transformation within the ranks was made eminently clear; there was an explicit attack on the Soviet Union, and the doctrine of the Lega was sharply restricted to aiding "friendly" nations and generating discontent in the Balkans.

Many things can be said of Eugenio Coselschi, but D'Annunzio perhaps summed the man up best one day in a letter to Giuseppe Piffer, his private secretary, who had written D'Annunzio to announce the arrival of an excited female nationalist who was desperate to see him. What should Piffer do? The comandante replied: "Have her flutter off to Coselschi, or some other literary figure with time on his hands."[50] The change from the passionately committed Kochnitzky to the opportunistic and rather mediocre Coselschi may well epitomize the situation in D'Annunzian Fiume as the first anniversary of the march of Ronchi approached: the quality of the enterprise had declined, and there was no real hope for an upswing in the fortunes of the Command.

10

The End of the Fiuman Adventure

While D'Annunzio's long delay in promulgating the new constitution was probably based on a realistic appraisal of the political situation both in Fiume and in Italy, the period of stasis had a grave impact upon the morale of his followers. The need for action was implicit in the utopian nature of D'Annunzio's adventure, and the longer he waited to proclaim "the march toward the future," the harder it became to discipline his impatient legionnaires. The situation would have been delicate even with the most mature group of legionnaires; but the Fiuman Legion had undergone substantial changes during the summer and early fall, and by September, the Command had a group of adventurers and fortune-seekers quite different from the original forces.

The seriousness of the decline in the quality of the legionnaires is demonstrated by numerous documents, perhaps the most interesting of which is a letter from De Ambris on 24 September outlining the progressive deterioration of the legions and the potentially explosive worsening of their relations with the citizenry.[1] De Ambris advised the comandante that a fratricidal struggle had broken out among the detachments, whose commanders had resorted to armed conflict over the enrollment of volunteers. The behavior of the commanders was so unrestrained, De Ambris said, as to exceed that of "drunken looters," and he suggested that such conflicts might explode into bloody confrontations on a large scale if decisive action were not taken: "You know that . . . I am not . . . an alarmist; but this is not a matter of bowing to outmoded forms of discipline, nor an alarmist generalization from isolated facts. This is a question of a tendency, which is demonstrated by so many facts as to constitute a system destructive of all that is most beautiful and most essential to our undertaking."[2]

It was like spitting into the wind to expect the comandante to impose rigid discipline on the legionnaires; indeed the tendency toward unrestrained licentiousness increased during the autumn and winter of 1920. In some cases, violence among the volunteers was elevated to the level of spectacle, as when the legionnaires staged a battle scene for Arturo Toscanini, who visited Fiume in late November with his orchestra. The scene itself was quite spectacular, but the use of live ammunition added a dimension to the "drama" that reinforced the apprehensions of De Ambris and others concerned with the efficacy of Fiume's armed forces. The decisive blow in the battle between the legionnaires and those who sought to discipline them came on 27 October, when a new "military code" was published.[3] Written by D'Annunzio and Captain Giovanni Piffer (who replaced Coselschi as private secretary to the comandante in June), the new Ordinamento dell'Esercito Liberatore called for a revolution in the organization of the armed forces. Henceforth, the value of ranks would be reduced to an absolute minimum; there would be only one supreme officer (D'Annunzio), and most major decisions would be taken by a military council. The new council would comprise all officers, including detachment heads, each of whom would have an equal vote. Moreover, the head of the council itself was to be elected by vote of all council members, thus giving the new army a democratic base and a fluidity of structure that would accurately reflect the actual relations between officers and soldiers in the Fiuman legions.

The new military code demonstrates once again the effect that the realities of life in Fiume had on the actions of the comandante. As Corrado Zoli (undersecretary of state in the *Reggenza*) rightly observed in his memoirs, the internal discipline of the armed forces "conserved precisely that deplorable license that had become the rule in the Fiuman militia."[4] Keller's world became institutionalized in the Ordinamento dell'Esercito Liberatore.

The notion of a democratized army did not appeal to the representatives of the "old order," and both Ceccherini and Sani left Fiume shortly after the promulgation of the code.[5] Moreover, the Ordinamento amply confirmed the fears of De Ambris that D'Annunzio was unwilling—or perhaps unable—to control his own troops. As we shall see, by the time the Ordinamento was published, De Ambris was engaged in a desperate struggle to salvage the few "radical" elements that had survived the summer, and in his eyes the new military code represented a further setback in his efforts to retain some control over the Fiuman situation. Although the ideas contained in the code undoubtedly appealed to the head of the cabinet, the practical effect of the document was to intensify the threat of an explosion from within the legions themselves. Such an explosion threatened to compromise the entire Fiuman adventure.

THE POLITICAL CRISIS

The summer of 1920 marked the apex of D'Annunzio's political fortunes. In addition to launching the League of Fiume and proclaiming the new constitution, he had the satisfaction of seeing Nitti fall from power in Rome. Yet the elimination of this ancient enemy proved to be a Pyrrhic victory, for the cunning and slow-moving Nitti was replaced by a far more decisive leader, Giovanni Giolitti. Whereas Nitti had hesitated to take decisive action, Giolitti was determined to bring the Fiuman episode to a speedy close. With the decision of the Allies at Versailles to let Yugoslavia and Italy settle their conflicts between themselves, and with the increasingly stable domestic situation in Yugoslavia, Giolitti had no need to use D'Annunzian Fiume as a lever in international negotiations. D'Annunzio thus became expendable, and from late summer onward, rumors reached Fiume of an imminent treaty with Yugoslavia. D'Annunzio knew that such a settlement would effectively end all hopes of a successful anti-Serbian insurrection in the Balkans, for without at least the tacit approval of the Italian government, the Yugoslavs could be expected to crush any uprising with little difficulty.

Giolitti's government sent a series of conflicting signals to Fiume in the middle of the summer; sources in the Foreign Ministry indicated support for the "Balkan intrigues," and Bonomi promised continued supplies of food and medicines.[6] At the same time, Giolitti made it clear to the comandante that he would not undertake a program to dramatically improve hospital care in the besieged city; no hospital beds or doctors would be provided.[7] Food continued to arrive, however, and Giolitti took no action to prevent Fiumans from recruiting volunteers for the legions within the kingdom.

Even before the new government was formed, De Ambris was dispatched to Rome to try to arrange a compromise with Giolitti over the Fiuman crisis (and simultaneously to attempt to raise funds for the Balkan insurrection). Yet at the very moment he was carrying on these delicate and important negotiations with Bonomi and Sforza, De Ambris discovered that there were other "official representatives" of the Command in Rome, engaged in similar efforts. Understandably, De Ambris reacted by writing an angry letter to the comandante, on the fifteenth of June: "the fact that various men, not even coordinated with each other, are in Rome to confer with the government, can produce problems which are neither negligible nor few in number. . . . I will not bemoan the matter if the choice should fall on another; but whoever has the task must be sure that he will not find others between his feet, at his side, or behind his back, who are acting on their own initiative . . .

giving the impression of uncertainty and discontinuity in the directives of the Command."[8]

De Ambris's rage at the existence of parallel activities that inevitably undercut his own actions was fully justified, and his appraisal of the situation within the Command was quite correct; the comandante, unable to decide on a single strategy, had decided to test all possible avenues. While it was possible that the new government would prove to be more sympathetic to the Fiuman enterprise (and its plans for foreign adventures) than its predecessor, it was also imperative to find money to finance the "Balkan intrigues." De Ambris was undoubtedly useful in both undertakings (in his quest for funds, he had contacted the likes of Torrigiani, Luzzatti, Costa, Lauro, and Borletti, in addition to the representatives of several leading Italian banks),[9] but he was also the spokesman for a revolutionary policy that D'Annunzio found increasingly untenable. The failure to establish a satisfactory link with the Socialists had convinced the comandante of the impossibility of embarking upon revolutionary adventures in Italy, and thenceforth he had concentrated his energies, as has been said, on the Balkan insurrection. De Ambris was of quite a different opinion, and the conflict between the two men may be described in geographic terms.[10] De Ambris desired an Italian revolution, based upon the principles of the Carta del Carnaro, in collaboration with the forces of interventionism. He thus believed, for example, that the utopian programs of the Lega di Fiume were detrimental to the overall strength of the Fiuman enterprise, and he reacted with satisfaction to the news of Kochnitzky's resignation in early July. "I am pleased," he wrote D'Annunzio, "that the crisis of the 'Relazioni Esteriori' has been resolved so 'graciously.' It will help us."[11] But De Ambris's happiness was destined to be short-lived, for the failure of the project for the league implied that the comandante was reconsidering *all* "revolutionary" projects, including those dear to De Ambris's heart.

De Ambris had come to Fiume because he believed that D'Annunzio was the man best suited to lead a revolution in Italy, and the comandante's cooperation in the Carta del Carnaro had encouraged De Ambris to maintain his faith in the prospects of revolutionary "Fiumanism." To be sure, the long delay in the promulgation of the constitution had undoubtedly bothered him, as had D'Annunzio's reluctance to challenge the National Council head-on over the Carta. Nonetheless, De Ambris had long believed that the fundamentally revolutionary principles of the constitution would eventually gain the upper hand, especially with its promulgation in early September. On 18 September De Ambris wrote D'Annunzio of his conviction that "the third act of the Fiuman drama" had begun: "I may be wrong, but everything comes together to make me believe that it is inevitable that 'Fiume will annex

Italy.' We do not conspire, but the facts conspire to this end."[12]

De Ambris's letter, although in the form of a confident prediction, was actually an impassioned appeal to D'Annunzio. De Ambris tied the future of Fiume to that of Italy, claiming that the destiny of the city would inevitably remain uncertain if the ruling class in Italy was not replaced with new elements. Italy, he said, was in crisis; all classes were deeply disturbed, and desired "a change that would install a new order." This new order could only come from Fiume:

> In Italy a saviour is demanded and awaited, and the most illuminated identify him as Gabriele D'Annunzio, the only man who could attract all the healthy elements of the proletariat, the bourgeoisie, and the military, creating the new order with the necessary and mandatory energy both at home and abroad.
>
> This expectation and this invocation can not remain without a response. It is therefore necessary that your genius as leader find itself in the best possible conditions to act. . . . Your Cabinet must provide for this. . . .

The second paragraph above points to an element that has heretofore received only scant attention, and it is necessary to expand upon it briefly. Much of the confusion and incoherence that emanated from the Command was due to D'Annunzio's desire to test all possible solutions to the crisis of the summer and fall of 1920. But a great deal of the chaos was also due to the nature of the comandante's behavior and to his choice of subordinates. With the steady decline in the quality of the legionnaires, D'Annunzio found himself more and more involved in the resolution of petty problems and day-to-day affairs, with the result that "he could not effectively direct the work of his secretaries of state; nor could he, except on formal occasions, preside over the all-too-frequent meetings of the rectors."[13] These words of Corrado Zoli, referring specifically to the period of September through December, are valid for the summer months as well, during which time great confusion reigned in the palace. The extent of the chaos can perhaps best be judged by a note of 15 June from Piffer to Colonel Dal Pozzo, in which Piffer observed that "the Command . . . has to wait for the newspapers in order to obtain information of the kingdom and from abroad."[14] The isolation of the Command had become so complete that there was no quick way to verify the innumerable rumors that swept through Fiume from one hour to the next, and Piffer was forced to establish regular telephone communications with his aides in Trieste (with a censor constantly on the line to advise the parties about information that could not be revealed to the public) in order to get reliable information. It is therefore not surprising that D'Annunzio felt obliged to dispatch numerous emissaries to Italy, for in addition to action on his various projects, he desperately needed to know what was going on in the world outside Fiume.

Increasingly isolated, desperately seeking funds for his Balkan
adventures, unwilling to follow either Kochnitzky along the path of
the League of Oppressed Peoples or De Ambris in the creation of
a new "order" in Italy, D'Annunzio simultaneously encountered
strong resistance from the Fiuman National Council, which viewed
the new constitution as the triumph of De Ambris's radical syndicalism. This rupture came, ironically, at a moment when D'Annunzio
was making serious efforts to enlist conservative leaders (in
particular, Nationalists like Maffeo Pantaleoni and Zoli) in his new
regency; but the rift was so profound as to be irrevocable. D'Annunzio
defiantly recognized the finality of the break in a letter to Grossich on
20 September:

> As a Fiuman citizen, I am guiding that which I call *la parte franca* toward the
> conquest of justice and liberty.
> *La parte schiava* is opposed to it, and dissents.
> Excellent.
> The struggle begins.
> We will fight.
> But the Directive Committee (of the National Council) . . . can not—it seems
> to me—collaborate with this work of life. It is like an amputated limb, from
> which vigor drains away. . . .[15]

If the rupture with the National Council was merely the last event
in a lengthy conflict of interests and political goals, the growing alienation of De Ambris represented a more profound change within the heart
of the Command. After his appeal to D'Annunzio to "annex Italy" to
Fiume, De Ambris found himself virtually eliminated from any decision-
making processes, even though D'Annunzio did not wish to make a clean
break with his head of cabinet. De Ambris recognized that the lofty
goals enunciated in the Carta del Carnaro were in grave danger of being
abandoned, and he took two important and closely related steps in September to attempt to "save the salvable." The first initiative, taken in
concert with other syndicalists in Fiume, consisted in printing various
articles in the weekly publication *La Conquista*.[16] The general thrust of
these articles was that "Fiumanism" was not restricted to, nor necessarily identical with, the public positions of Gabriele D'Annunzio. However, as De Ambris argued in a piece he wrote in September, the fact
that D'Annunzio ("free of all preoccupation of class as he is of all preju-
dice") embraced the principles of syndicalism in the Fiuman Constitution indicated that syndicalism was *"inevitably* the form towards which
society is headed. . . ."[17]

The obvious tactic on the part of the syndicalists was to attempt to
save the principles of the Carta while simultaneously arguing that D'Annunzio's political maneuvers had to do with different problems ("D'An-

nunzio is too unique an individual to be the partisan of a doctrine, whatever it might be").[18] In this manner, De Ambris and his associates sought to protect themselves from the imminent shift in the comandante's ideological stance. Foreseeing his possible involvement with forces of the Right, they also took pains to stipulate that while they would happily join D'Annunzio in fighting for liberty, they would not follow him if he marched under the banner of reaction.[19]

The second step De Ambris took in this period to salvage what he could of his brand of "Fiumanism" was more dramatic. Beginning in early September, he attempted to coordinate a seizure of power with Mussolini and other forces he hoped would be sympathetic to the scheme. The nature of the proposed action was completely in accord with the principles De Ambris had been enunciating for some time; Italy was in a revolutionary crisis, the solutions offered by the various political parties were all unsatisfactory, a radical solution was necessary, and D'Annunzio—as the author of the Carta del Carnaro—was the only man who could save the day. De Ambris took great pains to define the nature of the government he hoped D'Annunzio would lead:

> D'Annunzio is not to be confused with General Koltchak. There is no intention to take the workers' economic gains away from them, to narrow the political liberties of the citizens, or to restore the past. There is, on the other hand, a firm desire to establish that new order which the seditious revolutionaries do not know how to enact, offering the greatest possible guarantees of direct democracy to the citizenry, . . . [The Constitution of Fiume] defines our goals with great precision. Just as the liberal uprisings of '21 were accompanied by the cry, "long live the Spanish Constitution," our movement today must have as its war cry, "long live the Fiuman Constitution."[20]

De Ambris had reason to be encouraged by the response of the Fascists, for Mussolini posed a condition for his participation: the Fascists were to have the task of organizing the armed forces of the movement within Italy and would thus (in the words of De Ambris's final draft to Mussolini) control the "organic part of the movement." For De Ambris, this was acceptable, provided that Mussolini fully accepted the ideological basis of the operation: the Constitution of Fiume would be the model for the new Italian state, to be created following a popular uprising and a march on Rome by the combined forces.[21]

With a single stroke De Ambris hoped both to force D'Annunzio to focus his energies on the Italian crisis (it was unthinkable that the comandante could resist such an opportunity) and also to expand the base of support for the principles of the Carta del Carnaro. Yet he was unable to achieve either of his goals. Mussolini's support turned out to be entirely ephemeral—consisting primarily in a tactical stalling for time—and D'Annunzio was not dissuaded from his obsession with adventures in the

Balkans. Neither of these developments is particularly surprising; it was unthinkable that Mussolini would participate in a planned seizure of power that would be totally under D'Annunzio's control, even if the principles of the Fiuman Constitution had been acceptable to him. However, as is well known, the Carta del Carnaro was not to the Fascist leader's liking, and Mussolini had decided to adopt a parliamentary strategy (joining the majority) for the time being. Finally, D'Annunzio represented a serious menace to Mussolini, for the comandante might well be able to organize a revolutionary insurrection that would gravely compromise Mussolini's own chances of coming to power. But time was against D'Annunzio on both the national and international planes: the longer time passed with no dramatic change, the more disinterested in Fiume's destiny the Italian public became and the easier it was for the government to reach a compromise with Yugoslavia. Hence the Fascist tactic of stalling for time; of supporting (verbally) De Ambris's plans for a popular uprising but attempting to postpone the date (in mid-October, Mussolini suggested that the time would not be ripe for such an undertaking before the spring of 1921); and of supporting Giolitti's resolution of the Fiume crisis (the Treaty of Rapallo). Taken together, these decisions added up to a single maneuver—D'Annunzio was being abandoned to await his fate.

THE RETURN TO THE ORIGINS

The rupture with De Ambris and the attendant shift in the "foreign policy" of the Reggenza had important implications for the allies of the Command. D'Annunzio was returning to work with the selfsame forces that had collaborated in the march of Ronchi a year before—above all, the Nationalists (with their allies among the military) and those who favored the annexation of Dalmatia. These were the men and organizations that could be expected to support the Balkan adventures in both word and deed, and they gained strength within the Command throughout the late summer and fall. The leader of these conservative and imperialist elements in Fiume was Corrado Zoli, who became D'Annunzio's right-hand man during the final months of the adventure. Zoli had been deeply involved in the "Balkan intrigues" at least as early as February,[22] and had served as an important link to Nationalist circles in Italy. D'Annunzio's increasing involvement with the Nationalists was further demonstrated when, a parliamentary deputation having gone to Fiume on 5 December in a last-ditch attempt to find a way to settle the crisis, D'Annunzio entrusted his private thoughts to Federzoni alone of all the representatives.[23] Moreover, D'Annunzio's search for funds for his Balkan plans brought him into close contact with at least two major figures in the Italian industrial world whose names had been linked with expansionist policies: Salvatore Lauro and Senatore Borletti.[24]

These men were far removed indeed from Kochnitzky's vision of a League of the Oppressed, and further still from De Ambris's design for a radical new society. Their interests were more tightly linked to those desires for expansion which had played an important role in bringing about Italy's entry into the Great War and which had been frustrated at the peace tables in France. It is not surprising, therefore, that contacts between Fiume and Rome increased somewhat in the period following the fall of Nitti, or that they frequently revolved around the proposed Balkan insurrections.

The Fiuman ambassadors were Host-Venturi, Zoli, and Giuriati, and they circulated almost constantly between Fiume, Zara, Venice, Trieste, and Rome, talking with Balkan representatives, Italian financiers and political figures, secret agents and military leaders. Unfortunately, the crucial documents for this aspect of the Fiuman enterprise are not available,[25] and a bare outline must suffice. There was considerable verbal support for the project both from the Italian industrial world and from leaders of the Nationalist Party and the military (foremost among whom were Badoglio and Millo). For obvious reasons, the government could not openly support the project (although at one point Bonomi told Host-Venturi that there was a chance of this), and neither Nitti nor Giolitti wished to commit government funds to it. Industrialists were quite willing to raise funds for Fiume but were exceedingly reluctant to have the money spent for the Balkan adventures—a reluctance that is explained in a fascinating letter of 23 October from Senatore Borletti to D'Annunzio.[26] Borletti advised the comandante that news of the plot was too widespread and that too many people were involved in the matter. In order to raise the "millions and millions" required for the Balkan enterprise, the handful of wealthy Italians capable of furnishing such sums had to be certain that their involvement would remain a well-kept secret.

Given the environment around D'Annunzio, there was little hope of such contributions remaining secret, and the government was extremely well-informed about the discussions within the Command[27] (the same held for Fiuman knowledge about secret conversations in Rome, as will be demonstrated in the matter of the Treaty of Rapallo). The predictable result was transmitted by Host-Venturi to the comandante on 21 October: "I spoke, I insisted, but the financial group does not want any money diverted for the Balkan action. The funds Borletti has at his disposal have been given with specific requirements. Within two days . . . four hundred thousand lire will arrive for the command of the city."[28]

The failure to raise funds for the Balkan insurrection was of prime importance, for in the same letter Host-Venturi told D'Annunzio that the agreement with the Balkan representatives had been worked out by Zoli (most likely in Vienna, as other documents suggest)[29] and that it was impossible to wait any longer for the funds. In the meantime, Borletti was advised of the urgency of the situation, and he replied with a letter that must have been like an icy shower to D'Annunzio: "I judge the Balkan action to be inevitable as well as urgent, but I am not equipped [to fund the enterprise], nor could anyone have expected me to be able to furnish the nearly twenty million that is required. . . ."[30]

Borletti had been told that D'Annunzio was determined to sell the *Cogne* cargo to raise the twenty million, but he cautioned the comandante against this action, because it might damage Italian credit abroad, especially since the Fiume question had been viewed negatively by most major powers. Moreover, since Giolitti was trying to appear firm, Borletti feared that the government might attempt to exploit the sale of the goods and incur the wrath of large segments of the population. "This," said Borletti, "would undeniably paralyze our action."

In the end, D'Annunzio merely threatened the sale of the cargo, and Borletti raised twelve million lire to ransom the ship; but the agreement was not reached until late November, and the money was not forthcoming until early December. By this time, the Balkan revolution had been unalterably compromised, both by lack of money and by the Treaty of Rapallo.

The last desperate attempts to launch the Balkan insurrection took place in late October, and the tone of the enterprise can be judged from a letter of the twenty-seventh from Zoli to Vladimir Petrovich-Saxe formalizing a verbal agreement reached the preceding day with D'Annunzio.[31] The agreement provided that all proceeds from the sale of the cargo of the *Cogne* would be passed directly to Petrovich-Saxe. Yet the sale did not take place, and the funds were not transmitted to the group of "revolutionaries."

Shortly thereafter, the entire enterprise collapsed, as one might have expected, and the Command was faced with the unenviable necessity of having to pay off the various collaborators, hoping for a more propitious occasion in the future. The Balkan insurrection had been organized in Vienna (most probably with Zoli playing the key role), and sometime between late October and the end of November, Host-Venturi advised the comandante that the revolution could not be undertaken,[32] and that all the Balkan representatives had returned to Vienna. To make matters worse, the Macedonian emissary had requested a loan of ten thousand lire (fifty thousand had already been spent to organize the group of "revolutionaries" in the first place) to "satisfy all these emissaries," who would then keep themselves in a state of preparedness, ready to act when the Command gave the word.

Evidently, D'Annunzio continued to pass funds to his Balkan allies, for as late as the end of November we find Host-Venturi advising the Montenegrans in exile in Rome that the comandante had deposited twenty-five thousand lire to their account in the Banca di Sconto in the Capital.[33]

THE DIPLOMATIC CHECKMATE

For those who like to write history with "ifs," it is just barely possible to imagine that D'Annunzio might have managed to continue his Fiuman adventure if the Treaty of Rapallo had not been negotiated in November. The total failure of the comandante to achieve anything like a dramatic success in Fiume over the many months from early summer into late autumn, however, meant that the Treaty of Rapallo effectively ended any realistic possibility for "exporting Fiumanism." Once the Italians and the Yugoslavs had agreed—with a notable reservation—on the boundaries between the two countries, neither nation could long tolerate the existence of the Reggenza del Carnaro. From that moment on, the only remaining questions were when, and how, the end of D'Annunzian Fiume would come.

The precise nature of the end of D'Annunzian Fiume has been amply treated by other authors,[34] but it is important to dwell on D'Annunzio's psychological attitude during this dreary episode, for it was of a piece with everything that had gone before. Along with the explicit, formal terms of the Treaty of Rapallo (the definition of the boundaries between Italy and the kingdom of the Slavs, Croatians and Serbs; the cession of Zara to Italy; the establishment of Fiume as an independent city; the right of Italians living in Dalmatia to opt for Italian citizenship, even if remaining residents in Yugoslavia), there was a secret agreement between Sforza and Trumbic regarding the sovereignty of Porto Barros and the delta of the Enneo River.[35] In his official presentation of the treaty and in his representations to D'Annunzio through General Caviglia, Sforza claimed that the questions of Porto Barros and the delta would ultimately be resolved by a joint Italian-Yugoslav commission. Failing such an agreement, the president of the Swiss Confederation would be asked to arbitrate the dispute.[36] But in fact, Sforza had sent a letter to Trumbic in which he clearly indicated that the Italian government interpreted the treaty text to mean that Porto Barros and the delta would pass to Yugoslavia. There was, to be sure, a malicious ambiguity in Sforza's letter, which left open the possibility that subsequent Italian governments might read the clause differently, but at least for the moment this territory was clearly to be in the hands of Yugoslavia.

We now know, through an informant who had bugged the rooms of the Yugoslav delegation, that D'Annunzio was informed of this secret agreement, and that he flew into a rage. The areas of Porto Barros and the delta were themselves of considerable economic and commercial importance to Fiume, but the idea that the Italian government was trying to trick him was—as in the case of the modus vivendi negotiations of a year earlier—of even greater importance in determining D'Annunzio's posture. In the period that followed the treaty negotiations, D'Annunzio maintained a position of great pugnacity, and in early December, in the midst of the usual series of complicated negotiations with Rome for a settlement of the Fiume question, he proclaimed once again the necessity that Fiume be annexed!

That Giolitti had achieved a definitive checkmate with the Treaty of Rapallo is demonstrated by the rapidity with which D'Annunzio's most trusted supporters embraced the treaty: De Ambris, Mussolini, Pantaleoni, and Lauro, among others, all urged the comandante to accept it. In fact, it was possible to interpret the treaty as a great triumph for D'Annunzio, even though annexation had not been achieved. Was not the independence of Fiume from Yugoslavia a victory of sorts? And was it not possible, as De Ambris desperately advised him, to direct his energies toward Rome now that the Adriatic question had been temporarily resolved?

D'Annunzio's reaction to the checkmate was twofold: he withdrew into virtually total isolation, dealing almost exclusively with Zoli on matters of official policy, and then, from time to time, he erupted violently against the treaty and the Italian government. During this period, he seems to have again been awaiting some "sign" that new adventures were still possible, that he still had a card left to play. But even when opportunities presented themselves, the comandante was unable to exploit them. The most notorious opportunity was offered by Millo, who agreed in a secret meeting on 27 November with Giuriati, the comandante's representative, to provide arms and ammunition for an expeditionary force in Dalmatia. Giuriati enthusiastically carried the news to D'Annunzio, but nothing came of the matter.[37] Most likely, D'Annunzio was busy with other matters (he authorized De Ambris to reopen the question of an insurrectionary movement with the fascists in this period—an offer that was brusquely refused by Mussolini[38]) and believed that Millo would always be available. Yet Millo, too, accepted the finality of the Treaty of Rapallo and began the evacuation of Italian troops from Dalmatia on 2 December.

D'Annunzio, convinced at that point that he was surrounded by turncoats and cowards, filled with contempt for a government he was convinced was trying to deceive him and his supporters, unwilling to

The Municipal Palace after Shelling from the *Andrea Doria*, Bloody Christmas, 1920

believe what his closest advisers were telling him (that the Treaty of Rapallo was widely accepted, both in Fiume and in Italy, and that it was folly to oppose it), deluded by occasional defections to his side (in particular from the navy), decided to defy the course of events. Immediately following the negotiations for the treaty, he had his legionnaires occupy the islands of Veglia and Arbe without so much as consulting the members of the *Reggenza*. Indeed, D'Annunzio's isolation from the other regents was so pronounced that he was unable to obtain a unanimous vote against the Rapallo treaty from his own government—(at least two regents were in favor of accepting it)—and the *Reggenza* twice sent him formal protests against the occupation of the islands.[39]

As the weeks passed and his isolation became ever more complete, D'Annunzio passed from one extreme to the other—from defiant challenges to apparent willingness to negotiate with Giolitti; from flambuoyant proclamations of his willingness to die for "the cause" to vindictive attacks on a people and a government for which he was unwilling to spill even a drop of his blood.

Nonetheless, the myth of D'Annunzio remained potent, particularly among the armed forces, and there was considerable doubt about the reliability of Italian regulars in the event of armed conflict with the *Reggenza*.[40] D'Annunzio believed to the end that Italy would never attack Fiume, and the broadside that sent a cannonball through the wall of his Palace—narrowly missing the comandante—ended more than one illusion on both sides of the lines of combat during "Bloody Christmas." D'Annunzio not only failed to achieve the heroic death he had often wished for himself, but he was kept from the battlefield by his aides. Many would subsequently read this as a sign that D'Annunzio had not been equal to the occasion (and the comandante himself seems to have had similar emotions). So even though D'Annunzio returned to Italy as a great hero and a potent political symbol, his aura had been somewhat tarnished by the last days of the Fiuman adventure. On the other hand, his troops had now demonstrated a capacity that few had expected, and many would look to the legionnaires in the immediate future for further acts of heroism. Renzo De Felice has summarized the situation well indeed when he said that D'Annunzio's "personal prestige" had been greatly damaged but that the legionnaires "came out of it virtually unharmed, psychologically and politically."[41]

THE FIUMAN LEGACY

Of all the elements in the political and cultural maelstrom that characterized Italy in the immediate postwar period, D'Annunzian Fiume was undoubtedly the most bizarre and the most fascinating. Much has been written about this adventure, and, as has been suggested in these pages, much remains to be written. Yet enough is now known to enable a few general statements to be made that help shed light on the Fiuman enterprise.

In the first place, Fiume under D'Annunzio had a richness that few have ascribed to it. It is a gross oversimplification to treat the adventure as if it consisted in the imposition of the fruits of D'Annunzio's over-heated imagination upon a supine population. There was considerable interplay between leader and led, and the successful synthesis for most of the sixteen months was due to the vitality of Fiume and the creativity of the comandante. Without this vitality, D'Annunzian Fiume would have been just another colonial adventure. In fact, it represented a kind of preview of the twentieth century.

It is necessary to abandon one of the commonplaces most often repeated about the adventure: that D'Annunzio in Fiume paved the way for fascism, that D'Annunzian politics were essentially fascistic. This assumption must be thoroughly rejected, and it is encouraging to see that a recent work on the origins of Fascist ideology has put the matter very well indeed:

> The realistic ideology of Mussolini . . . was absolutely extraneous to the moral fervor, and to the libertarian and autonomist spirit that animated the work of De Ambris, and to the confused but sincere boiling cauldron of revolutionary ideas of the Fiuman environment. The fascists took the external apparatus from Fiumanism, that is to say, *a way of doing politics.* . . .[42]

This observation is of fundamental importance, for it is all too easy to confuse the style of D'Annunzian politics with the substance of both "Fiumanism" and the Fascism that came after it. As has been noted, the ritual of Fascism came in large measure from Fiume, and in this sense the comandante undoubtedly served as a model for the future Duce. Mussolini also "captured" many of those who supported the Fiuman adventure, whether by joining D'Annunzio at Fiume or by rallying to his support from afar. Yet with all of this, the substantial differences between Mussolini and the Poet make it impossible for one to claim that there was an important ideological continuity between D'Annunzian Fiume and Mussolini's Italy. It is unthinkable that D'Annunzio would have presided over the creation of a regime as reactionary and oppressive as that of Fascist Italy; the comandante's personality simply did not lend itself to the creation of a totalitarian state.

Many have seen an ineluctable process at work from the moment that D'Annunzio began to "orchestrate" the piazzas of Fiume, leading directly to the "oceanic" rallies under Mussolini's balcony in Piazza Venezia in Rome. This, too, is an oversimplification. It is important to recall that D'Annunzio himself experimented with several "political" positions in Fiume, from the hypernationalism tinged with militarism and imperialism of the first and last days, to the "Third World crusade" and the radical syndicalism of the Lega di Fiume and the Carta del Carnaro. One may agree or disagree with the various positions taken by D'Annunzio, but what remains of importance is that no single position, no single ideology came from D'Annunzio's *style*; the method remained constant, the particular theme was subject to change.

What makes D'Annunzian Fiume relevant to our world, rather than a piece of historical curiosity, is precisely this style, this melodramatic and poetic structuring of the crowd that became the "instrument" of D'Annunzio's rhetorical skill. Such was the power of the comandante that he could lead the Fiuman masses through the convolutions of his political shifts without losing their support. Such was the potency of the rituals and symbols he used in his political art that he could arouse the passions of the populace to support, variously, the annexation of Fiume to Italy, an alliance between an independent Fiume and other "downtrodden" peoples, and the creation of an independent Fiuman regency. D'Annunzian political style—the politics of mass manipulation, the politics of myth and symbol—have become the norm in the modern world. All too often we have lost sight of the point of departure of our political behavior, believing by now that ours is the normal political universe and that the manipulation of the masses is essential in the political process.

Finally, D'Annunzio offers us the possibility of viewing the fusion of "religious" and "political" themes at a moment when we can still perceive the two elements with a certain clarity. The radicalization of the masses in the twentieth century—the achievement of what George L. Mosse has called "the new politics"[43]—could not have succeeded without the blending of the "sacred" with the "profane." The timeless symbols that have always inspired men and women to risk their lives for higher ideals had necessarily to be transferred from a religious context into a secular liturgy if modern political leaders were to achieve the tremendous control over their followers' emotions that they have acquired. D'Annunzian Fiume seems to have marked a sort of watershed in this process, and that is perhaps the explanation for the fascinating symbiosis between themes of the "Right" and "Left" in the rhetoric of the comandante. It is of the utmost importance for us to remind ourselves that D'Annunzio's political appeal ranged from extreme Left to extreme Right, from leaders of the Russian Revolution to arch reactionaries.[44] How could this have been so unless the poet-warrior possessed the key to modern politics per se, regardless of their orientation? Perhaps, instead, radicals of both Right and Left found a common point of departure in D'Annunzio, a quasi-mythic figure who represented the heroic qualities of those who had fought in the Great War, along with the pacific striving for the good life in which every human being could fulfill himself in his own labor, while still retaining the ability to shine above his fellow-men by dint of his own genius.

Note on Archival Sources

There are six archives in Italy that proved to be indispensable in the research for this book and that will have to be consulted by anyone who wishes to pursue this subject further: Archivio Centrale dello Stato (Rome); Archivio della Fondazione del Vittoriale degli Italiani (Gardone Riviera); Archivio-Museo Fiumano (Romte); Archivio Centrale del Risorgimento (Rome), which has graciously allowed reproduction of the illustrations on pages 42, 70, 94, and 199; Archivio Ciraolo (Rome); and Archivio di Palazzo Giustiniana (the Masonic headquarters, Rome).

Notes

PREFACE

1. Renzo De Felice, *Intervista sul fascismo a cura di Michael A. Ledeen* (Bari: Laterza, 1975), pp. 30 ff. (In English, *Fascism*, trans. Michael A. Ledeen [New Brunswick, N.J.: Transactions, 1976].)

CHAPTER 1

1. Cited in Anthony Rhodes, *The Poet as Superman* (London, 1960), p. 162. This is one of the best biographies of D'Annunzio in English, even though it contains many inaccuracies.

2. Cited in Emilio Mariano, *Sentimento di vivere ovvero Gabriele D'Annunzio* (Milan: Mondadori, 1962), pp. 188-89. All translations from Italian primary and secondary materials are my own.

3. The most sensitive description of the Vittoriale is that of Tom Antongini, D'Annunzio's secretary of many years, in *Vita segreta di Gabriele D'Annunzio* (Verona: Mondadori, 1943), pp. 786 ff.

4. Cited in Rhodes, *Poet as Superman*, p. 50 (from a letter to the French poet Herelle).

5. Gabriele D'Annunzio, *Le vergini delle Rocce* (Milan: Mondadori, 1905), p. 73.

6. Nino Valeri, *Da Giolitti a Mussolini* (Florence: Le Monnier, 1958), p. 34.

7. *War, the Only Hygiene for the World* is the title of a famous work written by Marinetti in 1915.

8. Philippe Julian, *D'Annunzio* (New York: Viking, 1973).

9. Gabriele D'Annunzio, *Il Fuoco* (Rome, 1939), pp. 164-65. D'Annunzio was here reiterating Michelangelo's theory of sculpture: the artist "frees" the work of art encased in the marble block.

10. Gabriele D'Annunzio, *Prose di ricerca, di lotta, di comando, di conquista, di tormento, d'indovinazione, di rivendicazione, di liberazione, di favole, di giochi, di baleni*, 2 vols. (Verona: Mondadori, 1947), 1: 915-16.

11. Ibid., p. 21.

12. The League of Fiume is discussed at length in Chap. 9.

13. Antongini, *Vita segreta di Gabriele D'Annunzio*, p. 691.

14. Ibid., p. 12.

15. The most recent and provocative discussion of the Treaty of London and the attendant issues of postwar diplomacy is Arno J. Mayer's *Politics and Diplomacy of Peacemaking* (New York: Knopf, 1966).

16. I am indebted to Professor Henry Berger of Washington University for pointing out the intensity of the anti-Italian element in American popular culture during this period. Articles on Italian immigrants had titles like "The Scum of the Earth" even before the war. Wilson's anti-Italian prejudices are discussed in greater detail in Chap. 4.

17. Valeri, *Da Giolitti a Mussolini*, p. 36.

18. D'Annunzio, *Prose di ricerca*, 1: 803-19.

19. Ibid.

20. Ibid.

21. "General Records of the American Commission to Negotiate Peace (1918-1931)," Record Group 256, microcopy 820, roll 437, National Archives, Washington, D.C.

22. D'Annunzio, *Prose di ricerca*, 1: 857-58.

CHAPTER 2

1. The most useful source for the history of Fiume is the journal *Fiume* (Rome). The account I have given has been pieced together from many sources, the most important of which are: Aldo Depoli, "XXX ottobre 1918 (precedenti e prime ripercussioni del plebiscito fiumano)," *Fiume*, no. 7-12 (1958) (this invaluable discussion, along with other fundamental articles on Fiuman history, is reproduced in *Fiume prima e dopo Vittorio Veneto* [Venice: Edizioni della società di studi fiumani, 1968]); A. Luksich-Jamini, "Cinquantenario fiumano della guerra 1915-1918," *Fiume*, no. 1-8 (1967), and "Notizie sui partiti, circoli e organizzazioni sindacali marxisti di Fiume (1900-1945)," *Fiume* 1969-70; J. N. Macdonald, *A Political Escapade: The Story of Fiume and D'Annunzio* (London, 1924[?]); and Eduardo Susmel, *La marcia di Ronchi* (Milan: Fratelli Treves, 1941).

2. Giorgio Bombig, "Il porto di Fiume e la politica marittima dell'Ungheria fra il 1869 e il 1913," *Fiume*, no. 7-12 (1967).

3. Ibid., p. 146.

4. Ezio Pace, *Sicurezza sociale nel carnaro prima e con Gabriele D'Annunzio*, 2 vols. (Venice, n.d.), vol. 2, *Realizzazione*, p. 91.

5. Ibid., pp. 77 ff.

6. Macdonald, *A Political Escapade*, pp. 18-19.

7. Ibid., p. 16.

8. Bombig, "Il porto di Fiume," p. 130.

9. Macdonald, *A Political Escapade*, p. 18.

10. Armando Odenigo and Gian Proda, *La Giovine Fiume, rievocata nel cinquantesimo anniversario della sua fondazione* (Rome, n.d.). For a fascinating collection of documents and newspaper clippings, see Archivio-Museo Fiumano (Rome), busta "Giovine Fiume."

11. Salvatore Samani, *Il teatro nella storia di Fiume* (Padua: Lega fiumana di Padova, 1959), p. 25.

12. See Luksich-Jamini, "Cinquantenario fiumano," and also Enrico Burich, "Momenti della polemica per Fiume prima della guerra 1915-1918," in *Fiume prima e dopo Vittorio Veneto*, pp. 36-37.

13. See Giovanni Dalma, "Testimonianza su Fiume e Riccardo Zanella," *Il Movimento di Liberazione in Italia* (January-March 1965) for a pro-Zanella account. For a more critical picture, see Gian Proda, *Dal passato di Fiume* (Venice: Istituto tipografico editoriale, 1968), pp. 101-3. Finally, see the letters between Zanella and A. Ossoinak in Archivio-Museo Fiumano, busta "Riccardo Zanella."

14. See Luksich-Jamini, "Cinquantenario fiumano," for details of Hungarian policies toward Fiume during the war. In addition, the Archivio-Museo Fiumano has a collection of depositions by Fiuman citizens on various hostile acts performed by Hungarians and Croats during the war period.

15. In order to reconstruct the events of late October, one must read the accounts in the Fiuman newspapers. Two crucial issues are *La Bilancia*, 29 October 1918, and *Il Popolo*, 30 October 1918. In the former it appears that a passage of powers took place from Jekelfalussy to *both* Vio and the Croats. For the extreme points of view, cf. (for the pro-Italian version) Depoli, "XXX ottobre," and (for the pro-Croatian version) Macdonald, *A Political Escapade*.

16. Luksich-Jamini, "Cinquantenario fiumano," pp. 76-77.

17. This is the theme of the bulk of the literature written by the participants themselves: Giuriati, Susmel, Marini, etc.

18. For example, Macdonald and, as we shall see later, several of the more radical D'Annunzians: Keller, Kochnitzsky, and De Ambris. The quotation is from Macdonald, *A Political Escapade*, p. 27.

19. See Depoli, "XXX ottobre."

20. Luksich-Jamini, "Cinquantenario fiumano," p. 77.

21. Ibid.

22. Ferdinando Gerra, *L'impresa di Fiume*, 2 vols. (Milan: Longanesi, 1974-75), 1: 27 ff.

23. Depoli, "XXX ottobre," pp. 179-80.

24. Macdonald, *A Political Escapade*, p. 31.

25. Archivio Centrale dello Stato, *Presidenza del Consiglio dei Ministri (1940-1943)*, busta 316, fasc. 1.1.13, no. 210 (hereafter cited as ACS).

26. Ibid.

27. Cited in Susmel, *La marcia di Ronchi*, p. 239.

28. See Paolo Alatri, *Nitti, D'Annunzio e la questione adriatica* (Milan: Feltrinelli, 1959), *passim*, for official French attitudes toward the Fiume question. For a novel analysis of the roots of French foreign policy, see Mayer, *Politics and Diplomacy of Peacemaking*, esp. chaps. 2, 19, and 20.

29. The most important letters, chronologically arranged, are in ACS, *Pres. Cons. Min. (1940-1943)*, busta 316, fasc. 1.1.13, no. 210. This file contains the documents Mussolini approved for Susmel to consult in the preparation of *La marcia di Ronchi*. For a more complete collection of documents see ACS, *Pres. Cons. Min. Prima Guerra Mondiale*, busta 19-5-1/1 and busta 19-5-7/1 ("Questioni politiche"). See also ACS, *Ministero dell'Interno, Direzione della Pubblica Sicurezza (1916-1922), Categoria A5* ("Agitazione pro Fiume e Dalmazia") for reports of agents of the *pubblica sicurezza*.

30. ACS, *Pres. Cons. Min. (1940-1943)*, busta 316, fasc. 1.1.13, no. 210.

31. Ibid.

32. Ibid. There is also confirmation from Badoglio on the twenty-sixth: "Linee sono esercitate per conto comando francese, mentre comando italiano non dispone di una propria communicazione con Zagabria. . . ." ACS, *Pres. Cons. Min. Prima Guerra Mondiale*, busta 19-5-7/1, tel. no. 3112.

33. ACS, *Pres. Cons. Min. (1940-1943)*, busta 316, fasc. 1.1.13, no. 210.

34. See Alatri, *Nitti, D'Annunzio e la questione adriatica*, pp. 50-55.

35. See, for example, Giulio Benedetti, *La pace di Fiume* (Bologna: Zanichelli, 1924), esp. part 2, chaps. 2, 3, and 6. See also Ezio Pace, *Sicurezza sociale*, passim.

36. See Alatri, *Nitti, D'Annunzio e la questione adriatica*, pp. 59 ff., for the best single version of these incidents. See also Ferdinando Gerra, *L'impresa di Fiume*, 1: 61 ff,

CHAPTER 3

1. See Alatri, *Nitti, D'Annunzio e la questione adriatica*, pp. 86-88, 141 ff. See also the analysis of this issue as it pertains to *all* the soldiers in the Italian army in Roberto Vivarelli's review of Alatri's book in *Rivista Storica Italiana*, September 1961, pp. 588 ff.

2. The best short analysis of these conditions is in Federico Chabod, *L'Italia contemporanea (1918-1948)* (Turin: Einaudi, 1965).

3. Cited in Angelo Tasca, *Nascita e avvento del fascismo*, 2 vols. (Bari and Rome: Laterza, 1965), 1: 20.

4. Ferruccio Vecchi, *La tragedia del mio ardire* (Milan: Arti Grafiche Italiane, 1923), pp. 15-16.

5. Mario Carli, "Secondo appello alle Fiamme," *Roma futurista*, 10 December 1918. The entire question of the *Arditi* is discussed in a pioneering work by Ferdinando Cordova, *Arditi e legionari dannunziani* (Padua: Marsiglio, 1969). See also Paolo Giudici, *Reparti d'assalto* (Milan, 1928), for an eyewitness account of the phenomenon.

6. Enrico Caviglia, *Il conflitto di Fiume* (Cernusco sul naviglio: Garzanti, 1948), p. 65.

7. Cited in Cordova, *Arditi*, pp. 51-53.

8. Ibid.

9. Caviglia, *Il conflitto di Fiume*, p. 55.

10. Renzo De Felice, *Mussolini il rivoluzionario* (Turin: Einaudi, 1965), p. 484.

11. The order is dated 26 May 1919 and is reproduced in Eno Mecheri, *Chi ha tradito?* (Milan: Libreria Lombarda, 1947), p. 42.

12. ACS, *Min. Int., Dir. Gen. Pub. Sic.—Divisione affari generali e riservati, 1919, Categoria C2*, busta 50, fasc. "Roma, movimento sovversivo."

13. See Cordova, *Arditi*, pp. 97-100.

14. ACS, *Min. Int., Dir. Gen. Pub. Sic.—Div. aff. gen. e ris. (1916-1922), Categoria A5*, busta 1, fasc. 5, sottofasc. 3.

15. See Roberto Vivarelli, *Il dopoguerra in Italia e l'avvento del fascismo (1918-1922) 1: dalla fine della guerra all'impresa di Fiume* (Naples: Istituto italiano di studi storici, 1966), pp. 526-30. For the contacts between Zoppi and D'Annunzio, see Ferdinando Gerra, "I rapporti D'Annunzio-Zoppi per la questione adriatica," *Il Messaggero* (Rome), February 8, 1967.

16. Filippo Turati and Anna Kuliscioff, *Carteggio. V: Dopoguerra e fascismo (1919-1922)* (Turini: Einaudi, 1953), p. 147.

17. Archivio-Museo Fiumano, busta "Sinigaglia."

18. Susmel, *La marcia di Ronchi*, pp. 414-15.

19. See, for example, the correspondence in July between Sinigaglia and Giuriati in Archivio-Museo Fiumano, busta "Sinigaglia."

20. Susmel, *La marcia di Ronchi*, p. 284.

21. Ibid., p. 286.

22. ACS, *V. E. Orlando*, busta 1, fasc. "Movimento nazionalista e fascio dei combattenti," cited by De Felice, *Mussolini il rivoluzionario*, p. 526.

23. Cited by De Felice, ibid., p. 527, and Caviglia, *Il conflitto di Fiume*, pp. 118-21.

24. Valeri, *Da Giolitti a Mussolini*, p. 45.

25. Caviglia, *Il conflitto di Fiume*, pp. 65 ff.

26. Vivarelli, *Il dopoguerra in Italia*, pp. 462-63.

27. Giovanni Giuriati, *Con D'Annunzio e Millo in difesa dell'adriatico* (Florence: Sansoni, 1954), p. 9.

28. Ibid., p. 12.

29. Ibid., pp. 12 ff.

CHAPTER 4

1. Giovanni Comisso, *Le mie stagioni* (Milan: Longanesi, 1963), p. 21.

2. Vittorio E. Pittaluga, *In Italia, in Francia, a Fiume (1915-1919)* (Milan: Unitas, 1926), pp. 230-31.

3. Susmel, *La marcia di Ronchi*, p. 369.

4. "General Records of the American Commission," roll 436.

5. Gerra, *L'impresa di Fiume*, 1: 75.

6. *L'Idea Nazionale*, 23 June 1919.

7. ACS, *Segreteria particolare del Duce, carteggio riservato*, no. 537.471, "Prodam, Ing. Attilio."

8. Archivio Centrale del Risorgimento, busta 127, no. 60-62, "Carte di Umberto Gnata riguardanti l'impresa dannunziana, 1919-1920."

9. Cited in Gerra, *L'impresa di Fiume*, p. 86.

10. Ibid., pp. 88-89.

11. This account has been pieced together from dozens of sources, already referred to in the notes. This last bit of information, which is somewhat controversial, is confirmed both in Gnata's diary and in Mario Maria Martini, *La passione di Fiume* (Milan: Sonzogno, n.d.), p. 69.

12. Ibid., p. 70.

13. Ibid., p. 71.

14. Comisso, *Le mie stagioni*, p. 40.

15. Ibid., p. 43.

16. Cited in Susmel, *La marcia di Ronchi*, pp. 454-59.

17. I am indebted to George Mosse for much of this analysis.

18. Gerra, *L'impresa di Fiume*, 1: 100.

19. See Nino Valeri's brilliant discussion of this question in *D'Annunzio davanti al fascismo*, pp. 45 ff.

20. ACS, *Pres. Cons. Min. (1940-1943)*, busta 316, fasc. 1.1.13, no. 210. Nonetheless, there was still much work to be done, as Pittaluga wired from Fiume on 7 September. Pittaluga called for the replacement of several officers of the *carabinieri*, including Captain Rocco Vadalà, later a key figure in D'Annunzian Fiume. The cable is in the same file.

21. Francesco Saverio Nitti, *Rivelazioni* (Naples: Edizioni Scientifiche Italiane, 1948), pp. 329-30.

22. "General Records of the American Commission," roll 436.

23. Cited in Alatri, *Nitti, D'Annunzio e la questione adriatica*, pp. 200-202.

24. "General Records of the American Commission," roll 436.

25. Ibid.

26. Ibid.

27. "Io mi rivolgo dunque alle masse anonime, agli operai e ai contadini perchè la gran voce del popolo venga ammonitrice a tutti e tutti spinga sulla via della rinunzia e del dovere." *Atti della Camera dei Deputati–Discussioni*, 13 September 1919.

28. Susmel, *La marcia di Ronchi*, p. 356.

29. "General Records of the American Commission," roll 436.

30. See Valeri, *D'Annunzio davanti al fascismo*, p. 47.

CHAPTER 5

1. For this and other questions concerning relations between D'Annunzio and the National Council, see Guglielmo Salotti, *I rapporti fra il Consiglio Nazionale fiumano e Gabriele D'Annunzio* (thesis in modern history, University of Rome, Faculty of Letters, academic year 1969-70). Much of it is reprinted in *Fiume*, 1972, pp. 54 ff.

2. ACS, *Pres. Cons. Min. (1940-1943)*, busta 316, fasc. 1.1.13, no. 210.

3. Pietro Badoglio, *Rivelazioni su Fiume* (Rome: De Luigi, 1946), p. 157.

4. Ibid., p. 159.

5. ACS, *Pres. Cons. Min. (1940-1943)*, busta 316, fasc. 1.1.13, no. 210.

6. Badoglio, *Rivelazioni su Fiume*, p. 157.

7. ACS, *Pres. Cons. Min., Prima Guerra Mondiale*, 19-5-1/1.

8. "General Records of the American Commission," roll 436.

9. Salotti, *I rapporti*, pp. 65 ff.

10. This speech is known as "Qui rimarremo ottimamente." Along with the other speeches and essays from the Fiume period, it can be found in the most thorough collection of D'Annunzio's words in Fiume: Renzo De Felice, ed., *La penultima ventura* (Vicenza: Mondadori, 1974), pp. 128-29.

11. Ibid., pp. 139-43.

12. Emilio Mariano, *Sentimento del vivere ovvero Gabriele D'Annunzio*, p. 58.

13. See Michael A. Ledeen, *Universal Fascism* (New York: Howard Fertig, 1972).

14. "General Records of the American Commission," roll 436.

15. This is the title of Marinetti's work of 1915.

16. See Gerra, *L'impresa di Fiume*, 1: 115-16.

17. *La Vedetta d'Italia*, 26 September 1919.

18. Carlo Otto Guglielmino, *Una grande avventura* (Genoa: 1959), p. 55.

19. Archivio della Fondazione del Vittoriale degli Italiani, *Archivio Fiumano*, fasc. "Marinetti, F. T."

20. Ibid.

21. Ibid.

22. For the correspondence between D'Annunzio and Mussolini, see Renzo De Felice and Emilio Mariano, eds., *Carteggio D'Annunzio-Mussolini (1919-1938)* (Vicenza: Mondadori, 1971). For the letter in question see also Gerra, *L'impresa di Fiume*, 1: 81.

23. Ibid., 1: 113.

24. Ibid., p. 144.

25. The most complete discussion is in ibid., pp. 144 ff.

26. This will be treated in detail in a later chapter. See Nino Valeri, *D'Annunzio davanti al fascismo*, pp. 19 ff.

27. "General Records of the American Commission," roll 436.

28. Ibid.

29. Giovanni Dalma, "Testimonianza su Fiume e Riccardo Zanella," *Il Movimento di Liberazione in Italia* (January-March 1965), p. 62.

30. "General Records of the American Commission," roll 436.

31. Cited in Gerra, *L'impresa di Fiume*, 1: 121.

32. *Chicago Tribune*, 25 and 28 September 1919. There is a confirming telegram from Dodge in Belgrade dated 25 September. "General Records of the American Commission," roll 436.

33. This very important correspondence between Sinigaglia and Giuriati is in the Archivio-Museo Fiumano, busta "Oscar Sinigaglia."

34. See Alatri, *Nitti, D'Annunzio e la questione adriatica.*

35. Archivio-Museo Fiumano, busta "Oscar Sinigaglia."

36. Ibid.

37. Giuriati, *Con D'Annunzio e Millo*, pp. 53 ff.

38. Archivio-Museo Fiumano, busta "Oscar Sinigaglia."

39. See Gerra, *L'impresa di Fiume*, 1: 137 ff.

40. Ibid., pp. 129-30.

41. Ibid., p. 125.

42. Cited in ibid., p. 138.

43. Ibid., p. 139.

44. *La Vedetta d'Italia*, 9 October 1919. See also Adolfo Giuliotti, *Disobbedisco* (La Spezia: Tipografia Moderna, 1933), pp. 71-72.

45. *La Vedetta d'Italia*, 9 October 1919.

46. Giuseppe Maranini, *Lettere da Fiume alla fidanzata* (Milan: Pan, 1973), pp. 82-83.

47. "General Records of the American Commission," roll 436.

48. *Chicago Tribune*, 29 September 1974.

49. Comisso, *Le mie stagioni*, p. 428.

50. ACS, *Pres. Cons. Min. (1940-1943)*, busta 316, fasc. 1.1.13, no. 210.

51. Giuriati, *Con D'Annunzio e Millo*, p. 40.

52. See Walter Laqueur, *Young Germany* (New York: Basic Books, 1965).

53. Giuriati, *Con D'Annunzio e Millo*, p. 55.

54. See Tommaso Cartosio, *Vita eroica di Ernesto Cabruna* (Rome: Ufficio storico dello Stato Maggiore Aeronautica, 1972).

55. Guglielmino, *Una grande avventura*, pp. 60 ff.

56. Giuriati, *Con D'Annunzio e Millo*, p. 41.

CHAPTER 6

1. Giuriati, *Con D'Annunzio e Millo*, p. 49.

2. Ibid.

3. Ibid., 58 n.

4. Comisso, *Le mie stagioni*, p. 53.

5. Leon Kochnitzky, *La quinta stagione o i centauri di Fiume* (Bologna: Zanichelli, 1922), p. 24.

6. See Mario Carli, *Con D'Annunzio a Fiume* (Milan, 1920), p. 186.

7. Paolo Santarcangeli, *Il porto dell'aquila decapitata* (Florence: Vallecchi, 1969), p. 108.

8. Comisso, *Le mie stagioni*, p. 49.

9. Ibid.

10. Ibid., p. 70.

11. Maranini, *Lettere da Fiume*, p. 43.

12. Turati and Kuliscioff, *Carteggio*, p. 294.

13. ACS, *Min. Int., Dir. Gen. Pub. Sic.—Div. aff. gen. e ris. (1916-1922)*, *Categoria A5*, busta 6, fasc. 50: "Aside from financial interests, there are no ideals that inspire the people who have remained in Fiume for a variety of personal desires, above all for intimate reasons that take shape in a licentious, libertine, and immoral life. There is not an officer—and not even a legionnaire—at Fiume who does not have a lover among the poor Fiuman girls who are by now completely lost in the atmosphere of immorality. . . . Fiume therefore represents the earthly Eden, the Eldorado of all pleasures for the first group, . . . while for the other . . . volunteers . . . the land of abundance. . . ."

14. Comisso, *Le mie stagioni*, pp. 68-69.

15. Giuriati, *Con D'Annunzio e Millo*, p. 56. D'Annunzio himself probably took cocaine. Cf. A. Todisco, "C'è stata una donna nella morte di D'Annunzio," *Il Corriere della Sera*, 15 June 1975.

16. *Il Tappo*, 1 December 1919.

17. Santarcangeli, *Il porto dell'aquila decapitata*, p. 112.

18. *La Vedetta d'Italia*, 18 September 1919.

19. Ibid.

20. Archivio-Museo Fiumano, busta "Oscar Sinigaglia," and also Giuriati, *Con D'Annunzio e Millo*, p. 44.

21. Ibid., p. 43.

22. Nitti used the monetary crisis in an attempt to gain control over D'Annunzio. During the long and extremely complicated negotiations between Fiume and Rome (see Chap. 7), Nitti maintained that he would have examined the city's economic problems only after the political crisis had been satisfactorily resolved. See, for example, the correspondence on this subject with Giovanni Ciraolo, the president of the Italian Red Cross, in Archivio Ciraolo, "Carteggio fiumano (1919-1921)." On the other hand, Nitti permitted various Italian governmental institutions and several banks to negotiate loans with the city and with the Command, which further confirms the view that Nitti wanted the city to continue to live, even though he was not anxious to see it flourish.

Much of the activity of the Red Cross was due to the initiative of the Masons of Palazzo Giustiniani, of which Ciraolo was a member. Domizio Torriggiani, the Grand Master of the Grande Oriente d'Italia, made several trips to Fiume immediately following D'Annunzio's occupation and, once satisfied that the poet was not about to launch a "bolshevik" revolution in Italy, undertook to convince the government to supply the city with food and medical supplies. Throughout the D'Annunzian occupation of Fiume, the Masons continued to help the enterprise and simultaneously to prevent it from expanding into a more revolutionary phenomenon. See Archivio di Palazzo Giustiniani, *Grande Oriente d'Italia*, "Verbali, 1919-20."

23. *Il Tappo*, 1 December 1919. See also *La Vedetta d'Italia*, 4 and 21 November and 5 December 1919, for typical discussions of the monetary situation.

24. Archivio Ciraolo, "Carteggio fiumano."

25. Ibid.

26. ACS, *Pres. Cons. Min. (1940-1943)*, busta 316, fasc. 1.1.13, no. 210.

27. On the Danubius and the torpedo works, see *La Vedetta d'Italia*, 22 February 1920, and also Silurificio Whitehead di Fiume, *La storia del siluro* (Genoa,

1936).

28. *La Vedetta d'Italia*, 26 September 1919.

29. The handbill is in the Archivio-Museo Fiumano.

30. The letter is dated 19 October 1919. Archivio dell'Unione delle comunita israelitiche italiane, busta 1 (1919), fasc. 78, sottofasc. "Fiume, Trieste, Venezia."

31. Ibid.

32. *Israel*, 20 October 1919.

33. Ibid., 27 October 1919.

34. I am indebted for this information to Andrew Canepa, who is preparing a doctoral dissertation at the University of California at Los Angeles on Italian anti-Semitism at the turn of the century. On D'Annunzio's "anti-Semitism," see in particular *Il Corriere israelitico* 39 (1900-1901): 10, 35-37, and 51-52.

35. Cf. Santarcangeli, *Il porto dell'aquila decapitata*, esp. chap. 12.

CHAPTER 7

1. Archivio-Museo Fiumano, busta "Oscar Sinigaglia."

2. Ibid.

3. For the relationship between D'Annunzio and Giulietti, see G. Giulietti, *Pax mundi. La Federazione marinara nella bufera fascista* (Naples: Rispoli, n.d.); Cordova, *Arditi*; Gerra, *L'impresa di Fiume*, 1: 229-35; De Felice, *Mussolini il rivoluzionario*, pp. 553 ff.

4. The letter is reproduced in facsimile in Giulietti, *Pax mundi*, pp. 76-77. D'Annunzio misdated the letter a month earlier, as Gerra observes, *L'impresa di Fiume*, 1: 155.

5. Giuriati, *Con D'Annunzio e Millo*, p. 47.

6. According to Alatri (*Nitti, D'Annunzio e la questione adriatica*, p. 251) Vio had gone as far as to suggest to General Gandolfo (on 2 October) that "the existence of a Fiuman government not recognized by the central government placed the civic authorities in a very delicate situation; some differences of method and goal with respect to the D'Annunzian political and administrative criteria suggested that the Fiuman civic body establish contacts with the central government . . . thus Vio asked that Comm. Michele Castelli be officially recognized as the government's representative." (Accepted by Nitti in order to increase the rift between D'Annunzio and the National Council.)

7. De Felice, ed., *La penultima ventura*, p. xxxix.

8. Ibid., pp. 144 ff.

9. Archivio-Museo Fiumano, busta "Oscar Sinigaglia."

10. Ibid.

11. See Badoglio, *Rivelazioni su Fiume*, in particular Nitti's letters of 15 and 21 October (pp. 212, 204, and 211).

12. Comando di Fiume d'Italia, *Bollettino Ufficiale*, 11 October 1919.

13. Gerra, *L'impresa di Fiume*, 1: 160-61.

14. Cf. Alatri, *Nitti, D'Annunzio e la questione adriatica*, pp. 214 ff., and Gerra, *L'impresa di Fiume*, 1: 129.

15. Badoglio, *Rivelazioni su Fiume*, p. 217.

16. Badoglio was furious with Tittoni for having given the information to Pedrazzi (ibid., pp. 231-32). However, the telegrams the general reproduced in his book were only a fraction of the actual correspondence, and it is by no means impossible that he, too, knew of the rejection of the Tittoni compromise.

17. Badoglio, *Rivelazioni su Fiume*, p. 100. D'Annunzio confirmed the drastic state of affairs on 8 November: "There are about seven thousand unemployed workers. The port is squalid . . ." (ibid., pp. 235-36).

18. Archivio-Museo Fiumano, busta "Documenti di Giovanni Giuriati," fasc. "Millo."

19. Ibid.

20. Giuriati, *Con D'Annunzio e Millo*, p. 72.

21. Archivio-Museo Fiumano, busta "Doc. di G. Giuriati," fasc. "Millo."

22. Ibid.

23. Giuliotti, *Disobbedisco*, p. 102.

24. Archivio-Museo Fiumano, busta "Doc. di G. Giuriati," fasc. "Millo."

25. Ibid.

26. Luigi Albertini, *Epistolario (1911-1926)*, 5 vols. (Milan: Mondadori, 1968), 3: 1328 ff.

27. Badoglio, *Rivelazioni su Fiume*, pp. 103-4. As a matter of fact, the idea of an expedition to Zara had long been under consideration in Fiume and seems to have been supported by many of the "moderates." On 15 October, for example, Giuriati wrote to Luigi Ziliotto (the mayor of Zara) to assure him of the comandante's continued commitment: "When the opportunity presents itself, you will see that Gabriele D'Annunzio does not forget his promises . . ." (Archivio-Museo Fiumano, busta "Doc. di G. Giuriati").

28. "General Records of the American Commission," roll. 437.

29. Alatri, *Nitti, D'Annunzio e la questione adriatica*, p. 281.

30. Ibid., pp. 278 ff. Ceccherini and Tamaio were placed under tremendous pressure by Badoglio, who not only dispatched the head of the Masons to speak with Ceccherini but wrote an impassioned letter to the general as well (Badoglio, *Rivelazioni su Fiume*, pp. 226-30).

31. See the minutes of the conversations between Sforza, Salata, Sinigaglia, Igliori, and Raffaele Cantoni in Archivio-Museo Fiumano, busta "Oscar Sinigaglia."

32. Ibid.

33. See Giuriati, *Con D'Annunzio e Millo*, p. 48, and various letters from Sinigaglia (Archivio-Museo Fiumano, busta "Oscar Sinigaglia").

34. Alatri, *Nitti, D'Annunzio e la questione adriatica*, p. 336.

35. Archivio del Vittoriale, *Archivio Fiumano*, busta "Kochnitzky, Leon."

36. Archivio-Museo Fiumano, busta "Oscar Sinigaglia."

37. Ibid. For a good discussion of the negotiations regarding the modus vivendi, see Giovanni Preziosi, *Come l'on. F. S. Nitti tradi costantemente la causa di Fiume* (Rome, 1920).

38. Ibid., pp. 10-14.

39. This was clear from the conversation between Sforza, Sinigaglia, and Preziosi on 4 December. See Archivio-Museo Fiumano, busta "Oscar Sinigaglia."

40. *La Vedetta d'Italia*, 14 November 1919.

41. Ibid., 25 November 1919.

42. See Gerra's discussion of this point, *L'impresa di Fiume*, 1: 196-97.

43. The depositions at Reina's trial contain all the details of his attitudes and actions: Archivio del Vittoriale, *Archivio Fiumano*, busta "Sani, Mario."

44. ACS, *Pres. Cons. Min. (1940-1943)*, busta 316, fasc. 1.1.13, no. 210.

45. Comisso, *Le mie stagioni*, p. 58.

46. Archivio-Museo Fiumano, busta "Doc. di G. Giuriati," fasc. "Millo."

47. See *La Vedetta d'Italia*, 16 and 17 December 1919.

48. Gerra, *L'impresa di Fiume*, 1: 201.
49. De Felice, ed., *La penultima ventura*, pp. 184-87.
50. Renzo De Felice, ed., *La Carta del Carnaro* (Bologna: Il Mulino, 1974), p. 18.

CHAPTER 8

1. Renzo De Felice, *Sindacalismo rivoluzionario e fiumanesimo nel carteggio De Ambris-D'Annunzio* (Brescia: Morcelliana, 1966); *La Carta del Carnaro*; *La penultima ventura*; *Carteggio D'Annunzio-Mussolini·*
2. De Felice, *Sindacalismo rivoluzionario*, passim. The letter from Mussolini is in Eduardo Susmel and Duilio Susmel, eds., *Opera omnia di Benito Mussolini*, 20 vols. (Florence: La Fenice, 1954), 14: 479 ff.
3. In De Felice, *Sindacalismo rivoluzionario*, pp. 159-60.
4. See Gerra, *L'impresa di Fiume*, 1: 229 ff., and Giulietti, *Pax mundi*, pp. 82 ff.
5. The letter is reproduced in Giulietti, *Pax mundi*, pp. 84-86.
6. See, for example, the rueful observation of Leon Kochnitzky: "The presence of Alceste De Ambris in the Command of Fiume was sufficient to destroy, all by itself, the nascent sympathies, to dishearten the favorably inclined (socialists); there was a reciprocal hatred between him and the socialists that made any kind of agreement impossible."
7. In De Felice, ed., *La penultima ventura*, p. 185.
8. In De Felice, *Sindacalismo rivoluzionario*, p. 67.
9. The two most useful sources on the life of the legionnaires are Comisso, *Le mie stagioni*, and Kochnitzky, *La quinta stagione*. On the ascendancy of the more radical elements in 1920, see De Felice, *La penultima ventura*, intro., esp. pp. xliv-liv, and Caviglia, *Il conflitto di Fiume*, pp. 131-38, 144-48, 158-60, and 192-94.
10. *Yoga*, 27 November 1920.
11. This was the subtitle of the journal.
12 Mario Carli, *Con D'Annunzio a Fiume*, 138.
13. In D'Annunzio, *Prose di ricerca*, 1: 135 ff.
14. See H. Richter, *Dada* (New York: Praeger, 1954).
15. *Yoga*, 27 November 1920.
16. Comisso, *Le mie stagioni*, p. 62.
17. Osbert Sitwell, *Noble Essences* (London, n.d.), p. 135.
18. *La Vedetta d'Italia*, 15 and 16 May 1920.
19. Ibid., 16 July 1920.
20. For details, see Comando di Fiume d'Italia, *Bollettino Ufficiale*, 12 May 1920.
21. ACS, *Min. Int., Dir. Gen. Pub. Sic.—Aff. gen. e ris. (1916-1922)*, Categoria A5, busta 4, fasc. 32.
22. Ibid.
23. The letter is reproduced in Caviglia, *Il conflitto di Fiume*, p. 206.
24. Celso Costantini, *Foglie secche* (Rome: Tipografia Artistica, 1948), p. 364.
25. Ibid., p. 366.
26. *La Vedetta d'Italia*, 24 March 1920.
27. Ibid.
28. Ibid., 23 April 1920.
29. Cited in Gerra, *L'impresa di Fiume*, 1: 238.
30. Ibid., p. 230.
31. Nicola Francesco Cimmino, *Poesia e poetica di Gabriele D'Annunzio* (Flor-

ence: Centro Internazionale del libro, 1959), pp. 303-4.

32. Kochnitzky, *La quinta stagione*, p. 52.

33. In addition to the speeches by De Ambris cited later in this chapter (see notes 40 and 41), the best sources for the economic conditions in Fiume are the weekly reports from the Information Office of the Comando Generale delle RR. truppe della Venezia Giulia, in ACS, *Min. Int., Dir. Gen. Pub. Sic.—Aff. gen. e ris. (1916-1922), Categoria A5*, fasc. 32 busta 4, and *La Vedetta d'Italia*.

34. See *La Vedetta d'Italia* in the second half of January, esp. the seventeenth, twenty-third, and twenty-fourth.

35. Ibid., 22 February 1920.

36. This is the unanimous testimony of the more than fifty Fiumans or ex-legionnaires with whom I have spoken, as well as that contained in the autobiographical works by such authors as Kochnitzky, Comisso, Giuliotti, Guglielmino, Santarcangeli, etc., cited throughout this volume.

37. Archivio del Vittoriale, *Archivio Fiumano*, busta "Sani, Col. Mario."

38. Ibid.

39. Reproduced in Salvatore Samani, "Lettere di Gabriele D'Annunzio a Antonio Grossich (1919-1921), *Fiume* (July-December 1967), p. 115.

40. In De Felice, *Sindacalismo rivoluzionario*, pp. 264-65.

41. Ibid., p. 272.

42. See *La Vedetta d'Italia*, 26 February 1920.

43. See, in particular, De Felice, ed., *La Carta del Carnaro*, pp. 23 and 43.

44. Comando di Fiume d'Italia, *Bollettino Ufficiale*, 28 February 1920.

45. Salotti, *I rapporti*, pp. 118 ff.

46. Ibid., p. 120.

47. Ibid., pp. 122-23.

48. See his letter to D'Annunzio of 16 March, reproduced in Renzo De Felice, "Nuove lettere di Alceste De Ambris a Gabriele D'Annunzio," *Clio* (April-June 1973), pp. 213-15.

49. Comando di Fiume d'Italia, *Bollettino Ufficiale*, 10 February 1920.

50. In De Felice, ed., *La penultima ventura*, pp. 241 ff.

51. See Gerra, *L'impresa di Fiume*, 1: 263 ff.

52. Cited in ibid., p. 267.

CHAPTER 9

1. Comando di Fiume d'Italia, *Bollettino Ufficiale*, 13 April 1920.

2. The history of the drafts of the Carta del Carnaro, along with the texts of both versions, is contained in De Felice, ed., *La Carta del Carnaro*.

3. This and all other citations from the text of the constitution is taken from De Felice's work, where the two versions are printed on facing pages. Thus the reader can compare the version of De Ambris with that of D'Annunzio, section by section.

4. The use of *regency* instead of *republic* was undoubtedly due to D'Annunzio's desire to avoid provoking anti-Republican demonstrations. The change was made in the final galleys, a day or two before the constitution was printed. See De Felice, *La Carta del Carnaro*, intro.

5. Cited in ibid., p. 106.

6. Atlantico Ferrari, *Keller* (Rome, 1933), pp. 172 ff.

7. D'Annunzio, *Prose di lotta*, 2: 748.

8. Toscanini came in November and gave a concert for the legionnaires. Prior to the performance the legionnaires staged a mock battle for the maestro in which live grenades and ammunition were used, and several of the participants injured.

9. Caviglia, *Il conflitto di Fiume*, pp. 159 ff.

10. Cited in De Felice, *Sindacalismo rivoluzionario*, pp. 272 ff.

11. Archivio del Vittoriale, *Archivio Fiumano*, busta "Kochnitzky, Leon." The incident is cited in De Felice, ed., *La penultima ventura*, p. xxix. It should be noted that "bolshevism" in Fiume was not without its supporters. See, for example, Mario Carli, "Il nostro bolshevismo," in *Con D'Annunzio a Fiume*, pp. 105-10.

12. See Gerra, *L'impresa di Fiume*, 1: 286.

13. Ibid.

14. For this sequence of events, see Comando di Fiume d'Italia, *Bollettino Ufficiale*, 13 April 1920, and Archivio del Vittoriale, *Archivio Fiumano*, busta "Umanità Nova."

15. See Comando di Fiume d'Italia, *Bollettino Ufficiale*, 13 April 1920.

16. In Samani, "Lettere di Gabriele D'Annunzio," p. 113.

17. Archivio del Vittoriale, *Archivio Fiumano*, busta "Umanità Nova."

18. Ibid.

19. Kochnitzky wrote an article on his encounter, the original draft of which is in the Vittoriale: Archivio del Vittoriale, *Archivio Fiumano*, busta "Kochnitzky, Leon," fasc. "Uff. Relazioni Esteriori."

20. See also the article on this subject by Eugenio Coselschi in the *Bollettino Ufficiale*, 28 April 1920.

21. Kochnitzky, *La quinta stagione*, p. 212.

22. Archivio del Vittoriale, *Archivio Fiumano*, busta "Umanità Nova."

23. This was the thesis of *Umanità Nova*.

24. See De Felice, *Sindacalismo rivoluzionario*.

25. Unfortunately the original French text of Kochnitzky's memoir has not been found. The Italian version, *La quinta stagione*, is abridged.

26. The memoranda are reprinted in De Felice, ed., *La Carta del Carnaro*.

27. ACS, *Min. Int., Dir. Gen. Pub. Sic.—Aff. gen. e ris. (1920), Categoria A5*, busta 8, "Nazionalisti egiziani e irlandesi."

28. Ibid.

29. See n. 26.

30. Giuriati, *Con D'Annunzio e Millo*, p. 135.

31. De Felice, ed., *La penultima ventura*, p. lxi.

32. Both Giuriati and Alatri are of this opinion.

33. Cf. Giuriati, *Con D'Annunzio e Millo*, p. 131.

34. Archivio-Museo Fiumano, busta "Doc. di G. Giuriati."

35. Giulietti, *Pax mundi*, pp. 84-85.

36. Giuriati, *Con D'Annunzio e Millo*, p. 137.

37. See Archivio-Museo Fiumano, busta "Doc. di G. Giuriati," fasc. "Corrispondenza fra il Comandante Gabriele D'Annunzio e l'Ammiraglio Enrico Millo nel periodo ottobre 1919-novembre 1920." This correspondence, as yet unpublished in its entirety, is extremely important, particularly the letter dated 10 March 1920.

38. Alatri, *Nitti, D'Annunzio e la questione adriatica*, pp. 457-58.

39. Ibid., pp. 431-32.

40. Ibid., p. 457.

41. Giuriati, *Con D'Annunzio e Millo*, pp. 151 ff.

42. The original manuscripts were found in the Vittoriale or in the Archivio-

Museo Fiumano. I am grateful to Ferdinando Gerra for providing me with copies of the documents.

43. De Felice, ed., *La penultima ventura*, p. lxii.

44. See Gerra, *L'impresa di Fiume*, 2: 183 ff.

45. Archivio del Vittoriale, *Archivio Fiumano*.

46. Gerra, *L'impresa di Fiume*, 2: 185-88.

47. Archivio del Vittoriale, *Archivio Fiumano*.

48. Giuriati made no reference to the pact in his book, and Host-Venturi was surprised to hear of its discovery quite recently.

49. Archivio del Vittoriale, *Archivio Fiumano*, busta "Coselschi, Eugenio."

50. The correspondence between D'Annunzio and Piffer is in the Archivio Centrale del Risorgimento, busta 127.

CHAPTER 10

1. The letter is reproduced in De Felice, "Nuove lettere," pp. 237-38.

2. Ibid., p. 238.

3. The "Disegno di un nuovo ordinamento dell'esercito liberatore" in D'Annunzio, *Prose di ricerche*, 1: 135-55.

4. Corrado Zoli, *Le giornate di Fiume* (Bologna: Zanichelli, 1921), p. 133.

5. Sani, however, left "under a cloud." A government informant relayed the information that during the period in September when De Ambris had been in Italy, Sani had been the acting head of cabinet and had evicted various "persons of proven patriotic sentiment" from their homes. De Ambris had Sani removed from his position and transferred to Host-Venturi (rector for military affairs). ACS, *Min. Int., Dir. Gen. Pub. Sic.—Aff. gen. e ris. (1916-1922), Categoria A5*, busta 4, fasc. 32.

6. On Bonomi see Fernando Manzotti, "Bonomi e l'impresa di Fiume. Con lettere inedite di G. D'Annunzio, G. Giolitti e E. Caviglia," *Nuova Antologia*, October 1966, pp. 176 ff. For stories of support of the "Balkan intrigues," see Archivio del Vittoriale, *Archivio Fiumano*, busta "Host-Venturi, Giovanni."

7. See Archivio Ciraolo, "Carteggio Fiumano (1919-1921)."

8. De Felice, *Sindacalismo rivoluzionario*, pp. 195-96.

9. See the "key" to De Ambris's long letter of 9 April 1920 in De Felice, "Nuove lettere," p. 212 n.2.

10. The "geographic conflict" between D'Annunzio and De Ambris is extremely well analyzed by De Felice in *Sindacalismo rivoluzionario*, pp. 91 ff., and in *La penultima ventura*, pp. lxiv ff.

11. The letter is dated 8 July 1920. De Felice, "Nuove lettere," p. 229.

12. De Felice, *Sindacalismo rivoluzionario*, p. 209.

13. Zoli, *Le giornate di Fiume*, p. 127.

14. Archivio del Vittoriale, *Archivio Fiumano*, busta "Piffer, Giuseppe." See also the reports on the extreme state of disorder among the supporters of the Command in ACS, *Min. Int., Dir. Gen. Pub. Sic.—Aff. gen. e ris. (1916-1922), Categoria A5*, busta 4, fasc. 32. One of these reports states, for example, that the Command was forced to reject over half of the new volunteers in the fall because they were either AWOLs or "individuals of *cattiva fama*." Those who were accepted had to swear obedience. In addition, D'Annunzio had to personally intervene at one point to halt the mutiny of the sailors on board the *Cortellazzo*.

15. Cited in Salvatore Samani, "Lettere di Gabriele D'Annunzio," pp. 121-22 (letter dated 20 September).

16. Cited in De Felice, *Sindacalismo rivoluzionario*, pp. 92 ff.

17. Ibid., p. 93.

18. Ibid.

19. Ibid., p. 95.

20. Ibid., p. 101.

21. See De Ambris's proposal for the insurrection in ibid., pp. 103-7. The first paragraph indicates the importance that De Ambris ascribed to the Carta del Carnaro: "Assiduous and tenacious propaganda of the Fiuman Constitution, which must be illustrated and popularized in every way, by means of pamphlets, handbills, conferences, conversations etc., so that it becomes known above all to the friends of the Fiuman Cause, then to those who are neutral, and finally to its enemies."

22. See the letters from Zoli to D'Annunzio in February, Archivio del Vittoriale, *Archivio Fiumano*, busta "Zoli, Corrado."

23. ACS, *Min. Int., Dir. Gen. Pub. Sic.—Aff. gen. e ris. (1916-1922), Categoria A5*, busta 6, fasc. 50.

24. For Lauro, see several reports in ibid. As for Borletti, very little is known of the details of his relationship with D'Annunzio, but see n. 26.

25. To reconstruct the story of the Balkan intrigues, one would need considerable new information on the Masons, on the activities of Zoli, Borletti, and various banks, and of the government itself in this regard.

26. Archivio del Vittoriale, *Archivio Fiumano*, busta "Borletti, Senatore."

27. See in particular the letters from Captain Guido Taraschi, ACS, *Min. Int., Dir. Gen. Pub. Sic.—Aff. gen. e ris. (1916-1922), Categoria A5*, busta 6, fasc. 50. Taraschi was active in organizing support for sabotage within Fiume, trying to buy off legionnaires, supporting efforts by Zanella and Reina to generate anti-D'Annunzian uprising in the city, and so forth. Indeed, Valeri raises the question if it would not have been possible to overthrow the Command without resorting to bloodshed (Valeri, *D'Annunzio davanti al fascismo*, pp. 27 ff.).

28. Archivio del Vittoriale, *Archivio Fiumano*, busta "Host-Venturi, Giovanni."

29. The deduction that Zoli was in Vienna comes from repeated references to create a *centrale* for the Balkan uprisings in Vienna in the Vittoriale documents regarding Kochnitzky and Host-Venturi, plus Host-Venturi's later letter to D'Annunzio referring to a "return to Vienna" of the Balkan representatives. But there is no direct proof as such.

30. Archivio del Vittoriale, *Archivio Fiumano*, busta "Borletti, Senatore."

31. Archivio-Museo Fiumano, busta "Doc. di G. Giuriati."

32. Archivio del Vittoriale, *Archivio Fiumano*, busta "Host-Venturi, Giovanni."

33. Ibid.

34. On the last days of D'Annunzian Fiume see Gerra, *L'impresa di Fiume*; De Felice, *Sindacalismo rivoluzionario*, pp. 116 ff.; *La penultima ventura*, pp. lxvi ff.; I. E. Torsiello, *Gli ultimi giorni di Fiume dannunziana* (Bologna, 1921); Zoli, *Le giornate di Fiume*; Legioni di Ronchi, *Documenti delle cinque giornate di Fiume* (n.d. [but probably 1923]).

35. The text of the secret treaty has recently been published by Gerra, *L'impresa di Fiume*, 2: 193 ff.

36. It is important to note, however, that the president of the Swiss Federation was hardly likely to be well disposed toward the *Reggenza*, since a certain Adolfo Carmine had organized an irredentist movement in the Canton of Ticino, declaring himself to have been inspired by D'Annunzio. In a letter to the U.S. secretary of state in mid-December, the U.S. consul in Berne put the matter this way: "Swiss

public opinion is rather upset over the irredentist maneuvers of Mr. Carmine, and the entire national press condemns his activities in associating himself with D'Annunzio in the irredentist movement. . . . Mr. Motta, President of the Confederation, who is himself a citizen of the Canton of Tessin, during an interview in Geneva . . . authorized [the interviewer] to say that Switzerland considers any official protest against D'Annunzio's act entirely superfluous since the Italian government and the great majority of the Italian people condemn the fanatical aspirations of D'Annunzio. Mr. Motta further declared his conviction that any serious consideration of the message to the 'youth of the Tessin' would dignify the policy of D'Annunzio more than it deserved." *General Records of the Department of State*, Record Group 59, Decimal File, 1910-1929, National Archives, Washington, D.C.

37. Giuriati, *Con D'Annunzio e Millo*, pp. 171 ff.

38. See De Felice, *Sindacalismo rivoluzionario*, p. 114.

39. See De Felice, *La penultima ventura*, pp. lxxiv ff.

40. Lauro was quoted by a government informant as saying that if Fiume were attacked by regular troops, D'Annunzio was certain to win them over to his side. At the same time, however, Taraschi advised the government that in his opinion the new legionnaires were exceedingly unreliable. He noted that when, on a previous occasion, the rumor had spread that the *carabinieri* were preparing an attack on the city, many of the young legionnaires had defected to the government side. Hence, he concluded, this was likely to happen again when the actual assault took place, and he felt that a relatively small attacking force would suffice. ACS, *Min. Int., Dir. Gen. Pub. Sic.—Aff. gen. e ris. (1916-1922), Categoria A5*, busta 4, fasc. 50.

41. De Felice, ed., *La penultima ventura*, p. lxxviii.

42. Emilio Gentile, *Le origini dell'ideologia fascista* (Bari: Laterza, 1975), p. 184.

43. See George L. Mosse, *The Nationalization of the Masses* (New York: Howard Fertig, 1975).

44. There are many rumored contacts between D'Annunzian Fiume and Soviet Russia, but here one is constantly in the realm of "it is said." The most significant statement from the Soviet side about the importance of D'Annunzian Fiume comes from a statement attributed to the Hon. Bombacci in *La Tribuna* (Rome) on 30 December 1920: "The communist deputy declared that the D'Annunzian movement is perfectly and profoundly revolutionary, because D'Annunzio is a revolutionary. Lenin even said so at the Moscow Congress. And he added that if the socialists compile any document whatsoever against the comandante of Fiume, he will protest and vote against the document."

It is significant that in the same number of *La Tribuna*, a harsh judgment of D'Annunzio was cited from *Avanti!* : "D'Annunzio, the man of the patriotic Italian bourgeoisie . . . puts himself at the head of the work of destruction of the Italian state. . . ."

Index

Library of Congress Cataloging in Publication Data

Ledeen, Michael Arthur, 1941–
   The first duce.

   Translation of D'Annunzio a Fiume.
   Includes bibliographical references and index.
   1. Rijeka, Croatia (City)—History. 2. Annun-
zio, Gabriele d', 1863–1938. I. Title.
DB879.F5L3813   949.7'2   76-47376
ISBN 0-8018-1860-5